Public Sector Financial Control and Accounting

For M. Lourdes de Miguel García-Glynn

Public Sector Financial Control and Accounting

SECOND EDITION

John J. Glynn

First published 1987
Second edition published 1993

Blackwell Publishers
108 Cowley Road,
Oxford, OX4 1JF, UK

238 Main Street, Suite 501
Cambridge, MA 02142, USA

British Library Cataloguing in Publication Data
A CIP catalogue record of this book is available from the British Library.

Library of Congress Cataloging in Publication Data
Glynn, John J.
   Public sector financial control and accounting/John Glynn.—
2nd ed.
      p.   cm.
   Includes bibliographical references (p.   ) and index.
   ISBN 0–631–18191–1.—ISBN 0–631–18862–2 (paper)
   1. Finance, Public—Accounting.   2. Finance, Public—Auditing.
3. Finance, Public—Great Britain—Accounting.   4. Finance,
Public—Great Britain—Auditing.   I. Title.
HJ9733.G58   1993
657′.835—dc20   92–29621
CIP

Typeset in 10.5/11.5 Plantin by Pentacor
Printed in Great Britain by TJ Press (Padstow) Ltd
Printed on acid-free paper

Contents

Figures

Tables

Preface to the First Edition

This book is an introductory text on the topic of accounting and financial control in the public sector. Whereas most other books on this topic assume some prior knowledge of the area this does not. Its purpose is to provide short summaries on a wide range of topics across the rather broad spectrum of public sector activity. It is a book that should, hopefully, prove useful to two main groups of reader.

The first group comprises accountants and accounting students who, while conversant with fundamental accounting concepts and the application of financial control within the private sector, wish to understand more of their application in the, primarily, not-for-profit public sector. Only with respect to the nationalized industries is there broad similarity with the private sector. The first half of the book discusses broad issues while the second half of the book has a specific chapter on each of the main divisions of public sector expenditure. The style of each chapter is to provide a brief recent history of the issues under discussion together with a summary of present developments. The approach is principally to address policy rather than 'in-depth' technical issues. On advice received it was felt that this approach should also have broad appeal to a second group of readers, public servants not conversant with accounting issues who wished for such an overview in a public sector context.

Many readers will wish to pursue some of the issues raised in greater depth and it is for this reason that about 200 carefully selected references have been cited. This selection should be easily obtainable either from libraries or from direct application to the relevant government or research agency. Accounting developments in the public sector are constantly evolving. Indeed, many would argue the pace for change has noticeably quickened in recent years. As illustration to this last point, in the last month that this book was

completed (September 1986) three important developments occurred –
HM Treasury published a major report *Accounting for Economic Costs
and Changing Prices*, the DHSS announced that a new manual on
accounts and auditing was to be issued before the end of 1986 and the
joint Chartered Institute of Public Finance and Accountancy
(CIPFA)/Audit Commission working party announced that their
report on local authority accounting would be shortly released. On
reading this book readers will be aware that particular sources of
references are given prominence. Those wishing to keep abreast of
developments should keep up to date by reading: relevant government
publications including HM Treasury's *Economic Progress Reports;*
specialist journals such as *Financial Accountability and Management*
(Blackwell Publishers) and *Public Money* (CIPFA); and specialist
reports from such bodies as the Institute for Fiscal Studies and the
Urban Institute (Washington, DC).

This book was started in July 1985 while I was Visiting Fellow at the
Australian National University, Canberra. I am particularly grateful to
Professor Ron Bird, Department of Commerce, for allowing me this
second opportunity to visit Australia. While there I received valuable
assistance and advice from Michael McCrea and Mark Tippett. Upon
my return, in December 1985, I completed the outstanding chapters.
Special mention and thanks are due to Professor John Perrin,
University of Exeter, for reading my work and offering much
constructive advice and criticism. Also from Exeter, I should like to
thank Paul Collier and Professor Bob Parker for their assistance.
Grateful thanks are also due to all those who granted me permission to
reproduce various illustrations; in particular I should like to thank the
Controller of Her Majesty's Stationery Office and Cambridgeshire
County Council. Last, but by no means least, I would like to thank
Deloitte Haskins and Sells for their research facilities and technical
support. In particular I would like to mention two of their partners,
Tony Hazell and Michael Roberts, and two of their long-suffering
secretaries, Debbie Smith and Alison Stewart, who produced the final
manuscript.

JOHN J. GLYNN
Eliot College, The University of Kent at Canterbury

Preface to the Second Edition

When the first edition of this book was published in 1987, I remarked that several new developments were being introduced just as the book was about to be printed. Over the last five years the momentum for change in the financial management of the public sector has continued apace. At the local government level we have witnessed the introduction of the community charge (often popularly referred to as the poll tax). This policy has proven to be fraught with political and financial setbacks for the government, who now intend to introduce a new council tax, effective from April 1993. Major reforms in the field of healthcare have led to several changes that have included GP fundholding and 'self-governing' trusts. At the central government level the Next Steps initiative, a half-way house to the privatization of some central goverment services, is now in its third year of operation.

The country is also in deep economic recession. The latest (1992) ·Autumn Statement expects that the public sector borrowing requirement will rise to £37 bn this financial year, a significant increase on the Budget forecast of £28 bn. This compares to a forecast reduction of –£15 bn. in 1987 when the first edition was published. Many of the management reforms currently under way will be associated with an economic strategy that still seeks, despite short-term increase in public expenditure, to slim down the direct provision of public services. Most of the changes introduced during these five years effectively centre on a series of new contractual relationships.

Such changes have introduced new divisions of management practice that have created 'purchasing' and 'contracting' functions. For example, local authority social service departments are now increasingly in the role of brokers between their clients and the providers of the service they require. Increasingly, government at all levels is becoming an enabler rather than a direct provider of services. Largely unnoticed, constitutional changes are altering the very notion of public sector accountability. Ministerial accountability is now accountability to the Minister by a Chief Exectutive rather than accountability of the Minister to the House of Commons. All too often management reforms are also in danger of being associated with constitutional change, not by a pragmatic process but rather as a result of political faith. There is, therefore, the danger that managment reforms tend not to be evaluated in their own right. Good management is a politically neutral concept.

With this revision, I should like to thank Paul Sabin, Chief Executive, and colleagues at Kent County Council and Dr. David Perkins, formerly of the South East Thames Regional Health Authority and now at the Canterbury Business School, for their assistance. Also I should mention my secretary, Ann Hadaway, who assisted me with the production of the final manuscript.

JOHN J. GLYNN
Canterbury Business School
The University of Kent at Canterbury

1

An Introduction to Public Sector Financial Control

Introduction

This first chapter is designed to set in context the discussion of the ten succeeding chapters. Its purpose is to set out briefly the size and structure of the public sector, and to consider the broad objectives of accounting in the public sector.

The intention of each succeeding chapter is to discuss succinctly the various topics and to provide a guide to further reading. While every effort has been made to incorporate up-to-date references, the very nature of the public sector means that statistics, in particular, are often in need of revision. Whenever possible the reader is directed to ready sources of current information.

This book sets out the theory and facts as they relate to the UK. However, it is often useful to draw upon the comparative work of other countries. It is for this reason that, for example, the first section of chapter 4 reviews the application of programme budgeting in the USA.

Setting the Scene

Most modern, western-style economies are termed mixed economies; that is, a large proportion of their gross national products (GNPs) originate in the public sector. A mixed economy is a half-way house between a market economy and a centrally planned economy as typified in the former Soviet and eastern-bloc economies. In part, it reflects the fact that, if left to itself, the market system of any economy is unlikely to operate equitably. It also reflects the fact that the UK (along with Australia, New Zealand, western Europe, Canada and the USA) has expanded the socioeconomic functions of government; for example, with expanded programmes for education, health and welfare, social insurance and the protective services.

The growth of a mixed economy in the UK can be measured by expressing public expenditure as a percentage of gross national product (GNP). The figures at various times in the past 60 years are:

1932	1951	1970	1976	1980	1990	1992
29%	40%	45%	51%	53%	40%	42%

Taxation paid for a third of GNP in the mid–1950s, 48 per cent when the Conservative government came to power in 1979 and 77 per cent in 1992.

When the Conservative government came to power in 1979 public expenditure in Britain had risen steeply, often increasing by more than 10 per cent per annum. Indeed, for the financial year 1980–1, at £92.6 billion it was an increase on the previous year of more than 20 per cent. This was a period of high inflation and the government came to power with a manifesto which stated that they would improve efficiency and limit waste in the public sector. To achieve this, they enforced a strict financial climate that included the use of cash limits and cash planning (see chapter 7) to motivate public servants towards greater economy and efficiency. At present about 50 per cent of public expenditure is directly cash-limited. This includes the external financing limits imposed on those nationalized industries that currently remain. The balance represents 'demand-determined' services where, once policy is set and rates of payment determined, expenditure in the short term depends on the number of qualifying applicants (for example, social security benefits and local authority current expenditure).

Each year the Chancellor of the Exchequer presents to the House of Commons his autumn statement. As well as the agreed plans for public expenditure it also provides a short-term forecast of the UK economy. In recent years this publication has been expanded to incorporate much of the information that was formerly incorporated in the public expenditure white paper (PEWP). From 1991, the PEWP was replaced by individual departmental reports. The 1991 autumn statement revealed that the public expenditure planning total is to rise by 13 per cent between 1991–2 and 1992–3 to £26 billion, an increase on that forecast in the previous autumn statement. The estimate of privatization proceeds in 1991–2 and 1992–3 is forecast at £8 billion per year. The forecast outturn of the planning total for 1991–2 was given as £204.9 billion and the projection for 1992–3 was given as £226.6 billion. The effect of the recession which began in 1990 has been both to increase spending in areas such as social security and to reduce national income relative to trend. Hence the 2 per cent increase in GNP since 1990 After 1992–3 it is projected that this ratio will resume its downward trend. Table 1.1 analyses the planning total and general government expenditure over the period 1990–1 to 1994–5. Figure 1.1 sets out the relationship between the planning total and general government expenditure (GGE) for 1990–1, and shows the functional split of spending within GGE. The government's objective remains that, over time, public spending should take a declining share of national income. Equally important, all services are expected to make the best use of the resources available to them. It is the government's view (Cm. 1729) that the public, as both customers and taxpayers, are entitled to expect high-quality services, responsive to their needs, provided efficiently at reasonable cost.

The Citizen's Charter (Cm.1599), published in July 1991, is designed to provide further stimulus to greater efficiency improvements throughout the public sector with its emphasis on service standards and value for money (VFM). A forthcoming white paper will set out how the government proposes to secure better performance and increased VFM by further extending competition across the public services. In central government, the Next Steps initiative is also designed to improve VFM and deliver better services by the management reform of setting up executive agencies. Cm.1760 reviews the achievements of this initiative in 1991 The National Audit Office (NAO) continues to give a high priority to VFM studies, planning some 47 such investigations in 1992, increasing to around 50 in 1993 During 1991, some of its most influential reports were in the health and education areas and dealt with topics such as the use of hospital operating theatres (HC 306) and the repair and maintenance of school buildings (HC 648) For local authorities, and more recently the National Health Service (NHS), the Audit Commission plays an equally important role in spreading best practice and improving VFM.

Public sector manpower has been reduced by about a fifth since 1978–9. Table 1.2 shows that, over this period, there was a 23 per cent reduction in the number of civil servants and a 64 per cent reduction in those employed in nationalized industries. In the latter case most of this reduction represents a transfer to the private sector following on from privatization. In the NHS there was a 5 per cent increase in staffing over this period. The Office for the Management of the Civil Service (OMCS) has taken on responsibility for co-ordinating the response to employee training initiatives such as the Management Charter Initiative (MCI). The key management development word of the 1990s appears to be 'competence'. Efforts are underway in a

Table 1.1   The planning total and general government expenditure

	£ million Estimates of outturn	New plans/projections²				Changes from previous plans/projections¹		
	1990–91	1991–92	1992–93	1993–94	1994–95	1991–92	1992–93	1993–94
Central government expenditure¹	140,653	156,700	168,600	178,000	185,400	4,500	6,900	10,000
Central government support for local authorities¹	42,527	53,200	58,600	61,200	64,000	700	2,900	4,600
Financing requirements of nationalized industries	2,285	2,680	3,450	2,850	2,180	360	1,300	890
Reserve			4,000	8,000	12,000	−3,500	−3,000	−2,500
Privatization proceeds	−5,345	−8,000	−8,000	−5,500	−5,500	−2,500	−2,500	0
Adjustments¹	300	300				300		
Planning total	**180,119**	**204,900**	**226,600**	**244,500**	**258,000**	**−100**	**5,600**	**13,000**
Local authority self-financed expenditure¹	14,742	10,200	8,500	9,000	9,000	1100	−1000	−2,500
Central government debt interest	17,508	16,700	16,500	17,500	18,500	−100	−500	0
Accounting adjustments	3,767	4,300	4,500	5,000	5,500	400	−500	−500
General government expenditure	**216,136**	**236,100**	**256,300**	**276,500**	**291,100**	**1,300**	**3,900**	**10,200**
GCE excluding privatization proceeds as a percent of GDP	40	41½	42	41¾	41¼			

¹ For definition, rounding and other conventions, see notes in Annex A (page 25).
² The table shows new plans for the planning total and its constituents and projection for the other items in general government expenditure.
Source: Autumn Statement 1991 (Table 1.1), HM Treasury

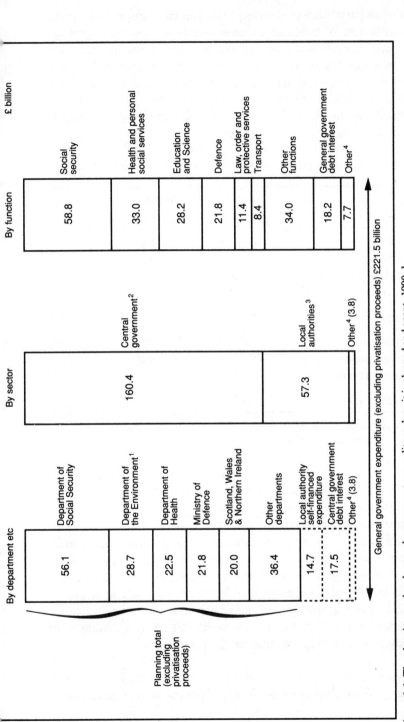

Figure 1.1 The planning total and general government expenditure: how it is planned and spent, 1990–1

1 Includes revenue support grant and non-domestic rate payments and certain transitional grants to local authorities in England. Comparable items are included in the figures for Scotland and Wales.

2 Includes grants, subsidies and net lending to public corporations, including nationalized industries. It also includes central government debt interest (£17.5 billion).

3 The total is made up of £42.5 billion financed by support from central government and £14.7 billion financed from local authorities' own resources. It includes local authority debt interest (£5.3 billion)

4 Includes the national accounts adjustments. The differences in these figures reflect the different treatment of local authority debt interest and market and overseas borrowing of public corporations in the analyses of GGE by function.

Source: Autumn Statement 1991 (Chart 1A.1), HM Treasury

number of departments to develop management competency frameworks and to attach standards to those competencies. Staff appraisal systems have been introduced and recruitment freedoms have been granted to a number of agencies, allowing them to proceed without reference to the old Civil Service Commission (now the Recruitment Agency) at the junior grades. The expected diversity in pay and employment conditions consequent upon the creation of executive agencies is now beginning to materialize.

Table 1.2   Public sector manpower: 1978–79 compared with 1990–91[a]

	1978–79 000 WTEs[b]	1990–91 000 WTEs	% Change
Civil service	734	560	−23
Armed forces	326	311	−5
National Health Service	923	970	+5
Other central government	211	213	+1
Total central government	2,194	2,054	−6
Local authorities	2,325	2,280	−2
Nationalized industries	1,843	665	−64
Public corporations	203	108	−47
Total public sector	6,565	5,107	−22

[a] Adapted from *Autumn Statement 1991* (Table 8.6), HM Treasury
[b] WTE = whole time equivalents

Because a department keeps within a predetermined cash target, or because a nationalized industry or hospital trust keeps within its borrowing limits, it cannot be assumed that, *ipso facto*, their programmes are both effective and efficient. It is for this reason that the public sector has also, in tandem with general management reforms, witnessed a number of attempts to reform the processes of financial management. These reforms are aimed at, on the one hand, providing better information to a wide variety of users and, on the other hand, making management more accountable for their actions. An important element in any management information system is its accounting procedures, accounting being defined as:

The process of analyzing and systematically recording in terms of money or other unit of measurement, operations or transactions and of summarizing and determining the results thereof. (CICA, 1983.)

The concern of this book is to examine the nature of financial control and accounting in the public sector; its purpose is to understand current practice, examine problem areas and consider the proposals designed to remedy these deficiencies.

The Objectives of Accounting in the Public Sector

The nature of public sector accounting is quite different from that adopted by the private sector. It is based on a quite distinctive financial and institutional structure. Nationalized industries aside, the majority of the public sector is budget-financed. Central government either provides services on a national basis or else redistributes funds which are managed on a semi-autonomous basis. Local authorities, for example, receive the largest proportion of their funds in the form of grants from central government. While the nationalized industries provide the closest analogy to the private sector, they are subject to a high degree of direct and indirect regulation on such matters as their level of funding and pricing policy, not to mention other directions that impinge upon their free market operation. Typical examples to illustrate this last point have included, at various times, directives to 'buy British' and the imposition of trade embargoes with certain countries. Private sector companies, even though they cover a diverse array of interests that range from manufacturing through to retailing and service industries, are all assumed to operate as profit maximizers. Within a classic normative microeconomic framework both owners and managers are assumed to have the same homogeneous expectation – that of maximizing the equity value of the firm (see Hirschleifer, 1958). All productive opportunities are undertaken so long as they maximize equity shareholders' welfare. The requirements of those in need of accounting information in the private sector are therefore fairly uniform.

In the public sector accounting information is also required, but by a wider and more diverse group of interested parties than in the private sector. While certain groups of users, such as creditors and employees, have common interests with the private sector, the public sector also has to present information to other interested parties, which include politicians, taxpayers, electors and the recipients of services. The needs and requirements of this latter group are heterogeneous, with individual user groups having conflicting interests. For example, council tax payers are, on the one hand, concerned with the efficiency of the services they receive from their local authority. On the other hand, they are concerned about the level of contribution required. In America, the report of the Committee of Concepts of Accounting Applicable to the Public Sector (1970–1, p. 80) stated that the primary objectives of accounting in public sector organizations are:

1. To provide the information necessary for faithful, efficient and economical management of an operation and of the resources entrusted to it. This objective relates to *management control*.
2. To provide information to enable managers to report on the discharge of their responsibilities to administer faithfully and effectively the programmes and use of the resources under their direction; and to permit all public officials to report to the public on the results of government operations and the use of public funds. This objective relates to *accountability*. [Emphasis added.)

Chapter 2 examines, at some length, the alternative concepts of accountability. An abridged summary of objectives contained in a National Council on Government Accounting research report (NCGA, 1979, p. 47) is as follows:

Overall goal
The overall goal of accounting and financial reporting for government units is to provide:

1 financial information useful for making economic, political and social decisions and demonstrating accountability and stewardship; and
2 information useful for evaluating managerial and organization performance.

Basic Objectives
The objectives of accounting and financial reporting for government units are to prove:

1 financial information useful for determining and predicting the flows, balances and requirements of short-term financial resources of the government unit;

2 to provide financial information useful for determining and predicting the economic condition of the government unit and changes
   therein;
3 financial information useful for monitoring performance under
   terms of legal, contractual and fiduciary requirements;
4 information useful for planning and budgeting, and for predicting
   the impact of the acquisition and allocation of resources on the
   achievement of operational objectives; and
5 to provide information useful for evaluating managerial and organizational performance:

   (a) for determining the costs of programmes, functions and
       activities in a manner which facilitates analysis and valid
       comparisons, with established criteria, amongst time periods,
       and with other government units;
   (b) for evaluating the efficiency and economy of operations of
       organizational units, programmes, activities and functions;
   (c) for evaluating the results of programmes, activities and
       functions and their effectiveness in achieving their goals and
       objectives; and
   (d) for evaluating the equity with which the burden of providing
       resources for government operations is imposed.

Point 5(d) of this American report is interesting since very often
government will direct agencies to provide a level of service for a
uniform charge. Consider the flat rate charged for prescriptions that
has no relation to the cost of the medicines dispensed, or a nationalized
industry that may incur additional costs on capital equipment because
of a directive to buy British.

Almost 12 months after this report the United States General
Accounting Office produced an exposure draft entitled *Objectives of
Accounting and Financial Reporting in the Federal Government* (1980). It
stated that (p. 24):

The primary objective of accounting and financial reporting in
the Federal Government is to provide useful information for
assessing management's performance and stewardship. Assessing
this, basically, involves determining what an entity has achieved
and what it can achieve in the future. In assessing past
performance, information must provide indications on:

– financial viability (the ability of the entity to provide the same
  level of resources);

- program activity (the degree of activity under various programs including costs of inputs and value of outputs);
- fiscal compliance (whether financial and related laws and regulations were followed).

The only comparable research in Britain that provides an insight to the objectives of financial reporting within the government sector is the report, in 1976, of the Layfield Committee (Cmnd.6453), but even then this was restricted to local authorities.

Cash and Accruals Accounting

When considering the objectives of financial reporting, it is necessary to appreciate that the present, traditional application of 'cash accounting' may not be entirely relevant for monitoring the efficiency and effectiveness of all departments or programmes. Cash accounting, recording the transactions by which revenue and expenses are reported in the period in which the related cash receipts and payments occur, is really only useful for short-term fiscal control. Particularly since the introduction of cash limits, there is an implied assumption that just may not be true; that is: keeping within a cash target denotes a well run department. Cash accounting only deals with fiscal compliance.

There is growing support, both internationally and in the UK, for the wider adoption of 'accruals accounting' in the public sector. In the words of the National Council on Government Accounting (NCGA) 1979, p. 11):

The accrual basis is the superior method of accounting for the economic resources of any organization. It results in accounting measurements based on the substance of transactions and events, rather than merely when cash is received and disbursed, and thus enhances their relevance, neutrality, timeliness, completeness and comparability. Accordingly, the Council recommends use of the accrual basis to the fullest extent practicable in the government environment. The cash basis of accounting is not appropriate.

This argument is supported in a recent report from the Joint Committee of Public Accounts of the Parliament of the Commonwealth of Australia (1982, p. 23):

the cash based system of the Commonwealth with its basis of appropriations and constitutional and parliamentary checks and balances is designed to protect the rights of taxpayers and citizens generally. This is recognized as fiscal compliance. Many authorities are set up to increase administrative efficiency and the effectiveness of services provided in discrete areas. Nevertheless, they see themselves as extensions of departments of state and thus conceive a cash basis of financial reporting to be legitimate in view of the structure of the financial system for the Commonwealth as a whole. This notion is misconceived.

The accruals convention makes the distinction between the receipt of cash and the right to receive cash, and the payment of cash and the legal obligation to pay cash. In practice there is often no coincidence in time between cash movements and the legal obligations to which they relate. Consider two transactions of an organization whose financial year coincides with the calendar year. In December 19x1, it pays rent on its offices for the first quarter of 19x2, and, amongst its year end accounts payable (creditors) is an amount representing PAYE income tax which has been deducted from employees. In the former transaction the organization has made a prepayment for a future economic benefit that will arise in the forthcoming financial year, 19x2. A cash accounting system would attribute this benefit in the current year, 19x1, in advance of it being received. In the latter transaction, a liability exists for the payment of tax to the government. It relates to the financial year 19x1 even though it will not be paid until 19x2. Under the accruals convention, therefore, revenue and costs are recognized as they are earned or incurred, irrespective of cash flows. This matching principle is recognized by Statement of Standard Accounting Practice (SSAP)2 as being one of the four fundamental accounting concepts.[1]

The distinction between the cash and accruals accounting conventions can best be illustrated in the following series of expressions:

1 Cash basis: cash receipts − cash payments = change in cash.
2 Accruals basis: revenue (income) − expenses = net profit/loss (surplus/deficit).
3 Revenue (income): cash received during a financial year − opening balance of accounts receivable (debtors) + closing balance of accounts receivable (debtors).
4 Expenses: cash paid out during a financial period − opening balance of accounts payable (creditors) + closing balance of accounts payable (creditors).

Accruals accounting in Britain was traditionally only mandatory for nationalized industries, whose accounting policies are expected to adhere to best commercial practice. In line with this matching principle, a variety of state controlled bodies provide for a provision for depreciation in their accounts. These include, in addition to the nationalized industries, such diverse bodies as the Cable Authority, the BBC and some minor public corporations. Local authorities generally adopt some form of modified accruals accounting which excludes the provision of depreciation.

The argument for including depreciation in financial statements is well put by Henke (1980, p. 186):

> The basic premise for the argument in favour of recognising depreciation as an element of cost is the contention that the responsibility of operational stewardship in non-profit organiz-ations extends through the acquisition and use of all assets. If this premise is accepted, it follows that the financial statements should disclose: (1) the consumption of all assets used in the operation of the entity; and (2) the changes in the net equity balances.
>
> Fixed assets are, in effect, nothing more than unexpired units of service. As these units expire through usage, they should be accounted for as part of the full cost of services rendered by the organis-ation. This practice can best be accomplished through the recording of depreciation.

The main argument here is that depreciation is a cost of operation, and that management should be accountable for all assets under their stewardship. Depreciation is an estimate of the expiration cost of fixed assets over the financial year.

The counter-argument is that since departments operate under a budgetary system using appropriations of centrally raised revenue for their various programmes, including the original acquisition and replacement of capital assets, the reporting of depreciation is not necessary. Anthony's report for the Financial Accounting Standards Board (FASB) (1978, p. 141) states that:

> the acquisition of fixed assets by means of capital appropriations or donations represents a commitment by past generations to provide for capital needs. Correspondingly, when the needs for additional fixed assets arise in the future, future generations have an implied commitment to provide for these needs. Current users

should not be expected to provide for future needs, which would be the case if user charges included depreciation expense.

Some who argue against depreciation believe that if it is a notional charge for future replacement then it should be identified as an appropriation. Alternatively, if fixed assets were purchased from debt finance these proponents would argue that depreciation is irrelevant, and that the cost should be the debt repayment and interest charges. There are also problems with certain assets that do not have a market value (such as roads and sewers), or other assets that are donated (for example, a renal dialysis machine presented to a hospital). Certainly most research on this point remains equivocal, with opinions being based on the particular circumstances in which an asset came into operation and the future policy decisions relating to replacement.

This author would generally argue for the inclusion of a charge for depreciation (albeit an imperfect system) whenever practical and meaningful, so that the true costs of operation can be measured. Indeed, there are now signs that the argument in favour of recognizing depreciation as an element of cost is beginning to be accepted within local government and the NHS (see chapters 8 and 9).

Central government's requirement for information which primarily shows fiscal compliance has meant that cash accounting has percolated down to all levels within the public sector. Problems arise with the wider introduction of accruals accounting; for example, the unresolved debate on depreciation (just mentioned) and other arguments, such as whether there should be a wider adoption of accounting standards. There is clearly much more research work required into the whole structure and content of public sector financial reporting.

Conclusion

Political choice determines the variety and scale of the activities carried on in the public sector. The funding of these activities depends primarily upon taxes, but limited finance is also provided from charges and prices. Funding aspects will not be the prime concern of this book, which concentrates on the financial management and control of public sector activities so that they can offer the best service and provide value for money.

The elements of diversity in the public sector are great. On the one hand, nationalized industries and some executive agencies are expected to operate commercially as trading entities. Broadly, one might expect that they should therefore have the same financial information needs as private sector organizations. On the other hand, central government departments, local authorities and health authorities do not exist by selling goods and services; nor do they have shareholders. As stated, their activities are funded by compulsory levies. (However, it is important to note that internal markets, with the creation of the purchaser/provider split within local government and the NHS, are a partial move in this direction.)

Chapter 2 will examine the need for greater accountability in the public sector. While set in a partially theoretical and partially comparative framework, this chapter provides an important background to the discussion of later chapters. Chapters 3 to 6 range over the key areas of management control, investment appraisal and auditing in the public sector. The next three chapters are devoted to the main segments of public sector expenditure: central government, local government and the NHS. Chapter 10 discusses the financial management, by central government, of the nationalized industries. The scale of change in the public sector over the last decade has been enormous. The aim of this book is to review the financial management aspects of these changes against the two themes set out in chapters 2 and 3: financial accountability and management control.

Notes

1. Note that responsibility for the development of accounting standards now resides with the Accounting Standards Board (ASB). SSAP 2 was published by the former Accounting Standards Committee (ASC). The ASB will update existing accounting standards as required.

2

Financial Accountability

Introduction

The theme of accountability is crucial to the operation of both the private and public sectors. It is a fundamental concept that can be traced back to earliest times. In the New Testament, Matthew (25:14–30) relates the parable about the man who entrusted his property to three servants. Two of the servants doubled the funds entrusted to them and were praised for their efforts. The third servant simply buried the funds entrusted to him in a hole in the ground for safekeeping and was condemned for his worthlessness because he had not even taken the (virtually riskless) alternative of leaving the money on deposit with the bankers. Even earlier, Aristotle wrote in *The Politics*: 'To protect the treasury from being defrauded, let all public money be issued openly in front of the whole city, and let copies of the accounts be deposited in the various wards' (Sinclair, 1984). Both of these references relate to one particular concept of accountability, namely that of 'financial accountability'. The former reference can be thought of as a private sector illustration of financial accountability. The master expected his servant to increase his own personal wealth, a situation that is exactly analogous with the generally accepted microeconomic concept that management should seek to maximize the wealth of their ordinary (equity) shareholders. The latter question is, obviously, a reference to public sector financial accountability, which is, in practice, a vaguer and less tangible concept.

Johnson (1971, p. 283) points out that, historically, the emphasis 'in Britain has been almost exclusively on procedures which would enable Parliament to exercise a *post facto* check on the manner in which monies had been spent for the purposes approved by (but not proposed by) Parliament'. But Normanton (1971, p. 312) points out that 'public accountability is capable of much more: it is actually, or potentially, a rich and open source of knowledge about how government services function in actual practice, and hence of ideas about how they ought to function'. The opening paragraphs of this chapter discuss alternative concepts of accountability in order to recognize that, while financial accountability is important, it is but part of a larger canvas. The concept of financial accountability and how it should be achieved externally, through financial reporting, and internally, through managerial accountability is then considered in greater detail. This chapter, therefore, mainly concentrates upon the theory of what should be done as opposed to what is done. Such an analysis is an important prerequisite to much of the discussion that follows in succeeding chapters.

Alternative Concepts of Accountability

Public accountability is an essential component for the functioning of our political system. Glynn (1985, p. 143) states that 'public sector accountability means that those who are charged with drafting and/or carrying out policy should be obliged to give an explanation of their actions to their electorate'; the electorate being a composite group that includes clients, employees and taxpayers. As Heald (1983, p. 155) states:

> The growth in the public sector, both in terms of its scale and the diversity of its activities, has outstretched the traditional machinery of public accountability, heavily dependent upon the formal relationship between the executive and the legislative. There have emerged alternative views of what accountability entails, involving different answers to both the substance and form of the account. The concepts of accountability which now dominate the debate are *political* accountability, *managerial* accountability and *legal* accountability.

In developing his argument Heald (1983) incorporates his three classifications of accountability with the nine types of accountability distinguished by Smith (1980). Both views are incorporated in table 2.1. Sociologists and political scientists have devoted much time to developing a variety of theories on the determination of public sector expenditure. They have been concerned with certain aspects of accountability listed under Divisions I and III. Likewise, economists have discussed at length technical aspects of economic policy, particularly macroeconomic policy. They have been concerned with certain aspects listed under Divisions I and II. However, accountants, who also ought to be concerned with the concepts of accountability listed under Divisions I and II, have not traditionally played a major role. On the one hand this can be attributed to an unwillingness by politicians to provide for a greater disclosure of information. On the other hand the accountancy profession has only contributed, to a limited extent, to improving commercial and professional accountability. Further work needs to be carried out in order to improve the present level of constitutional, decentralized and resource concepts of accountability.

To public administrators and political scientists the word accountability generally relates to the separation of power and responsibility. Because of the nature of the public sector, the term 'acting in the public interest' is often used when considering the question of responsibility for what and to whom. It is a phrase that underlies nearly all discussions on public policy, political action, social value and individual interest, yet there is no agreement as to what we mean when we use the term. Schubert (1960, p. 223) states that:

> It may be somewhat difficult . . . to accept the conclusion that there is no public interest theory worthy of the name and that the concept itself is significant as a datum of politics. As such, it may at times fulfil a 'hair shirt' function, to borrow Sorouf's felicitous phrase; it may also be nothing more than a label attached indiscriminately to a miscellany of particular compromises for the moment. In either case, *the public interest* neither adds to nor detracts from the theory and the methods presently available for analysing political behaviour.

This view is shared by Downs (1962, p. 1) when he states:

> the term public interest is constantly used by politicians, lobbyists, political theorists, and voters, but any detailed enquiry about its exact meaning plunges the inquirer into a welter of platitudes, generalities, and philosophic arguments. It soon becomes apparent that no general agreement exists about whether the term has any meaning at all, or, if it has, what the meaning is, which specific actions are in the public interest and which are not, and how to distinguish them.

In more general terms (see Held, 1970) we can say that the term 'public interest' is used to express approval or communication of

Table 2.1 Concepts of public sector accountability

Division	Subdivision	
I Political accountability	(a) Constitutional accountability	the hallmark of parliamentary systems
	(b) Decentralized accountability	the devolution of control and accountability, e.g. to local authorities
	(c) Consultative accountability	the involvement of interested parties and pressure groups
II Managerial accountability	(a) Commercial accountability	publicly owned organizations, financed by user charge and not by budgetary appropriations
	(b) Resource accountability	adopting managerial practices that will promote the efficiency and effectiveness of non-commercial entities; by the establishment of an appropriate budgetary control framework

Table 2.1 cont.

Division	Subdivision	
	(c) Professional accountability	self-regulation by professional groups employed in the public sector
III Legal accountability	(a) Judicial accountability	a review of executive actions at the instigation of an aggrieved individual; decisions should not be *ultra vires* those required by statute
	(b) Quasi-judicial accountability	the control of administrative discretion, e.g. by review tribunals
	(c) Procedural accountability	a review of decisions by an external agency, usually by an ombudsman

Source: Glynn (1985), p. 145

policies adopted or proposed by the government. In order to demonstrate the accountability for policies there is a need to develop quantitative measures that demonstrate that they have been carried out efficiently and effectively. Heald (1983) would also stress the need to demonstrate equity. Accountability, therefore, requires a clear definition of the objectives of a policy or programme and the development, if practicable, of measures of output and outcome.

Accountability is all about responsibility relationships, both externally and internally. Particularly for the concepts of accountability outlined in Divisions I and II of table 2.1, an important way to communicate accountability is through the provision of financial, and related, information – financial accountability. It is the accounting system that is charged with 'keeping a record of all legal authorisations as well as commitments, agreements, encumbrances, obligations, and expenditures that use any part of the authorisation granted' (AAA, 1970–1, p. 81). While legal accountability is primarily directed towards providing protection for the individual against administrative discretion, political and managerial accountability are concerned more with the provision of an account of why funds were disbursed in a particular manner and what results or benefits thereby resulted.

Langenderfer (1973) suggests a normative view of accounting which considers three aspects: the nature of the information it provides; to whom the information is provided; and the purposes for which information is to be provided. He states (p. 50):

> Accounting is a measurement and communication system to provide economic and social information about an identifiable entity to permit users to make informed judgments and decisions leading to an optimal allocation of resources and the accomplishment of an organization's objectives.

Users of Accounting Information

In this section we consider the potential users of public sector accounting information and the kinds of information they need. Drebin et al. (1981) identify ten different user groups: management; legislative bodies; voters; taxpayers; service recipients; oversight bodies; investors (lenders); employees; vendors (suppliers); and grantors. The first two of these groups cover the need for a policy-making function and an administrative function, the former being the responsibility of the legislative body and the latter being the responsibility undertaken by management. The legislative body represents the public interest and determines (or plans) service and programme objectives. Management have the responsibility for accomplishing these objectives; it is their responsibility to motivate staff and direct activities. The results of these activities are subsequently evaluated by the legislative body in order to determine whether objectives have been met. Management therefore need information that helps them determine the cost and effectiveness of alternative programmes given a variety of resource constraints (typically the imposition of cash limits and target staffing levels).

Voters are interested in assessing the performance of their elected representatives. In financial terms, information can be provided in three areas: the level of taxes and charges, efficiency, and stewardship of resources. Drebin et al. (1981, p. 42) also state that 'non financial information concerning effectiveness of programs and equity of service delivery is necessary to properly evaluate the performance of incumbent administrators'. They go on to state that 'whilst to a large extent, voters may depend on their own experience with service delivery . . . information concerning overall objectives and service activities would provide a more balanced view'. Voters can also be taxpayers and recipients of various services. As taxpayers it might be useful to have information helpful in predicting future tax levels. Service recipients are concerned with the equity and quality of the service they receive. There is, therefore, an implied need to provide information that measures the inputs (resources) and outputs of individual programmes. In order to gauge the equity of service, information is required on such matters as demography, geographical location, age, sex and race of service recipients.

Oversight bodies represent a number of relationships. For example, there is the central/local government relationship whereby central government, as grantor, passes legislation that delegates the responsibility and provides the funding for the provision of various services to local authorities. Central government, therefore, requires information that local authority expenditure has been legitimate and that minimum service provisions have been met. Other oversight bodies would include Select Committees and audit agencies. Their information requirements would be similar and all oversight bodies should also require financial and related statistical information in order to determine that the particular organization being reviewed has provided value for money.

Lenders' information needs are concerned with the ability of the government to meet its contractual obligations, as well as information that enables them to compare the return they receive with alternative investments. Suppliers have similar information needs. In the short term they need assurance that the payment for past services will be forthcoming. In the longer term they require more general financial information in order to assess whether or not there is likely to be an increase or decrease in requirement for the goods or services they supply. Employees require information to determine whether, in the first place, to work for a public sector agency and subsequently to determine when to press for salary increases or an enhancement of conditions of employment.

Grantors exist within the government sector, as with the central/local authority relationship discussed above. They can also exist, for example, when a government agency makes a grant to a private sector not-for-profit organization such as a charity. The information requirements from the grantee to the grantor are therefore as previously outlined. Figure 2.1 expresses the complexity and interrelationships of these groups. It illustrates the point made by Drebin et al. (1981, p. 43) that:

> Many users act in multiple roles. Individual citizens, for instance, in their capacity as voters legitimize the Government through the election of public officials. As taxpayers, the same residents provide financial resources. Some residents may be employees of the government or invest in its securities.

Drebin et al. (1981) therefore follow the orthodox approach, previously developed in the private sector, by outlining a conceptual framework for accounting for users' needs. Their analysis leads to the following (abridged) summary of objectives (vol. 1, p. 110):

1 To provide financial information useful for determining and predicting the flows, balances and requirements of short-term financial resources of the governmental unit.
2 To provide financial information useful for determining and predicting the economic condition of the governmental unit and changes therein.
3 To provide financial information useful for monitoring performance under terms of legal, contractual and fiduciary requirements.
4 To provide information useful for planning and budgeting, and for predicting the impact of the acquisitioning and allocation of resources on the achievement of their organizational objectives.
5 To provide information useful for evaluating managerial and organizational performance.

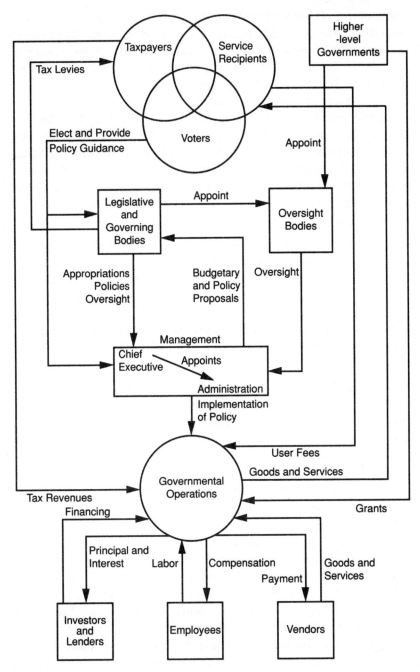

Figure 2.1   Potential users of financial information and their relationship
Source: Drebin et al. (1981)

These objectives are supported by the United States General Accounting Office (GAO) (1980, p. 24) in its exposure draft *Objectives of
Accounting and Financial Reporting in the Federal Government* (see page
11). Both of these sets of objectives support the contention,
introduced in the previous chapter, that cash accounting is an
inadequate accounting base for performance evaluation.

Another useful contribution to this debate is provided by Anthony
(1978). His report, *Financial Accounting in Nonbusiness Organisations*,
was commissioned by the United States Financial Accounting Standards Board (FASB) as an attempt to redress their traditional
preoccupation with accounting principles and standards in the private
sector. In his study Anthony distinguished three alternative classifications of organization:

1 Profit-orientated: private sector organizations that have as their
  primary objective the pursuit of profit.
2 Type A nonprofit: a nonprofit organization whose financial resources
  are obtained entirely, or almost entirely, from revenues from the sale
  of goods and services.
3 Type B nonprofit: a nonprofit organization that obtains a significant
  amount of financial resources from sources other than the sale of
  goods and services.

Nationalized industries or agencies such as the UK Passport Agency
would be classed as Type A organizations, while local authorities, for
example, would be classed as Type B organizations. The purpose in
defining these three classes of organization was to consider the
question (Anthony, 1978, p. 165): 'How, if at all, would business
organizations be distinguished from other organizations for the
purposes of developing accounting concepts?' He considered three
alternatives: 'the profit/nonprofit approach and the "sources of
financial resources" approach', followed by a discussion on 'the
considerations relating to the questions of whether there should be a
separate set of accounting concepts for non business organizations'.

While profit is the dominant goal for profitorientated organizations
the dominant goal of nonprofit organizations is to render services to
society (either in general or to qualifying applicants). For profit-
orientated organizations accounting reports emphasize the measurement of profit as an indication of the success of the organization. The
published, external reports of such entities are largely designed to
inform the equity shareholders about the returns on their investment.
The management accounts of such bodies are likewise concerned with

the attainment of this single goal. Anthony (1978, p. 167) points out that:

> Since a nonprofit organization exists to render services, users of its financial statements are interested in how much services of various types were performed. These types of services correspond to programs. Thus, the (external) financial statements of a nonprofit organization often report spending by programs; whereas, there is less need for such a spending classification in profit-orientated organizations.

Both nationalized industries and local authorities publish a good deal of information on their various and diverse activities (see chapters 8 and 10) In Type A nonprofit organizations the level of revenue raised is often regarded as indicative of the value that recipients place on an organization's services. However, many Type A organizations are monopolies which challenge the validity of this argument. If, for example, postage prices rise, many customers have little alternative, at least in the short term, but to pay these charges. In some individual cases the number of items posted will decrease and in other cases there will be a change in the pattern of consumer spending, customers perhaps making use of private sector delivery services. Government intervention can likewise influence the demand for a particular nationalized industry's services. Type B nonprofit organizations have no market test for the level of services provided. They must comply with a far greater degree of control (and restrictions). The funds they receive are for specific services – hence the term 'fund accounting'.

Having discussed the distinguishing features of these three organizational groups, Anthony (1978, p. 173) considers that 'differences between Type A nonprofit organizations and profitorientated organizations are primarily in the way accounting information is used, not in the concepts governing how it is reported'. For Type B organizations three differences (without solutions) are cited that affect accounting:

1 How to account for non revenue resource inflows. (Should, for example, a health authority account for donated assets and voluntary labour?)
2 How to account for restrictions on spending, including the need to distinguish between operating resource inflows and capital inflows.
3 The fact that there is no counterpart, in the private sector, to the power to impose taxes.

With respect to this last point, Anthony (1978, p. 173) cites the following, abbreviated comments by Smokovich:

> taxation is simply a way of getting cash. Other ways of getting cash include earning profits, borrowing and issuing stock. The similarities are obvious. Profits are limited by market forces, by laws, and by conventions; the power to tax is limited also. . . A tax does have unique characteristics, but none of them are overwhelming. It could also be argued that the power to tax should be assigned a value in a governmental balance sheet. A counter-argument is that the taxing power is conceptually akin to the earning power of a business. Although earning power is, in effect, a franchise, it has never been recognized for balance sheet purposes. . . , except in the limited extent of purchased goodwill.

The importance of this FASB-sponsored report is, therefore, that it recognizes that accounting concepts are essentially the same for both profit-orientated and nonprofit organizations. Both need to distinguish operating transactions from capital transactions. Both need to maintain their capital base in monetary terms. For the profit-orientated organization this is achieved when the difference between revenues and expenses at least equals dividends. Type A nonprofit organizations maintain their monetary capital when the difference between their revenues and expenses at least equals zero, while, Type B nonprofit organizations maintain their monetary capital when the difference between operating inflows and expenses at least equals zero.

Financial Accountability in the UK Public Sector

Figure 2.2 outlines four formalized chains of financial accountability to Parliament. These are: central government; local authority; health authority; and nationalized industry. The solid arrows represent formalized channels by which financial information is provided on a regular basis. The broken arrows represent relationships whereby information can be requested, but on an *ad hoc* basis. These four diagrams can only represent a simplified overview; in practice accountability relationships exist via a variety of direct and indirect routes. For example, while the head of a central government department, the Chief Secretary, is directly responsible to Parliament, the chairman of a nationalized industry is accountable via a sponsoring department.

(a) Central Government Department

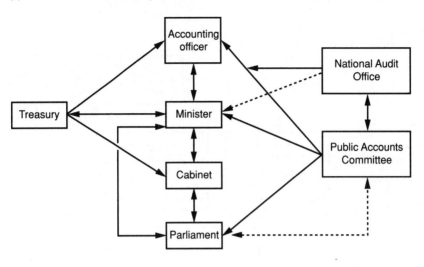

(b) Local Authority

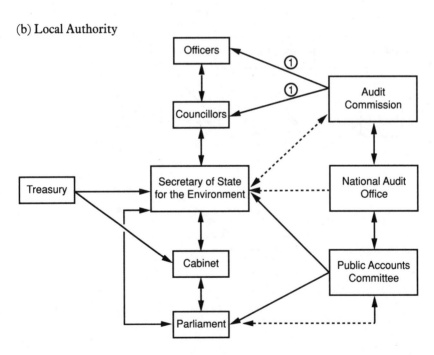

(c) Health Authority

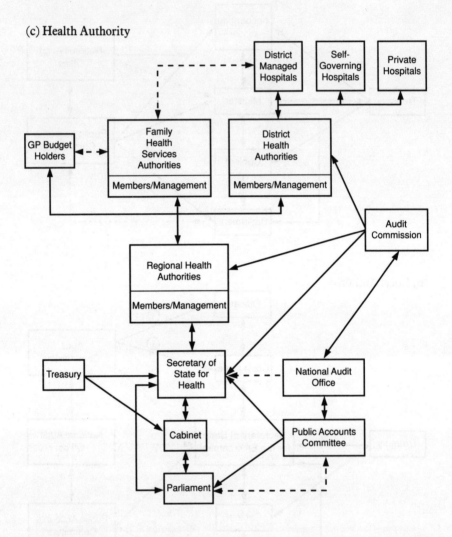

(d) Nationalized Industry

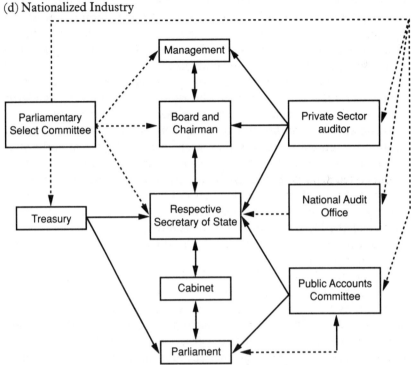

Figure 2.2   Accountability chains in the public sector

Parliament determines overall objectives for all four of these groups. Broad objectives are set out in enabling legislation and are subsequently amplified as a result of statutory instrument; ministerial directions; discussions of the House of Commons Select Committees; Committees of Enquiry; consumer councils; and so on. The accounts presented to Parliament, in the form of Estimates and Appropriation Accounts, are statements of cash receipts and payments during a year regardless of whether they are in respect of current or capital expenditure and, if current, whether benefit of the related goods and services was received during that year. For each central government department the permanent (civil service) head of each department is its 'Accounting Officer' and is nominally responsible for the legal *regularity* of payments from his department. This, however, is a rule that has not been enforced since the 1920s. The Westminster model of government accounting is structured on a system of centralized financial and economic authority. In this model there are two distinct functions carried out by the Treasury: economic policy, planning and advice; and financial management control. The Treasury is a duolithic department. The Prime Minister is First Lord of the Treasury and the

Chancellor of the Exchequer is the Treasurer. With this model there has been a tendency, historically based, for the domination of the budgeteer/economic approach at the expense of the accountant/ financial management approach, which has led to accounting practice being strongly influenced by the budgeteer.

Local authorities probably face the most complex set of responsibilities. Certain services, such as education, have minimum standards imposed by Parliament. Due to increased fiscal control by central government, local authorities are limited as to the volume and quality of any discretionary services they wish to provide. Local authorities must also respond to requests for information from a variety of interested groups. For example, a district county council has responsibilities to: its electors and ratepayers (who may not necessarily be the same group); the county council; central government departments (in particular the Department of the Environment) and Parliament; not to mention pressure groups such as the local Chamber of commerce and local action groups.

Traditionally, only local authorities and nationalized industries were required to publish annual reports. Local authorities receive their direction by Section 2(2) of the Local Government Planning and Land and Land Act, 1980, while nationalized industries have this requirement included in their enabling legislation. Typical, for nationalized industries, is the requirement that accounts and other records be in 'a form which shall conform with the best commercial standards'. This can be interpreted as complying with generally accepted accounting practice; professional regulations as enunciated by the Accounting Standards Board (ASB); requirements of the various Companies Acts; and Stock Exchange requirements (even though such industries have no Stock Exchange quotation). Chapters 8 and 10 respectively examine these external reports in greater detail. Now that the annual public expenditure white paper is no longer produced, individual central government departments have to produce annual reports (see chapter 7).

Normanton (1971, p. 313) discusses the balance between accountability and autonomy, particulary with respect to local authorities and nationalized industries. He takes the view that:

in Britain the balance of accountability has in varying degrees become lost. . . There is too much independence (which means in effect the power to work in secrecy) in the case of the nationalized industries and the local authorities both have become enormous spenders of taxation without its counterpart in public accountability.

Since Normanton (1971) wrote this there have been important moves to improve the information provided by local authorities, though Tomkins (1977) points out that the standards of reports vary, some being elaborate while others are simply extracts from the accounts. However, the problem of accountability for the nationalized industries remains in conflict. This conflict arises because any directives towards making nationalized industries more fully accountable would, on the one hand, lead to the release of commercially confidential information that would be readily available to private sector competitors, and, on the other hand, would provide for potential political exploitation by those either for or against the concept of nationalization.

Certainly the nationalized industry chairmen are in no doubt that secrecy avoids several problems, and it remains the case that detailed knowledge about how these major industries perform remains very limited. Normanton (1971, p. 325) suggests that consideration should be given to the expedient adopted by France, in 1948, when the Commission des Enterprises Publiques was established. This body, which is closely associated with the Cour des Comptes (or the national audit authority), examines all aspects of managerial efficiency as well as reporting upon the accounts. It publishes reports at two levels: (1) a general report that avoids controversial issues; and (2) a limited circulation report that is available only to responsible ministers, the Cour des Comptes, and (upon request) to the parliamentary finance commissions. Normanton (1971, p. 325) regards such 'security measures as realistic in the circumstances'.

Central government provides information on its activities when it publishes its various expenditure statements. However, such information is only of limited use when trying to assess the performance of the public sector. While, increasingly, information is provided that enables the reader to consider output measures on the volume of service provided, little information is provided on the quality and effectiveness of services. Central government is hamstrung on the notion of secrecy, which is the major impediment to any meaningful development of accountability. Since the early 1970s, when government first introduced internal efficiency reviews, successive administrations have refused to make these reports public. Heald (1983, p. 168) refers to one occasion when this refusal 'degenerated to the level of farce'. This was in 1976, when the Expenditure Committee of the House of Commons was refused access to a programme analysis and review (PAR) study on educational planning which had been made available to the organisation for Economic Co-operation and Development (OECD) and referred to at length in one of their publications. As Heald (1983, p. 168) stated: 'Parliament, the press and the public are thus denied the information essential to a proper assessment of executive actions. Much can always be learned from the policy options that are reflected.'

One common occurrence, as a consequence of this obsession with secrecy, is that we now have a system of government by leaks. Such leaks can be made by ministers or civil servants in order to alert public opinion to a proposed action to which they are opposed. The unfortunate side of such a policy is that those responsible for such leaks may, on other occasions, be perfectly happy to follow the status quo or actively participate in a policy of nondisclosure if such disclosure is likely to reflect upon themselves.

Health authorities have no requirement to publish annual reports, but as explained in chapter 9, it would appear that one or two do, and that many finance officers are now more prepared to entertain personal enquiries on an individual basis. Increasingly this is done, voluntarily, with Department of Health (DOH) encouragement. Nevertheless, there would appear to be a case for each authority to provide an annual report in the same way as local authorities.

Financial accountability is also important for management control. The American Accounting Association (AAA, 1970–1, p. 85) states that: 'One of the greatest challenges to accountants in government at all levels is to help managers more effectively utilise the resources available for accomplishing the intended objectives.'

The AAA (1975) report considers that information is required on a threefold basis: to evaluate management progress and performance; to assist in determination of programmes designed to accomplish objectives; and to render a report on the accountability of management. The accountant fulfils an important service function by providing information that assists management to better perform the tasks assigned to them; as such, information should be timely, accurate and, above all, appropriate to management's needs. The next two chapters consider management control, and in particular budgetary control, in some detail.

Accounting Standards in the Public Sector

Information, whether it is prepared for external or internal purposes, should be objective. In part this is assisted by the establishment of accounting standards. Until August 1990, responsibility for the preparation of accounting standards rested with the Accounting Standards Committee (ASC). Originally known as the Accounting Standards Steering Committee, it was established by the Institute of Chartered Accountants in England and Wales in January 1970. By February 1976 the ASC was reconstituted as a joint committee of the six major professional accountancy bodies, through the Consultative Committee of Accountancy Bodies (CCAB). This standard setting body produced Statements of Standard Accounting Practice (SSAPs), the explanatory foreword to each of which states that they 'describe methods of accounting. . . approved for application to all financial accounts intended to give a true and fair view of financial position'. They are, therefore, standards, primarily drafted with private sector entities in mind. In addition to issuing accounting standards the ASC have issued Statements of Recommended Practice (SORPs), which are not mandatory, and 'franked' SORPs which have limited application for specific industry groups. Examples of two such industry groups would be the Oil Industry Accounting Committee and the Building Societies Association.

Despite the bias of SSAPs towards private sector profit-making organizations, this should not preclude their applicability, when appropriate, to the public sector, or for that matter, to private sector not-for-profit organizations such as charities. This contention is supported by Bird and Morgan-Jones (1981, p. 92), who state that 'as far as possible all SSAPs, excluding of course those not relevant, are intended to apply to all enterprises, including charities and other non-profit organizations' and Hepworth and Vass (1984, p. 43), who believe in 'a common approach where there are common elements'. Indeed in 1983 the ASC established a Public Sector Liaison Group (PSLG). The ASC had franked on the recommendation of the PSLG the following public sector SORPS:

- Accounting Practices for Scottish Local Authorities (January 1987, March 1983);
- Application of Accounting Standards (SSAPs) to Local Authorities in England and Wales (April 1987);
- CIPFA – Local Authority Accounting (the Code of Practice) (November 1987);
- Accounting in UK Universities (May 1989);
- Application of Accounting Standards (SSAPs) to Local Authorities in Great Britain (July 1990).

In 1987 the CCAB set up a committee under the chairmanship of Sir Ron Dearing to review the accounting standard setting process. This committee reported in September 1988 and the government incorporated the main proposals of this report into the Companies Act 1989. This move has greatly strengthened the regulatory force of accounting standards. On 1 August 1990 the ASC was replaced by the Accounting Standards Board (ASB). It is the ASB that now issues accounting standards. The standard setting process and the financing of the ASB is overseen by the Financial Reporting Council (FRC), which covers a wide range of constituency interests. The task of monitoring compliance with accounting standards is undertaken by a Review Panel (RP), which reports to the ASB and which, if deemed necessary, has powers to take a company to court for noncompliance. The FRC is chaired by Sir Ron Dearing and has 20 members and three observers (the Comptroller and Auditor General (C & AG) plus one representative each from the Treasury and the Bank of England). The FRC's role is to produce guidance on broad policy issues but not to approve individual accounting standards. The chairman of the ASB is David Tweedie, a former technical partner of KPMG Peat Marwick McLintock. He is assisted by a technical director, Allan Cook, formerly head of accounting research at Shell, and seven other members. Professor Geoffrey Whittington of Cambridge University acts as academic adviser. The RP is chaired by Simon Tuckey QC, with the former chairman of the ASC, Michael Renshall, acting as his deputy. Under the provision of the Companies Act 1989 the Secretary of State has powers to seek a ruling from the courts, under a new civil procedure, on whether a company's accounts comply with the provisions of the Companies Act 1985. He is empowered to authorize the use of these powers to a properly constituted body and the RP is seen as fulfilling this role. Approved accounting standards adopted or issued by the ASB have, effectively, the force of law. Companies are required to state that their accounts are prepared in accordance with approved accounting standards. The effects and reasons for any departures from this have to be clearly disclosed.

Table 2.2 lists those SSAPs currently adopted by the ASB and deemed applicable for local authorities, health authorities and nationalized industries. Central government departments are expected, alternatively, to comply with the provisions of *Government Accounting: a Guide on Accounting and Financial Procedures for the Use of Government Departments*. This manual is prepared by the Treasury because standard setting by the accountancy profession is framed around the accruals accounting concept, rather than the cash accounting concept adopted by central government. As will be clear from table 2.2, SSAP 3 (Earnings Per Share) has no relevance to local

Table 2.2 Statements of Standard Accounting Practice applicable to the public sector as at June 1992

SSAP	Title	Local authorities	Health authorities	Nationalized industries
1*	Accounting for the Results of Associated Companies	×	×	✓
2	Disclosure of Accounting Policies	✓	✓	✓
3	Earnings per Share	×	×	×
4	The Accounting Treatment of Government Grants	✓	ø	✓
5	Accounting for Valued Added Tax	✓	✓	✓
6	Extraordinary Items and Prior Year Adjustments	ø	ø	✓
7	Accounting for Changes in the Purchasing Power of Money (provisional and superseded by SSAP 16)	×	×	×
8	The Treatment of Taxation under the Imputation System	×	×	✓
9	Stocks and Work-in-Progress	✓	✓	✓
10	Statement of Source and Application of Funds	✓	✓	✓
11	Accounting for Deferred Taxation (replaced by SSAP 15)	×	×	×

Table 2.2 cont.

SSAP	Title	Local authorities	Health authorities	Nationalized industries
12	Accounting for Depreciation	×	×	√
13	Accounting for Research and Development	√	ø	√
14*	Group Accounts	×	×	√
15	Accounting for Deferred Taxation	×	×	√
16	Current Cost Accounting (mandatory status suspended 6 June 1985)	×	×	√
17	Accounting for Post Balance Sheet Events	ø	ø	√
18	Accounting for Contingencies	√	√	√
19	Accounting for Investment Properties	ø	ø	√
20	Foreign Currency Translation	ø	×	√
21	Accounting for Leases and Hire Purchase Contracts	ø	ø	√
22	Accounting for Goodwill	×	×	√
23	Accounting for Acquisitions and Mergers	×	×	√
24	Accounting for Pension Costs	ø	ø	√
25	Segmental Reparting	×	×	√

Key

√ = appropriate or required to be adhered to
× = not applicable/relevant
ø = partially applicable
* = SSAPs 1 and 14 have been amended by an ASB Interim Statement: Consolidated Accounts

authorities. The same also applies, for reasons outlined in chapter 8, for SSAP 12 (Depreciation) and SSAP 16 (Current Cost Accounting). Other accounting standards, such as SSAP 2 (Disclosure of Accounting Policies) and SSAP 17 (Accounting for Post Balance Sheet Events) are either wholly or partially relevant. Nationalized industries are expected to comply with all SSAPs. Only with respect to SSAP 16 was there a specific mention, at paragraph 51, of an exemption from compliance. It states that 'no adjustment should be made in the profit and loss accounts of Nationalized Industries in view of the special nature of their capital structure'. The technical arguments underlying this exemption are discussed in chapter 10.

Audit and Public Accountability

Audit is an expost event and improvements in this important function may be of little longterm value if they are not coupled with more general reforms of the accountability of government. The expanded audit mandates discussed in chapter 6 mean that auditors are no longer solely concerned with fiscal compliance; rather they are now charged with assessing and reporting on management's efforts to develop effective programmes as efficiently as possible.

One consequence of the National Audit Act 1983 is that the Comptroller and Auditor General (C & AG) has adopted a new publishing policy. These reports are now published separately and not, as previously, treated as appendices to the reports of the Public Accounts Committee or the Appropriation Accounts. The intention behind this policy is to reach a wider audience, with consequently greater publicity and public awareness of the investigations undertaken. This is a great improvement. However, while some reports are well drafted, others could do with being both more complete and more pointed in terms of their recommendations.

Gordon Downey (1986), a former C & AG, notes that as the amounts of money being voted by Parliament grow larger and larger, so too is there increasingly less attention being paid to the fact that billions of pounds a year have been voted automatically. Funds for major projects and programmes have been approved virtually on the nod. He states (p. 36): 'a Parliament which *de facto* gives up its control of supply gives up much of its constitutional control of government and accountability'. The balance of power is, therefore, clearly weighted in favour of the government of the day. Downey (1986, p. 37) goes on to say that:

The irony is that in recent times, Parliament as a whole has demonstrated its interest in accountability as a constitutional principle. But – with exceptions of course – it has at the same time been unable or unwilling to devote enough time and effort to understanding and pursing financial and accounting matters, perhaps because these often lack the immediate and general glamour of other aspects of policies.

Conclusion

Commitment and firm action are necessary in order to improve the standard of financial accountability in the public sector. Historically there has been too much reliance on expost financial accountability in the form of audit reports and *ad hoc* investigations. Many of the developments outlined in succeeding chapters are relatively new, and only time will tell whether politicians, management and the public at large are, as a result, better informed on the activities of government. It is one thing to recognize the present weaknesses in financial accountability; it is another to devote time, money and effort to remedying these defects. A major (and fundamental) reform of public sector accountability is long overdue and needs to start from the top down; that is, with constitutional accountability. Prime Minister John Major's Citizen's Charter initiative, launched in the summer of 1991, represents an attempt to apply some of the tenets of total quality management to the civil service, transport, health and education. Only time will tell if this is a serious effort at improving both public sector accountability and overall performance.

3
Management Control in the Public Sector

Introduction

This chapter considers the general framework of management control and its importance to the public sector. It also considers the importance of budgeting in linking planning with control. Chapter 4 outlines some of the more important budget innovations of recent years – new ideas promoted on the basis of criticisms of the traditional, line-item budgetary process.

The public sector is primarily composed of nonprofit-making organizations. For such organizations it is a matter of balancing the demands for their services against the limited resources available.

Central government departments, the National Health Service and so on depend directly on the Exchequer for all their funds. If charges are made for certain services they are usually nominal and have little impact on the level of services offered. Equally, so-called autonomous bodies are subject to a high degree of central government control. Local authorities receive by far the largest proportion of their funds via the community charge/council tax.[1] While they can raise revenue locally, primarily by levying, the extent of their powers is strictly monitored by central government. Even public sector business entities, such as the nationalized industries, find that although they may have a very dominant profit or financial target, they often have to take account of wider exogenous implications. Central government has, from time to time, legislated on such matters as their pricing policies, external funding limits and trade with certain overseas countries.

Management control, in its broadest context, is the means by which an organization carries out its objectives effectively and efficiently. Public sector organizations can generally be distinguished as having hierarchical structures composed of responsibility centres: units, sections, departments and divisions. Except at the unit level, each responsibility centre consists of aggregations of smaller responsibility centres. Indeed each organization can itself be described as a responsibility centre. The function of executive management is therefore to plan, coordinate and control the work of these more or less autonomous responsibility centres. Note that this general use of the term unit is different from that used in the NHS, where a unit is defined as an administrative subdivision of a health district and may itself consist of several hospital sites, each of which would be subdivided into cost/responsibility centres.

By far the greatest number of responsibility centres, trading organizations such as the nationalized industries excluded, can be described as 'expense centres'. Traditionally the management control system has only measured the expenses (or inputs) incurred by a responsibility centre rather than the monetary value of its outputs. Measuring the costs of outputs and outcomes has more recently received greater attention and succeeding chapters will illustrate those areas of the public sector where some progress has been made. For now, suffice it to say that the present state of the art is such that while some areas are capable of producing meaningful output measures, it is proving difficult to develop appropriate measures in other areas. While readers might accept that the National Health Service could produce useful output measures such as the number and cost of various treatments, they might wish to consider what appropriate output measures could meaningfully be produced to measure, for example, a police force's community liaison programme.

Control and Responsibility

Most studies on the management control process have been carried out in the private sector with profit-orientated organizations. As a consequence most descriptions of the management control process are framed around the primary objective of earning profits. However, as Anthony and Young (1984, p. 4) argue, 'the basic control concepts are the same in both profit-orientated and nonprofit organizations, but because of the special characteristics of nonprofit organizations, the application of these concepts differs in some important respects'.

The control structure of any organization consists, by and large, of a definition of the relationships between controllability and responsibility, or more precisely a specification of which managers are responsible for which resources in the organization. While every organization exists to carry out various programmes it is not necessarily the case that the responsibility structure matches the programme structure. For example, an objective of a local authority may be the care of the mentally ill in the community. Such a programme would involve more than one local authority department; in this case the social services department and the housing department. Additionally, some programmes would also involve more than one organization. With this example, the local authority would also have to liaise, and possibly share some costs, with a district health authority. In many instances, though, the responsibility structure matches the programme structure.

Anthony and Young (1984, p. 239) define a programme as 'some definable activity or group of activities that the organization carries on, either directly in order to accomplish the organization's objective or indirectly in support of other programme elements'. Each programme is operated by a group of people all working towards some organizational objective and headed by a manager who is responsible for their actions.

Anthony and Young (1984, p. 10) suggest that there are four principal components to a formal management process: programming; budget formulation; operating (and measurement); and reporting and evaluation.

Programming

Programming, the first stage, is composed of five steps: (1) initiation, (2) screening, (3) analysis, (4) decision, and (5) selling. In order to encourage the internal generation of ideas, senior management must provide a clear mechanism for bringing ideas to their attention. Ideas only find favour once an influential person(s) has been convinced of their practicability. Obviously it is necessary to screen ideas to decide whether they are compatible with the objectives of the organization. There are two aspects to this analysis: technical and political. A technical analysis involves estimating the costs of a proposed programme, attempting to quantify its benefits, and, if feasible, assessing alternative ways of carrying it out. A political analysis, in a non-party sense, involves consideration of how the proposal is likely to be viewed by the parties who are affected by it, in particular the resource providers. The final step is to submit the proposal to senior management for a decision on its acceptability. Usually a proposal will be composed of a number of variants rather than a single 'take-it-or-leave-it' proposition.

Budget formulation

The budget provides the essential link between the important elements of programming and operation. It is a statement that expresses future plans in financial terms; the plans become firm commitments for which funds have been allocated. The budget also provides a basis for evaluating performance. Wildavsky (1975, p. 5) describes budgeting as 'attempts to allocate financial resources through political processes to serve differing human purposes'. This theme will be further examined in chapter 4.

As such, an apparently straightforward procedure is not as simple as it might at first seem. Budgets are generally of two types – the 'revenue budget' and the 'capital budget'. Revenue budgets have traditionally been referred to as line-item budgets; that is, budgets which focus on expense elements such as salaries, materials and other consumables, rather than on the reason for the expenditure. This latter approach is known as programme budgeting and it identifies amounts allocated to individual services. While many public sector organizations divide their budgets into the activity centres that they operate, they do not undertake programme budgeting. For example, a local authority's education programme may be subdivided into pre-school education, primary education, secondary education and adult education. This is nothing more than a deaggregation of larger line items. No information is provided on the individual programmes undertaken within each of these divisions. It could be that adult literacy is an important programme undertaken in the adult education budget. There would obviously be other important programmes undertaken but the line-item approach to budgeting does little to improve managerial planning and control. Two alternative approaches to programme budgeting will be considered in the next chapter.

While many new ideas have been promoted for budgetary reform it remains the case that they have generally failed to gain general acceptance. As Jones and Pendlebury (1984, p. 130) state:

> The irrationality of taking last year's budget as the base for the current year's, and arguing only for and against increments, has been repeatedly pointed out.

The traditional line-item budget has the following defects:

(a) The budget is subdivided on the basis of department or activity centres, each of which may operate several programmes either individually or as joint ventures.
(b) It is usually drawn up on an annual basis by comparing the previous year's expenditure and adding increments, or perhaps decrements.
(c) There is a natural tendency, when dealing with inputs on an incremental basis, to favour existing programmes. New programmes have to compete with each other for limited resources, regardless of their priority.
(d) Control is primarily exercised on the budget inputs rather than its outputs. That is, it provides data on what government consumes rather than data about what government does or about the purposes for which money is spent.

Despite these problems the traditional budget continues to serve its original purpose, that of ensuring *compliance* with the conditions set out in appropriations. In part this has been due to budget reformers making overenthusiastic claims for overelaborate systems. Traditional line item budgeting exists despite its defects because:

1 It is an ideal mechanism for limiting expenditure to the amounts and to the items voted in the appropriations.
2 It provides flexibility when across-the-board cuts have to be made for macroeconomic purposes.
3 It is a fairly uncomplicated system that avoids any conflicts about objectives and the methods of achieving them, particularly when budget preparation follows a tight timetable.
4 It is adaptable, so its supporters claim, to all economic situations.

As Wildavsky (1975, p. 42) states: 'It is not so much that traditional budgeting succeeds brilliantly on every criterion but that it does not entirely fail on any one that is responsible for its longevity.'

A whole range of strategies tend to be adopted by those seeking budget appropriations. It is necessary therefore for the providers of funds to understand the ploys that will be used to obtain funds in what some authors term 'the budget game'. Anthony and Young (1984,pp. 376–86) illustrate some 30 ploys used in the game of budgetary control.

In addition to the revenue budget, most public sector organizations attempt to budget separately for items of a capital nature. The Chartered Institute of Public Finance and Accountancy's publication *Local Authority 1: Accounting Principles* (1985, p. 11) proposes the following rule for identifying capital expenditure: 'Any outlay which is of value to the Authority in the provision of these services beyond the end of the year of account should be recorded as a capital asset provided there is no legal constraint.'

While new capital assets, such as buildings, clearly provide benefits beyond one fiscal year, certain situations can arise when such a classification is less obvious. Repairs and maintenance could merely maintain an asset at its present state (revenue expenditure) or could add improvements to an asset (capital expenditure). The funding of capital expenditure is usually spread over the years that benefit will accrue. Certainly, as far as central and local government are concerned, this philosophy has long been accepted. If a local authority wished to open a new senior citizens' home it would seem unreasonable to burden the current year's community charge/council tax payers with the full cost of an asset that might have, say, 50 years' useful life. Instead, a loan is raised and its repayment, including interest, shared by future generations of local taxation payers. Local authorities have an unusual approach to recording their assets as they make no provision for depreciation – see chapter 8.

Other public sector bodies have adopted a similar approach, although recent years have witnessed a growing tendency, particularly in the nationalized industries, for an increasing proportion of capital expenditure to be financed out of current expenditure. According to *The Government's Expenditure Plans to 1984/85* (Cmnd.8494, 1982) it is the government's aim that the customers of the nationalized industries will have charges levied against them sufficient to fund 75 per cent of capital expenditure.

The Chartered Institute of Public Finance and Accountancy's research report, *Capital Budgeting* (CIPFA, 1977a, (pp. 11–15), has identified the following objectives of capital budgeting:

1 To express in financial terms capital works necessary to meet the objectives expressed or implied of an organization within an accounting period or periods.
2 To set out the agreed priorities of capital schemes.
3 To facilitate coordination of plans and resources by:

   (a) allocating the financial resources between departments;
   (b) assisting in the implementation of capital schemes;
   (c) providing a basis for forecasting capital cash flows and financial requirements;
   (d) providing a basis for forecasting revenue implications;

(e) providing a basis for budgetary control of outturn against forecast;

(f) to satisfy government control requirements.

Measuring and reporting

The final two components in any system of formal management control involve measuring the resources consumed and reporting thereon to management so that they can investigate adverse variances and initiate corrective action. Accounting information should, where possible, be supplemented with a variety of other information. Reports should provide useful information for evaluating both management and programmes. The evaluation of performance can result in a revision of a programme, or a revision of the budget, or a modification in operations. It can also lead to a reconsideration of the organization's strategies for achieving its goals. Figure 3.1 provides an overview of these phases of management control.

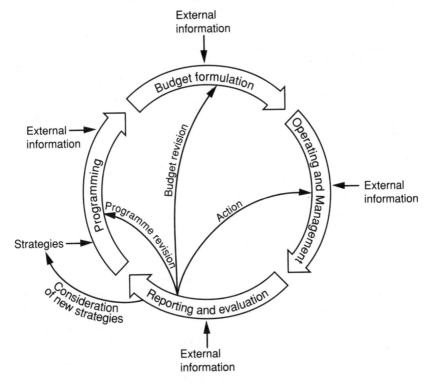

Figure 3.1   Phases of management control
Source: Anthony and Young (1984) p. 10

The Role of Accounting in Public Sector Management Control

The distinctive patterns and processes of government accounting and budgeting are largely a product of the public sector infrastructure. In this context executive financial integrity is institutionalized. Accounting as a means of collecting and reporting on patterns of expenditure has played a not insignificant role in shaping the policies pursued by the various public sector organizations.

As will by now be apparent to the reader, recent discussions on the advancement of public sector accounting continue to stress economic measurement. As Hopwood (1984, p. 172) states:

> Continued economic restraint has given a new urgency to demands to improve the efficiency of management in the public sector. More and more accusations of waste, maladministration and inefficiency have been made. High staffing levels have been pointed out. The traditionalism and sluggishness of the decision processes in the public sector is noted repeatedly. Although it is sometimes realized that the demands of public sector accountability and decision making in a political context can serve to limit the extent to which concepts of efficiency derived from the private sector can be applied uncritically in the public sector domain, there nevertheless remains a feeling that much more could be done to improve resource utilisation. Efficiency remains a very real and persuasive dream.

While greater demands are, from time to time, made for the right to assess public information, attend meetings and, more generally observe and question the machinery of state, successive governments remain preoccupied with administrative rather than public accountability.

Because accounting provides information on the pattern of resources used, and has the potential to make visible what was previously unknown, it has the potential to shape the pattern of power and to influence an organization. Accounting systems of financial control expand the flow of information, so enabling closer monitoring for planning and control. Accounting tends to supersede direct observation because the units to be controlled are usually many and they are also probably geographically dispersed. Management control thereby has a tendency to become more centralized.

It should not be forgotten that, in addition to those being regulated, there are those who have the power to influence the composition of the accounts, thereby manipulating the directions for change that they consider desirable. With the present depressed economic climate, economic rather than social costs tend to be stressed and it is noticeable that even though accounting is masked in its own technical language it can have quite profound consequences in the political sphere. Again to quote Hopwood (1984, p. 179): 'Accounting, by shaping the realm of the visible, can have a major impact on the significance that is attached to both organizational life as it is and the directions of change which are considered desirable.'

Certainly the technical aspects of accounting can have a major influence when comparing the cost of one unit of activity with another. *Accountancy*, the journal of the Institute of Chartered Accountants in England and Wales (ICAEW), provides an interesting example of these kinds of problems in its January 1985 edition. In the journal, Berry et al. (1985) argued that the accounting policies presently adopted by British Coal (BC), formerly the National Coal Board (NCB), have led to certain pits being incorrectly selected for closure. In reaching their conclusions they were critical of BC's practice of allocating central administrative overheads to individual pits. They also criticized their policy of allocating proceeds (based on production) rather than revenue (based on quantity sold). Their contention was that BC management should consider the contribution, rather than the profitability, of each pit (i.e. income earned less variable costs – see glossary of terms). This article was followed by a reply from BC's finance director, in which he argued for the appropriateness of the Board's accounting policies. BC also commissioned Custis et al. (1985) to reply to the criticisms.

These arguments appear technical. They are, but it must be recognized that by adopting certain accounting policies over others, management can influence the future expansion and direction of (as in this case) a major nationalized industry. It is important, therefore, that all those in receipt of accounting information appreciate the underlying policy implications that could possibly ensue depending on the particular treatment of various items of expenditure. Succeeding chapters will introduce further examples of conflict arising out of the adoption of alternative accounting policies.

Management need to adopt a modern approach to financial reporting, one that focuses attention on the need to provide useful information rather than on mere compliance with any particular set of established procedures. In the words of *The Corporate Report* (ASSC 1975, p. 28): 'The fundamental objective. . . is to communicate economic measurements of and information about the resources and performance of the reporting entity useful to those having reasonable rights to such information.' Such an objective should apply to external as well as internal reporting. The needs of the user groups of these two divisions were discussed in the previous chapter.

Value for Money

In recent years the phrase 'value for money' has entered the vocabulary of government. It is a phrase that has a wide and ambiguous meaning. Politicians and the media commonly use it when presenting political arguments for expenditure cuts, particularly in conjunction with other phrases such as 'cash limits'. The intention in this chapter is to present a more considered view on the objective of attaining value for money in the public sector. To say that a particular department (or programme) provides value for money means that those who strive to provide the service do the best they can, within the resources that are available and the environment within which they operate.

Value for money can be thought as consisting of three elements: 'economy', 'efficiency' and 'effectiveness'. The first two of these elements are fairly uncontroversial but the third element, effectiveness, is both hard to define and difficult to measure. Control over the effectiveness of government activities involves the fulfilment of political goals by effective administration. Figure 3.2 provides a brief illustration of this process. The diagram depicts the development of political goals into parliamentary legislation or ministerial direction in order to provide the plans from which devolved departments (or agencies) proceed to day to day implementation. The diagram also shows the various stages at which the three elements of value for money enter the cycle. The use of the word 'devolved' is intentional since, while formalized channels of communication exist for the conveyance of policy, service implementation is often determined at local level.

Until recently there would normally have been two interpretive stages. While the first is mainly the result of political debate and inevitable compromise the second arises as a result of translating diffuse policy decisions into concrete plans for action. The third stage, which leads to a review of effectiveness, is a new stage that is becoming increasingly demanded. These three elements can be defined as follows:

Economy: acquiring resources of an appropriate quality for the minimum cost.

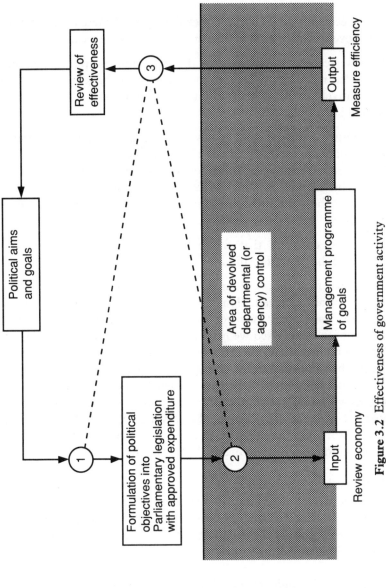

Figure 3.2 Effectiveness of government activity
Source: Glynn (1958), p. 19

A lack of economy could occur, for example, when there is overstaffing or when overqualified staff or overpriced facilities are used.

Efficiency: seeking to ensure that the maximum output is obtained from the resources devoted to a department (or programme), or alternatively ensuring that only the minimum level of resources is devoted to a given level of output.

An operation could be said to have increased in efficiency either if fewer inputs were used to produce a given amount of output, or a given level of input resulted in increased output. Inefficiency would be revealed by identifying the performance of work with no useful purpose, or the accumulation of an excess of (or unneeded) material and supplies.

Effectiveness: ensuring that the output from any given activity is achieving the desired results.

To evaluate effectiveness we need to establish that approved/desired goals are being achieved. This is not necessarily a straightforward procedure; some goals may not be initially apparent. Once a set of goals has been established we need to examine whether these goals are being accomplished. While these elements have been ranked in order of comprehensibility, they are clearly interrelated to one another.

A conflict can arise between efficiency and effectiveness. For example, community charge/council tax payers are, on the one hand, concerned with the efficiency of the services they receive from their local authority. On the other hand, they are concerned about the level of contribution they have to make. As Hepworth (1980, p. 239) states:

> The conflict between efficiency and effectiveness, particularly in sensitive services like education and social services, is extremely difficult to resolve, and is best left to individual judgments, which really means the judgment of those most concerned with the development of the service.

The *Audit Guide: Auditing of Efficiency* (1981), produced by the Office of the Auditor General of Canada, draws an important distinction between efficiency and productivity. The terms are often used (though quite wrongly) as synonyms for each other. The guide (p. 2) states:

- Productivity is the arithmetical ratio between the amount of goods or services produced and the amount of resources used

in the course of production; the ratio between output and input.
– Efficiency is the relationship of actual output/input (productivity) to a performance standard. This relationship is usually expressed as a percentage.

The efficiency of an operation should therefore be compared to a predetermined standard or target. Efficiency can be measured in terms of the rate of return of production, the work content measured over time, or the unit cost of an output. Consider the following example (from Glynn, 1985) in relation to the dispensing of prescriptions by a hospital pharmacy.

Example. A hospital employs two pharmacists who each work a 35 hour week. The standard *rate of production* is 6 prescriptions/hour; which in terms of *work content in time* is 10 minutes/prescription. Each pharmacist is paid £8.40 per hour so that the *unit cost per prescription* is £1.40. Statistics show that on average 924 prescriptions are dispensed each month.

Efficiency can be measured as follows:

(i) $\dfrac{\text{Actual rate per hour}}{\text{Standard rate per hour}} = \dfrac{6.60 \text{ prescriptions}}{6 \text{ prescriptions}} \times 100 = 110\%$

(ii) $\dfrac{\text{Standard time/prescription}}{\text{Actual time/prescription}} = \dfrac{10 \text{ minutes}}{9.09 \text{ minutes}} \times 100 = 110\%$

(iii) $\dfrac{\text{Standard cost/prescription}}{\text{Actual cost/prescription}} = \dfrac{\pounds 1.40}{\pounds 1.27} \times 100 = 110\%$

Various points arise from this simple example. In comparing actual costs with standard costs management should first consider the economy of operations. Efficiency measures are only possible when outputs can be separated from each other and possess uniform characteristics. A repetitive process, as in our example, meets these criteria. There are instances when efficiency measures are either not practicable or not possible. An example, previously referred to, could be a community police programme. Though tasks may be clearly stated (school visiting, crime prevention enquiries, contact with ethnic minorities, etc.), outcomes, not being tangible, cannot be measured.

When an agreed standard of performance does not exist it might be useful to compare present performance with some previous base period (e.g. the same month last year). Such a base period output/input ratio is termed an historical standard or target. This assumes that past performance is indicative of future performance and this may not always be so. For instance, if a new service is building up a clientele base then one could naturally expect the efficiency ratio to improve over time.

A useful list of comparison measures was provided by Hatry et al. for the Urban Institute, Washington DC (1979):

1 Comparisons over *time*.
2 Measurements compared *between* geographical areas.
3 Comparison of actual performance with *standards* particularly in relation to standardised procedures.
4 Comparison of actual performance with performance *targeted* at the beginning of the year.
5 Comparison with similar *private sector* activities.
6 *Inter-authority* comparisons.

Efficiency should not be measured for efficiency's sake. Improving efficiency is the objective. By developing efficiency measures management can contribute to improving efficiency and to determining the expected gains from suggested improvements. Concern by management to monitor efficiency should serve to focus regular attention on the subject rather than attract *ad hoc* attention.

The 1981 Canadian Audit Guide (p. 5) discussed the importance of efficiency measures in the following terms:

Standards and performance data are used for different purposes in various information and control systems. These are to:

– demonstrate achievement of results by comparing performance data to standards, targets and goals;
– plan operations and budget resource requirements by providing data for comparing present and proposed methods and procedures;
– provide a rational basis for pricing goods and services (when charges are made);
– make trade-off decisions between efficiency and the level of service; and
– indicate to employees and supervisors what results are expected.

(Therefore standards are useful both in appraising the performance of managers and groups of employees and in motivating them.)

The key elements for management that arise from adopting efficiency measures are therefore:

1 an awareness of, and the determination to accomplish, programme goals in the most economical and efficient manner;
2 the need to plan operations as efficiently as possible for a given level of resources (or budgeted level of income if a statutory authority is expected to largely generate its own income);
3 the need to have a structured organization whose administration should follow prescribed work measures and procedures in order to avoid duplication of effort, unnecessary tasks, idle time, etc.; and
4 the provision of work instructions, in sufficient detail, to employees who are suitably qualified and trained for the duties they are required to perform.

Effectiveness involves an examination of the relationship between the output and objectives of the department. The management control process should endeavour to measure whether predetermined goals are being achieved. Effectiveness indicates whether results have been achieved, irrespective of the resources used to achieve those results. It could be that effectiveness could be obtained more efficiently. Assessing the effectiveness of programmes in a systematic and regular way is the newest and most difficult area of work that public sector management must adapt to.

A useful example of a management control system that incorporates performance measures comes from Thunder Bay in Ontario, Canada. The city is committed to the advancement of modern management systems and performance measurement. In 1980 the city's chief administrative officer received the International City Management's Innovation Award for Organization and Management. The city's corporate planning and development division have categorized performance measures into three groups:

1 workload/demand measures: to indicate the amount due or to be done;
2 efficiency measures: to measure how well resources are utilized; and

The City of Thunder Bay
1980 PERFORMANCE MEASUREMENT PROJECT

DEPARTMENT	PROGRAM AREA	SIGNATURE	DATE December 31, 1980
SOCIAL SERVICES	HOSTELS AND CRISIS HOMES	Jim Dolph - Social Services Administrator	PAGE 4

PROGRAM DESCRIPTION
To provide temporary living accommodations to transient, unhouseable clients, problem male youths and female family heads in crisis.

COLLECTION FREQUENCY CODE
1 Annual   4 Monthly
2 Bi-annual   5 Weekly
3 Quarterly   6 Daily

	PERFORMANCE MEASUREMENTS	SOURCE AND HOW COLLECTED	HOW ANALYSED OPTIONS	COLL. FREQ CODE
WORKLOAD/ DEMAND	Number of clients serviced by program and by caseworker	Internal Records	Manual	4
	Number of days service provided per program	"	"	4
	Number of days of occupancy of Crisis House	"	"	4
	Number of Crisis Homes	"	"	4
EFFICIENCY	Gross and Net Cost per day service by program	Approved Budget, Internal Records	Manual	4
EFFECTIVENESS	Occupancy percentage for all Crisis Homes and per Home	Internal Records	Manual	4
	Percentage of eligible clients served by program	"	"	4

61

T02061A

Figure 3.3 Performance measurement project
Source: Corporate and Development Division, City of Thunder Bay, *Performance Measurement Manual and Catalogue*, Ontario, Canada, 1980

3 effectiveness measures: to measure how well a goal or objective is being achieved.

Under this system each department is divided into programme areas and a detailed programme description is provided. The performance measures are provided under each category together with details of the source of the information; how it is to be collected; how it is to be analysed (manual/computer); and the frequency of data collection (which ranges from annually to daily). Each programme is discussed with the responsible manager and agreed by him or her. One department covered by this exercise was that of social services. Four of the programmes identified were: adult services; child day-care centres; field eligibility; and hostels and crisis homes. The information provided on the fourth of these programmes is shown in figure 3.3 Similar approaches have yet to be adopted in Britain. While this Canadian experiment attempts to provide as many performance measures as possible, it is admitted that it is not practical to provide measures for all programmes.

Currently most of the impetus for developing efficiency and effectiveness measures arises out of recent legislation to expand the traditional role of the auditor (see chapter 6).

Conclusion

This chapter has provided a brief introduction to the principal components that are necessary in order to establish a system of management control in the public sector. The approach has been normative; that is, theoretical rather than practical considerations have been discussed. In order to evaluate more critically the proposals for budget and management reform outlined in chapters 4 and 7 , it is important to remember that accounting information is very much a product of the public sector infrastructure. Hopefully, if the management information system in an organization is one that reflects control and accountability, rather than the narrow concept of compliance, then the accounting information thereby generated should demonstrate the attainment or otherwise of value for money from public services.

Notes

1 At the time of writing it is the government's intention to replace the community charge with the council tax (see chapter 8). Hence the use of the term 'community charge/council tax'.

4

Budget Innovation and Reform

Introduction

The previous chapter outlined the irrationality of the traditional, line-item approach to budgeting. This chapter considers two of the more widely reported approaches to budgetary reform that focused on programmes: the planning, programming, budgeting (PPB) system, and zero-base budgeting (ZBB). While both of those systems were initially developed in the USA, and have since been used in other countries with varying degrees of success, many of the claims made on their behalf have failed to materialize. Nevertheless, a review of both systems provides important insights into the problems associated with budgetary reform. PPB and ZBB are largely ignored in the UK and, as a prelude to part of the discussion in chapter 7, this chapter concludes by outlining the strategy adopted by central government since the mid-1960s.

Budgeting is an important part of management control, particularly in the public sector. Table 4.1 provides an overview. It indicates the significant aspects of budgeting in the public sector, the influences from the different social sciences, and the areas covered. The table divides the purposes and associated features of the budget into three aspects: as a tool of accountability; as a tool of management; and as an instrument of economic policy. Premchaud (1983, p. 36) states:

> Budgeting in the final analysis. . . is a political exercise. From this point of view, a budget is expected to state clearly the purposes of expenditures and provide them in a form that will be useful for legislative action. In addition, the budget is the instrument for accountability, in that the government agencies are responsible for the proper management of funds and programmes for which funds are appropriated. It is also a tool for

management, because a budget, as an operational budget, specifies either directly or implicitly the cost, time and nature of expected results.

Budgeting as an instrument of economic policy has more varied functions. First, in policy terms, it indicates the direction of the economy and expresses intentions regarding the utilisation of the community's resources. In operational terms, it leads to the determination of the national growth and investment goals. . . Second, a major function of the budget is to promote macro-economic balance in the economy. The policy choices in this regard include the specification of the amount of growth that is compatible with employment, price stability, and balance in the external sector. Third . . . the budget has become a vehicle for reducing inequalities. . . Fourth, the budget should be so organized as to permit a quick and meaningful measurement of its impact on the national economy as a whole.

All of these functions are composite in the budgetary process, which can be described as a two-stage process. First, there is the establishment of goals in the light of available data and with the recognition of economic, political and administrative constraints. Second, there follows the development of plans and programmes for the short, medium and long term. The traditional budget ensures compliance with the conditions set out in the appropriations; that is, it acts as a control mechanism. It stresses inputs rather than outputs by providing data on what government consumes instead of data about what government does or the purposes for which money is spent. Budgets in the public sector should serve a number of purposes rather than the single and rather narrow concept of compliance. The line item/input approach prevents proper political choice amongst objectives and the rational allocation of resources. In addition it limits public understanding of government ability, inhibits the explicit establishment of public sector planning programmes, and leads to inefficiency and lack of accountability on the part of departmental and programme managers. An alternative approach is programme budgeting.

Planning, Programming and Budgeting (PPB) System

PPB is a programme orientated, as opposed to an organization orientated, management approach which examines needs over a medium- to long-term period. It worked with some success in the early

Table 4.1   Approaches to the study of budgeting

Aspects of budgeting	Discipline	General areas covered
Accountability control	Public administration	Description of internal working administrative agencies; stages of budget cycle, etc.
	Political science	Legislature–government relationships; political processes for determining allocation of resources; pressure groups; conflicts.
	Accounting	Efficiency audit; management accounting; adaptation of commercial accounting principles to government.
Efficiency control	Economics	Allocative efficiency; production and distribution functions.
	Accounting	Cost measurement (out-puts as well as inputs).
	Public administration	Normative aspects of modern management systems and their application to government.
	Political science	Boundaries of government; limits on spending; privatization.
Economic control	Economics	Approaches of fiscal policy; economic framework of annual budget; incidence of taxes and expenditures; distributional concerns.

Source: Premchaud (1983), table 4

1960s within the US Defense Department, but when applied in other departments it proved too arduous.

Programme budgeting was first recommended in the US by the Hoover Commission in 1949 (*Report to Congress on Budget and*

Accounting). The approach envisaged three elements: programme and activity classification by government departments; performance measurement and performance reporting. The recommendations of the Commission were not entirely adopted, but they did have an impact on the Budget and Accounting Procedures Act 1950, which provided for a federal budget based on the functions and activities of the government. However, numerous difficulties were encountered and it was not until 1961 that a relatively successful programme budgeting system was introduced into the US Department of Defense by the Rand Corporation. This system was then extended to all federal government departments in 1965, under the Johnson administration, and the terminology changed from programme budgeting to planning, programming, budgeting (PPB) system.

Nichols (1969, p. 12) views PPB as following five processes which accord to the three elements outlined in the previous paragraph. The processes are:

1 The overall objectives and goals of the organisation and of the various agencies and departments within the organisation are formulated. Priorities are determined for the attainment of the goals and objectives.
2 The possible alternative programmes which may be used to fulfil the desired objectives are compared based on the effectiveness of each in achieving the organisational objectives.
3 The total cost of each programme is related to the total benefits that would be derived from the programme to determine the efficiency of the programme.
4 The most effective and efficient programmes are selected, integrated into a comprehensive programme, and implemented.
5 The results of this programme, once initiated, are reviewed and judged on the basis of performance. The purposes of this review are control in the implementation of the programme and procurement of information for future decisions and forecasts.

Each programme cannot, of course, be reviewed each year. But the analytical steps of PPB call for a periodic review of fundamental programme objectives, costs and accomplishments to date. Table 4.2 illustrates the basic division of a programme undertaken by the (mythical) Barchester District Council. The programme is planning and development, and it is the responsibility of the council's planning and development committee. The programme has three basic elements and eleven subdivisions. Each of these headings would then have to be costed.

Table 4.2   Barchester District Council committee: planning and development

Basic programme: planning and development

Overall objective: To shape and co-ordinate the land-uses and the physical redevelopment of BDC; to provide a satisfactory urban environment sustained by adequate economic activity.

Programme	*Sub-Classification*
1 Land-use planning	(a) Development plan
	(b) Development control
	(c) Processing applications and appeals
2 Environmental improvements	(a) Conservation areas
	(b) Environmental improvements areas
	(c) Care of trees
	(d) Grants to historic buildings
	(e) Traffic measures
3 Commercial redevelopment	(a) Industral estates
	(b) Other industrial locations
	(c) Shops and offices

Source: adapted from an original illustration in Nicholson (1973), p.56.)

Culver (1973, p. 185) provides a useful illustration of a trial PPB system with respect to the allocation of expenditure in a police force, although he prefers to call this approach 'output budgeting', a term used in the UK civil service (see below). Figures 4.1 and 4.2 summarize this example, with the former depicting gross expenditure on the police force distributed on a line item/input basis and the latter distributing expenditure according to major programmes on an output basis. Whereas the line item approach bears no relation at all to the activities of the police force it is possible to identify various functions carried out by the police and thereby determine suitable programmes. A list of police functions might include: maintenance of law and order; prevention of crime; detection of criminals; interrogation and prosecution of offenders; road traffic control and so on. On the basis of such objectives major police programmes could be grouped as follows:

1 Protection of persons and property from:

  (a) criminal activities
  (b) traffic hazards
  (c) miscellaneous hazards.

2 Treatment of offenders:

  (a) detection and apprehension
  (b) process and trial
  (c) training.

One problem highlighted in figure 4.2 is that it may not always be possible to allocate all of the costs meaningfully to a category.

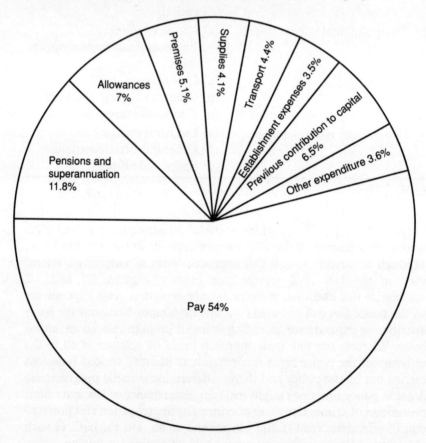

Figure 4.1 Gross expenditure on police force distributed by conventional budget categories

Source: adapted from Culyer: (1973), p. 186

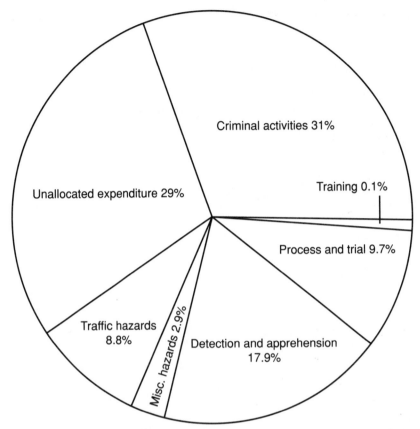

Figure 4.2 Output budget for police force
Source: adapted from Culyer (1973), p. 186

Figure 4.2 is based on work in the Home Office, but 29 per cent is left unallocated. Culyer (1973) suggested a possible compromise in order to allocate all inputs; that is, to allocate in terms of activities rather than in terms of the end product of those activities. Such an approach involves less intensive data collection and generally conforms to the managerial form of the organization (see figure 4.3). This approach, though, has little merit since a genuine PPB system should, in theory, identify competing or complementary activities that are designed explicitly to cut across traditional organizational lines. The emphasis should be on objectives, programmes and programme elements, all stated in output terms.

The US National Association of Accountants (1981, p. 66) cites the following advantages of using a PPB system. A PPB system:

1 provides a framework of accountability;

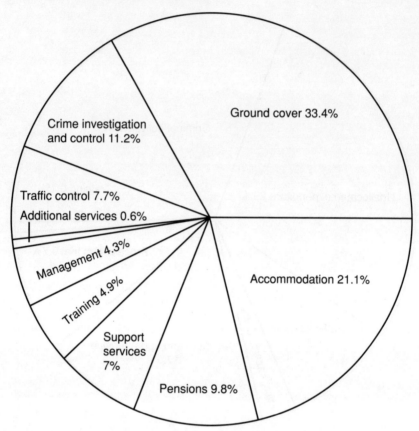

Figure 4.3   Programme budget for police force
Source: adapted from Culyer: (1973), p. 186

2 provides opportunity for long-range planning;
3 promotes an optimization of resources;
4 assists in acquiring government funds;
5 provides opportunities to the programme staff to give their inputs in the decisionmaking process;
6 compels organizational selfstudy and analysis.
7 promotes rational decisions.

The implementation of PPB failed to deliver the reforms that it promised. In part this was due to the haste in which the system was introduced. President Johnson announced the general introduction of PPB into all federal agencies on 25 August 1965 This was followed some nine weeks later, in October, by a timetable for implementation, issued by the Bureau of the Budget. This timetable allowed only 19 days for agencies to agree to a tentative list of programme categories with the Bureau. Agencies then had to develop procedures for the implementation of PPB by the end of December 1965 By 1 April 1966 agencies were expected to have developed a comprehensive, multi-year programme and financial plan. Thus PPB was adopted on a totally unrealistic time-scale of some five and a half months from the date of the original instructions. Wildavsky (1969) supports this view by pointing out that it took the Rand Corporation over five years to develop the pilot system adopted in the US Department of Defense. Other difficulties were also encountered. There was a lack of suitably qualified staff to implement the system and it became costly and timeconsuming to implement. The development of programme structures was seen as an additional administrative responsibility rather than a substitute for previous ones. Difficulty was also encountered in adequately defining programmes. What had seemed practicable in the US Defense Department proved illusive in many of the other civil agencies. In some areas, such as social policy, it was not always possible to develop meaningful output measures. As illustrated in figure 4.2, it was also not always possible to relate fully all input costs to programmes. While the practical impact of PPB can best be described as marginal, it has provided an important contribution in terms of new ideas for the potentiality of a system of output budgeting.

PPB was all but abandoned by the incoming Nixon administration and in 1973 the US government adopted a system of management by objectives (MBO). This was another system adopted from the private sector and was essentially one in which objectives were specified and quantified, potential conflicts identified, and opportunities provided to management to monitor progress and to evaluate results. Whereas the emphasis of PPB could be thought of as being economic and financial, the emphasis of MBO was managerial. Only in the US Department of Defense does PPB continue to be applied with any great degree of success. Puritano and Korb (1981) report the directions of the Secretary of Defense to improve the effectiveness of the PPB system. They also report the abandonment of zero-base budgeting, which had been added to, rather than integrated with PPB.

Zero-Base Budgeting (ZBB)

Yet another change in the US administration heralded yet another programme budgeting reform: that of ZBB, introduced by President Carter in 1976 following its earlier implementation in his home state of Georgia. (Gordon and Heivilin (1978), however, point out that the origins of ZBB can be traced back at least until 1924). ZBB required government departments and agencies to evaluate all of their programmes and activities anew, at basezero, each and every fiscal year. ZBB involves five basic steps: (1) determination of decision units; (2) development of 'decision packages' that describe each decision unit; (3) ranking decision packages at the operational level of the organization; (4) consolidation of rankings at higher levels within the organization; and (5) allocation of funds.

A decision unit could be a project or a cost centre, though Herzlinger (1979, p. 3) narrows this definition to 'an organizational entity that has an identifiable manager with the necessary authority to establish priorities and prepare budgets for all activities within the unit'. A 'decision package' is jargon for the documentation (typically a proforma) that is used to describe a decision unit and its cost of operation. Typically, the manager will have to provide information on the activity to be undertaken, any possible alternative strategies, and the advantages and consequences of nonfunding. An example of the type of information required is shown as table 4.3 It is an important part of the philosophy of ZBB that all possible alternative strategies are presented. Depending upon the decision unit being assessed, alternatives can be either mutually exclusive to the strategy proposed or else a preferred level of activity compared with alternative levels of service provision. Once each set of packages are prepared they are ranked in descending order of importance; that is, the more important the package the higher the ranking. Once this ranking process has taken place, respective managers sends their ranked packages to their superiors and so the process continues upwards through the hierarchy of the organization. Finally, at departmental or agency level, the funds are allocated. Figure 4.4 summarizes this process.

Unlike incremental/line-item budgeting, ZBB does not automatically assume that existing programmes will continue in succeeding years. The status quo is ignored and all existing and proposed activities must be presented anew each year. Gordon and Heivilin (1978, p. 59) summarized this approach as 'an analytical or rational economic approach, as opposed to a political process'. It is a process that forces line management to consider their operational priorities and also allows for decentralized decisionmaking.

Despite the fact that ZBB was adopted by the majority of federal government agencies, it was quickly amended because it too, like PPB, proved almost unworkable in practice. In fact, since President Reagan came to office in 1981 the system itself has remained in virtual limbo. Why was this so? Once again the rhetoric failed to produce tangible

Table 4.3   Example of decision package

Department: Division:	Prepared by: Approved by:	Date prepared: level of rank:	
Objective:	Resources/costs required	Current year	Budget year
Activity description:	Personnel number Personnel Internal costs External costs Costs Total	$ $ $ $	

Alternatives:

Advantages/benefits:

Consequences of not funding:

Source: Pattillo and Mimmier (1977), p. 21

results. ZBB in its pure form created a paper mountain that greatly increased the workload of line management. Many of the benefits of programmes, or decision units, were unable to be quantified so that the ranking process could not always take place.

Letzkus (1980) and Anthony (1977) both criticize ZBB. Letzkus (1980, p. 181) states that 'it appears that the concept of ZBB has been oversold. Although not without its unique merits, ZBB does not differ that greatly from the illfated PPB experiments'. He points out that, for the financial year 1981, only one quarter of the US federal budget could be regarded as controllable. The majority of the budget consisted of relatively uncontrollable expenditure; uncontrollable in the sense of outlays for entitlement programmes, such as social security and unemployment benefits, and outlays that arose from previous electoral obligations. In many cases it proved unrealistic to cast aside previously initiated electoral promises.

Anthony (1977, p. 9) was quite adamant in his criticism of ZBB when he stated: 'The new parts are not good, and the good parts are not new. . . zerobase budgeting is a fraud.' In a short, but pithy, article Anthony (1977) reviewed the application of ZBB in the state of

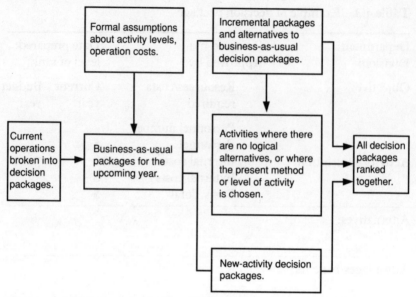

Figure 4.4 Zero-base budgeting: formulation of decision packages at the lowest operational level, or cost centre.

Note: Business-as-usual packages present operations in terms of the next financial year's costs.

Source: Reprinted by permission of the *Harvard Business Review.* An exhibit from "Zerobase Budgeting" by Peter A. Phyrr (Nov–Dec. 1970). Copyright © 1970 by the President and Fellows of Harvard College; all rights reserved.

Georgia, the home state of President Carter and the original public sector pilot scheme for this approach to budgeting. One previously stated problem with ZBB was that of the paper mountain it created. In Georgia there were over 11,000 decision packages. 'If the Governor set aside four hours every day for two months he could spend a minute on each decision package, not enough time to read it, let alone make an analysis of its merits' (Anthony, 1977, p. 19). In fact before the first year of this trial was completed, some 80 per cent of decision packages were approved almost automatically and resources were directed at the remaining 20 per cent of packages. More recently, many states have enacted 'sunset legislation', whereby all departments and programmes are subject to an in-depth review on a rolling-programme basis. For example, a department may be subject to a base-zero review every five years, while another department may be subject to review every three years. The social services of Kent County Council can be cited as an example of a local authority which has adapted the key elements of ZBB so that key programmes are reviewed not annually but on a five yearly cycle.

Politics and Budgeting

The initial claims made on behalf of PPB and ZBB failed to materialize. In principle both systems have merit. Indeed, they both have certain similarities. Table 4.4 summarizes the comparative features of PPB and ZBB. Both systems were termed revolutionary in that they were both expected to radically influence the financial decision-making of government. Both systems stressed the need for an analysis of objectives and outputs. Both systems called for increased management participation; while with PPB the approach was top-down, with ZBB the approach was bottom-up; whereas PPB stressed horizontal equity, ZBB stressed vertical equity. Brief descriptions of each system have been provided, together with some of the criticisms of their practicality. Despite their demise valuable lessons can be learned. The basic problem with budgetary reform is that it not only requires administrative reform, but also strong political support.

Table 4.4 A comparison of PPBS and ZBB characteristics

Characteristics	PPB	ZBB
Annual zero-base review of all ongoing programmes		×
Annual zero-base review of selected ongoing programmes	×	
Annual zero-base review of all new programmes	×	×
Priority ranking for all programmes/activities		×
Developed as a counter to incremental budgeting	×	×
Programme-orientated	×	×
Consideration of incremental changes in costs and benefits	×	×
Benefits quantified	×	×
Planning function stressed	×	×
Identified and examination of goals and objectives in each major area of activity	×	×
Analysis of programmes in terms of objectives	×	×
Measurement of total, long-range costs	×	×
Foundation of long-range objectives	×	×
Analyses of alternative methods of accomplishing objectives	×	×
Costs compared to benefits	×	×

Source: Letzkus (1980), p. 187

Writers such as Schick (1969) and Wildavsky (1964) view politicians as examining budgets from their individual perspective positions. That is, budgeting is a process that finances existing commitments or new commitments (or increments). Politicians are deemed to have a bias for stability and continuity. To change to a process of programme budgeting might imply the unwelcome potential for larger annual budget shifts in priority than might be derived from the traditional line-item budget process. Schick (1969, p. 138) terms the traditional budgetary process a strategy that accommodates 'process politics' and 'process budgeting'. It is a process whereby scarce resources are allocated among competing powers and claimants. Process politics and budgeting tends to favour departments, agencies and other groups. By contrast 'systems budgeting', as with some forms of programme budgeting, considers the allocation of funds as necessary to attain future objectives. For such a system to work, it is argued that 'systems politics' is required. For systems politics to work, politicians need to take a relatively holistic view of objectives compared to the partisan view associated with process politics.

Wildavsky (1964, p. 127) is very critical of budget reformers, typically accountants, economists or systems analysts who fail to consider the political consequences of their reforms. He states:

> There is little or no realization amongst reformers, however, that any effective change in budgetary relationships must necessarily alter the outcomes of the budgetary process. . . proposed reforms inevitably contain important implications for the system; that is, for the 'who gets what' of government decisions.

The present line-item budgeting system is not an economic system but a political one biased towards the government of the day. Politicians, once in government, tend to favour a budgetary system based on legal checks and balances, rather than one that is non-partisan and consists of social checks and balances. The process approach offers a convenient escape from difficult value questions. A systems approach to budgeting that focuses on the outcomes and objectives of government policy cannot avoid controversy. Politicians tend to support the traditional approach to budgeting. They take the distribution of resources as Pareto optimal because they have arisen out of a group barter system at cabinet and departmental level. It is politicians who tend to determine and legislate for policy objectives. Objectives, for example in the area of educational policy, are often multi-purpose and disagreements constantly arise as to what these objectives are or should be. Approaches such as PPB and ZBB place a heavy emphasis on quantitative measures of output which are then translated into financial consequences. The traditional line item approach to budgeting, is, in this respect, expedient since it can easily accommodate a myriad of views as to what the objectives should be.

Budgetary Reform in the United Kingdom

Programme budgeting in the UK has generally followed a very different path from that of the US. In part this reflects the political and constitutional environment in which our government operates. Bridgeman (1973, p. 89) offers three distinctions:

> First, while parliament has to vote the annual Estimates, the party system in the House of Commons is such that it is virtually unknown for Parliament to amend the Estimates put to it by the government. That is not to say that Parliament does not have a significant influence on the pattern of public expenditure, but it is exercised in various indirect ways at the formative stage of determining the pattern of public expenditure, and not through variations in the government's proposals once they have been laid before the House. Second, successive governments since World War II have used taxation and public expenditure as instruments in their management of the level of demand in the economy. Finally, central government has sufficient influence over expenditure by local government. . . that it can realistically plan for the total of central and local government expenditure and not just for its own expenditure.

While in more recent years central government's efforts at budgetary reform have centred around the Public Expenditure Survey Committee (PESC), there were efforts in the 1960s to adopt the PPB system of budgetary control. Two of the more widely reported exercises, in addition to the police illustration referred to earlier, concerned the Ministries of Defence (1964) and Education and Science (1970). In the Ministry of Defence, the programme was known as the functional costing system and was closely modelled on the programme structure then in use by the Pentagon. Fifteen main programmes were developed and these were divided into over 600 sub-elements. The main programmes were (Bridgeman, 1973, p. 92):

Nuclear Strategic Forces
European Ground Forces
General Purpose Combat Forces: Army
General Purpose Combat Forces: Navy
General Purpose Combat Forces: Air Force
Air Mobility
Reserve and Auxiliary Formations
Research and Development
Training
Production
Repairs and Associated Research Facilities in the United Kingdom
Contingencies
Other Support Functions
Miscellaneous Expenditure and Receipts
Special Materials

The development of this system was complemented by the development of analytical techniques for evaluating weapon systems and other alternative defence strategies. For this purpose the Defence Operational Analysis Establishment was formed, thereby bringing together specialist staff from the three service departments. This (since revised) version of PPB is used purely inhouse. The annual estimates are presented on an input, lineitem basis with some brief analysis of programmes in the accompanying white paper.

The sheer growth of central and local government spending on education in the 1960s caused the Department of Education and Science to investigate the possible adoption of programme budgeting. The programme structure for education was published in *Output budgeting for the Department of Education and Science* (Department of Education and Science, 1970). A two dimensional structure was proposed that analysed programmes according to: (1) the groups for whom education is provided; and (2) different factors affecting changes in resource allocation. Once again the results of this exercise remained inhouse. CIPFA (1977b) provides further illustrations of local authority efforts to adopt PPB.

Programme budgeting was never formally introduced by the government. Instead, when budgetary reform took place it took the form of a three tier decision making unit. Its elements were: the Public Expenditure Survey Committee (PESC); the development of programme analysis and review (PAR) and the creation of the Central Policy Review Staff (CPRS). This development was effected by a government white paper, *The Reorganisation of Central Government* (Cmnd.4506) issued in October 1970 PESC, PAR and CPRS were seen as basically administrative procedures for facilitating political decisionmaking and subsequent managerial control of implementation. In the words of Cmnd.4506 (p. 3):

> The administration has pledged itself to introduce a new style of government. More is involved than bringing forward new policies and programmes: it means. . . improving the efficiency of the machinery intended to achieve the aims it sets itself. . .

> The review of government functions and organizations which has been carried out. . . is intended to lay the necessary foundations. The aims in that review have been:

> (i) To improve the quality of policy formulation and decision-taking in government by presenting ministers, collectively in Cabinet and individually within their departments, with well defined options, costed where possible, and relating the choice between options to the contribution they can make to meeting national needs. This is not confined to new policies and new decisions, but implies also the continuing examination, on a systematic and critical basis of existing activities of government.

> (ii) To improve the framework within which public policy is formulated by matching the field of responsibility of government departments to coherent fields of policy and administration.

> (iii) To ensure that the government machine responds and adapts itself to new policies and programmes as they emerge, within the broad framework of the main departmental fields of responsibility.

The need to undertake expenditure forecasts was recognized by the Plowden Committee Report (1961) *Control of Public Expenditure* (Cmnd.1432). The Plowden Committee took the view that the efficiency and management of public services, as well as the evaluation of ongoing and new policies, could be greatly improved. As Premchaud (1983, p. 207) states: 'the responsibility for decisions on the totality of public expenditure was divided between central or local governments and nationalised industries'. There were a large number of decision-makers, whose concerns were not always properly captured by the budget coverage and the budgetary process. The government supported the Plowden Committee's recommendations and the new system came to be known as the Public Expenditure Survey Committee (PESC). PESC is chaired by a deputy secretary of the Treasury, and its three-year forecasts are published twice a year, under schedule 5 of the 1975 Industry Act. PESC does not embody detailed analysis of policy operations; its purpose is primarily for macro-economic planning. For each year of the forecast the previous year's level of service is taken as the base; that is then modified by additions representing new policies and subtractions reflecting the closure of activities that have already been agreed to during the year. Proposals over and above the levels so indicated constitute new policy proposals. This process implies that forecasts effectively became the annual budgets. Since 1982–3 cash planning has replaced the previous system of constant prices. The change to cash planning arose, in part, because estimates in constant prices implied that cash had to be provided, regardless of the rise in prices, in order to maintain the agreed levels of services in real terms. In a time of rising inflation this had the potential of depriving the government of control over cash expenditure. The advantages of cash planning as perceived by the present government, are set out in chapter 7.

PESC is an important instrument of demand management and financial control, but as the 1970 white paper (Cmnd.4506, p. 14) pointed out:

> There are two important respects in which it [PESC] does not provide all the information that is needed. . . It does not call for explicit statements of the objectives of expenditure in a way that would enable a Minister's plans to be tested against general government strategy: nor can it regularly embody detailed analysis of existing programmes and of major policy options on them. Much work has been undertaken in special *ad hoc* policy reviews and in long-term studies, but it has become increasingly clear that the public expenditure survey system should be further strengthened.

These deficiencies were to be remedied by PAR, which was established to examine individual programmes in detail. Each autumn, collective ministerial choices of about a dozen topics for PAR studies were to be made in co-operation with the CPRS. In the main, these decisions arose out of interests raised in the annual PESC review cycle. The responsibility for preparing a particular PAR report rested with the particular department, the Treasury, the CPRS, and any other affected government departments. The first meeting was usually convened by the Treasury in order to discuss the general scope of the study; thereafter the work of the report was prepared by the particular department concerned, and submitted to the appropriate Cabinet committee. PAR reports, as with so many other government reports, are classified and are not available to anyone except a small number of ministers and senior civil servants. In the January 1972 hearings of the Select Committee on Expenditure of the House of Commons, repeated requests made by Members of Parliament for a list of the programmes subject to analysis and for copies of the reports so far prepared were denied. The objectives of PAR were rather too ambitious, for essentially they sought to review the major policies of government. Ministers proved reluctant to side with the Treasury in an attack on other ministers' programmes. Departments tended to volunteer for study either their strongest programmes or ones that were politically sensitive, the ploy being to protect their more vulnerable programmes (see Heald (1983, pp. 186–9)). While it was a Conservative government, under Edward Heath, that initiated the PAR review mechanism, it was the 1979 Conservative administration, under Margaret Thatcher, that formally abandoned PAR and instituted an alternative strategy of 'scrutinies' under the (then) direction of Sir (later Lord) Derek Rayner – see chapter 7.

The third administrative procedure established by the 1970 white paper was the establishment of the CPRS, a small multidisciplinary unit which remains as part of the Cabinet Office. Its role is to assist ministers and the Cabinet to:

> take better policy decisions by assisting them to work out the implications of their basic strategy in terms of policies in specific areas, to establish the relative priorities to be given to the different sectors of their programme as a whole, to identify those areas of policy in which new choices can be exercised and to ensure that the underlying implications of alternative courses of action are fully analysed and considered. (Cmnd.4506, pp. 13–14.)

The major role of the CPRS is to overview the totality of government policies; its members initiate inter-departmental studies and are closely involved with the work of PESC.

Conclusion

The Plowden Committee Report (1961, Cmnd.1432) was the main influence that led to the development of the PESC system of forward planning. It is a system that remains influential but, at the same time, it is one that has caused much controversy, with resultant strains in relationships between the Treasury and central government departments, and between central and local government. In the latter case, by including local government expenditure within the public expenditure totals, it effectively means that Cabinet makes decisions without reference to local authorities. This strain in central-local government relationships has been further hardened by the imposition of charge-capping and other fiscal controls that are designed to keep local authorities within central government's expenditure plans.

PESC is clearly an improvement on the system that existed in the 1950s, but it has defects. While it provides invaluable information about the resources used in public sector programmes, it says little about the output that is expected. While the public sector pay explosion in the mid-1970s led to the demise of volume planning, the imposition of cash planning has proven a blunt instrument. Both Else and Marshal (1981) and Likierman (1981) point out that the imposition of cash limits has structurally altered the entire PESC system. The volume of government activity has therefore become a passive residual in a planning cycle that has been reduced from five to three years.

The UK remains exceptionally centralized in its fiscal affairs, with the Treasury and its ministers opposed to all changes which would release its grip (Heald, 1983, p. 203).

The dominance of the Treasury in the determination of public sector spending priorities looks set to continue until better management information systems are available for the civil service. Various management techniques have been introduced and then abandoned. Among these were PPB, which survived in two departments until the mid 1970s, PAR and MBO, which flourished in a few pilot studies. Chapter 7 briefly reviews the developments instituted in the 1980s.

5

Investment Appraisal

Introduction

Although in recent years total government capital spending has been of
the order of £20 billion per annum, Brown and Jackson (1983, p. 138)
point out that this represents a real reduction of approximately one half
over the past 20 years. Stabilized at 1970 prices, they calculated public
sector capital expenditure at 5.1 per cent of GNP in 1966 but only 3.0
per cent of GNP in 1980. While total public expenditure on goods and
services (at 1970 prices) as a share of GNP has remained relatively
stable, this reduction in capital expenditure has been necessary in
order to offset rises in current expenditure. Nevertheless, the sheer
magnitude of public investment should still demand that appropriate
appraisal techniques are adopted. The reality is that only until
relatively recently have appropriate techniques been more generally
adopted throughout the public sector.

This chapter is in three sections. The first section reviews the major
methods of capital project appraisal currently used by private sector
companies. It concludes that the most appropriate method is one that
considers future discounted cash flows – the net present value
technique – and argues that this is also the most appropriate technique
for the public sector. In the second section there is discussion as to
what is an appropriate discount rate for this technique. Finally, we
consider cost-benefit analysis because often the costs and benefits of
many public sector projects are not directly quantifiable in monetary
terms. While the consideration of, say, what is an appropriate
replacement bus is relatively straightforward, the benefits of a new
motorway scheme are far less easy to evaluate.

Techniques of Investment Appraisal

In the private sector productive opportunities are undertaken in order to enhance the wealth of investors, principally the equity investors. The techniques used to evaluate these opportunities can be classified under two headings: traditional methods of investment appraisal and discounted cash flow (DCF) methods of investment appraisal. The academic literature has long advocated the use of DCF evaluations. Kennedy and Sugden (1986, p. 34) refer to seven recent surveys carried out in Britain and the USA that 'confirmed an ever-increasing acceptance of these techniques by businesses, so that utilisation rates of more than 75 per cent amongst the surveyed firms are commonplace'. Only brief attention will be given to traditional methods of appraisal as they have little to offer to either the public or private sector.

The two most commonly referred to traditional techniques are the accounting rate of return on capital employed (ROCE) and the payback period. Numerous definitions of ROCE can be devised but essentially it can be defined as:

$$\frac{\text{Some measure of accounting profit/surplus}}{\text{Some corresponding measure of capital employed}}$$

The numerator in this calculation is taken from an organization's profit and loss account or income and expenditure account while the denominator is taken from the organization's balance sheet. The most commonly used measure for assessing overall performance in the private sector is to divide profit before the deduction of interest and a provision for taxation by capital employed, defined as share capital plus longterm debt.

The problems with ROCE are two-fold. First, the figures used are based on accruals accounting concepts and include noncash items such as depreciation and a provision for bad debts. Second, ROCE measures are single period and take no account of the time value of money. This latter point is particularly important since the further into the future the benefits of projects are deferred the less they are worth in today's values. Basic microeconomic theory suggests that investors will forgo present consumption and invest (cash) in the expectation of a future higher return (initial cash outlay plus dividends or interest) that will provide for greater future consumption. The foundations of this theory have long been established, see for example Hirschleifer (1958).

The payback period is a simple concept which, though dealing with cash flows, is principally flawed by the fact that it too disregards the time value of money. Consider, for example, the choice between two mutually exclusive investments, A and B, both of which involve an investment outlay of £50,000. As shown in table 5 .1, Project A has a payback period of two years as opposed to Project B's 2⅔ years payback period. However, an inspection of both projects' cash flows might cause most readers to query this preference since the total cash inflows of Project B exceed those of Project A by £20,000. Two defects are found with the payback technique. First, no account is taken of cash flows arising after the payback date. Second, the cash flows are not presented in present value terms (that is, future cash flows re-expressed in today's value). Project B remits larger cash inflows spread over a five-year period as opposed to the three years of cash inflows from Project A. Discounted cash flows would provide a rational basis for comparing these two projects on an equitable basis.

Table 5.1   The payback period

	Project A (£000)	Project B (£000)
t_0	−50	−50
t_1	+25	+20
t_2	+25	+20
t_3	+10	+15
t_4	−	+15
t_5	−	+10
Payback period	2 years	$2^{2/3}$ years

All cash flows are assumed to occur at the end of each time period of 12 months, except 't_0' which denotes a cash outflow at the beginning of the project.

Negative (−) signs denote estimated net investment of funds and positive (+) signs denote estimated net cash inflows from an investment.

The two commonly used methods of DCF investment appraisal are the net present value (NPV) approach and the internal rate of return (IRR) approach. The NPV approach discounts future cash flows by use of an imputed discount factor which should reflect the opportunity cost of capital. Future cash flows are thereby expressed in present value (today's) terms. The initial investment outlay is deducted from the sum of these present value cash flows to produce the NPV of a project; the decision rule is that all projects yielding a positive NPV should be accepted and all projects yielding a negative NPV should be rejected. In theory, with a certain knowledge of future events and a perfect capital market, it should be possible for a firm to borrow sufficient funds to finance all those projects that meet this acceptance criterion. In practice, we live in an uncertain environment where future events cannot be predicted with certainty and capital markets are far from perfect. It is not possible to deal at length with all of these problems in this single chapter. Specialist textbooks, such as Lumby (1984) and Collier, Cooke and Glynn (1987), provide further analysis of these problems.

Let us continue by reconsidering our two mutually exclusive projects, A and B, and assume that 10 per cent represents a fair assessment of the opportunity cost of capital. In such circumstances a firm with surplus funds would have three investment opportunities: Project A, Project B or investing £50,000 on the capital market to earn compound interest at 10 per cent per annum. (A more technical discussion on the topic of a suitable discount factor is deferred until the next section of this chapter.)

Table 5.2 summarizes the necessary calculations for these three options. If the firm were simply to invest £50,000 on the capital market it would only produce a zero NPV. By contrast both productive opportunities yield positive NPVs; that is, they provide a return to investors over and above that offered by the capital market. As these projects are mutually exclusive only one can be chosen, and therefore Project B is the preferred option as it has a positive NPV of £12,430, which is 14 times greater than the return earned by Project A.

The second commonly used method of DCF appraisal is the IRR approach. The IRR can be defined as that rate which discounts future cash flows to produce a NPV of zero. In other words, it is the rate that equates future net cash flows to the initial investment outlay. The acceptance criterion for this method is that, to be approved, a project's IRR should be greater than the opportunity cost of capital. The IRR can be approximated by linear interpolation. The approach is to choose two discount rates to apply to a project, so that one produces a positive NPV and the other a negative NPV. Discounting Project A by 8 per cent and 14 per cent produces this result: whereby an 8 per cent discount factor produces a negative NPV of £2,025 and a 14 per cent discount factor produces a positive NPV of £2,515. We can therefore approximate the IRR for Project A as follows:

$$0.08 + \frac{£2,515}{£2,515 + £2,025}(0.14 - 0.08) = 0.11, \text{ or } 11 \text{ per cent}$$

Table 5.2 DCF investment appraisal – the net present value approach

	Cash flows (£000)				Present values (£000)			
				10%				
Project A	Project B	Capital market	DCF	Project A	Project B		Capital market	
							3 years	5 years
t_0 −50	−50	–	1.000	–	–		–	−5
t_1 +25	+20	–	0.909	+22.73	+18.18		–	–
t_2 +25	+20	–	0.826	+20.65	+16.52		–	–
t_3 +10	+15	+66.55	0.751	+7.51	+11.27		+50	–
t_4 –	+15	or	0.683	–	+10.25		–	–
t_5 –	+10	+80.53	0.621	–	+6.21		–	+50
			NPV	(£)0.89	12.43		0	0

Discounted cash flow (DCF) factors at 10 per cent are calculated as follows:

$$\frac{1}{(1.10)} \quad \frac{1}{(1.10)} \quad \frac{1}{(1.10)} \quad \frac{1}{(1.10)} \quad \frac{1}{(1.10)}$$
$$= 0.909 \quad 0.826 \quad 0.751 \quad 0.683 \quad 0.621$$

For ease of presentation all present values have been rounded off to two places of decimals. Note that, with respect to investment on the capital market, two scenarios are considered: an investment of three years and an investment of five years. In either case, as the opportunity cost of capital is 10 per cent, both investments return a zero NPV.

By similar analysis the IRR for Project B can be calculated to be 20.5 per cent. Readers can confirm these results by selecting suitable discount rates from the table provided in appendix 5 .1 As Project B's IRR is almost double that of Project A it is once again the preferred option.

While in practice the IRR is a commonly used method and usually gives the same answer as the NPV method, it can be criticized on both practical and theoretical grounds. As Bromwich (1976, p. 87) states: 'knowledge of a project's internal rate of return is neither necessary nor sufficient for optimal investment decisions'. On its own the IRR of a project gives no information about either a project's present value or the effect of its acceptance on the value of the firm. Whereas the NPV provides an absolute value the IRR does not. On occasions the NPV and IRR methods can provide conflicting advice. Consider the position of two further mutually exclusive projects, C and D (see table 5.3).

Table 5.3   NPV calculations on two projects (with DCF 10 percent)

	Project C	Project D
t_0	−£20,000	−£30,000
t_2	+£24,000	+£35,000
IRR	20 per cent	18 per cent
NPV	+£1,818	+£2,179

While, under the IRR acceptance rule, we would accept Project C and the incremental project (D minus C), the same rule rejects the sum of the two projects, Project D. The incremental project is accepted because its IRR of 14 per cent is greater than the opportunity cost of capital of 10 per cent. Readers can check this result by subtracting Project C's cash flows from Project D's cash flows and solving for the IRR as outlined in the previous paragraph. If the incremental project can be accepted then the logical conclusion is to accept Project D in the first instance. By *automatically* examining and comparing the incremental cash flows against the cost of capital, the NPV method ensures that the firm will reach the optimal level of investment.

In contrasting the NPV rule with the IRR approach it is interesting to examine the *implicit* assumptions made by both regarding the reinvestment of interim cash flows, remembering that the technique of discounting is simply that of compound interest in reverse. Rather than saying that £100 invested today at an annual rate of 10 per cent will yield £110 in 12 months' time, we say that £110 due in 12 months' time has a present value of £100 today. The annual rate of 10 per cent is assumed to represent the investor's time preference for money. The IRR method implicitly assumes that a project's annual cash flows can be reinvested at the project's internal rate of return; the NPV method assumes that the cash flows can be reinvested at the firm's opportunity cost of capital. It is probably highly unlikely that a firm which earns, say, 20 per cent from one productive opportunity can earn the same return from all other productive opportunities.

Often there are projects whose cash flows do not follow the conventional pattern of an initial net outflow followed by a series of net cash inflows. For example, it could be that after initial investment has taken place further capital investment may be required in a subsequent period which, in that year, is greater than the firm's net trading cash inflows. Alternatively, it might be that a negative cash flow occurs at the end of the project's life cycle. This could occur if the project concerned an extractive industry and it was a condition of the contract that the site be landscaped upon completion. Simply expressed, every time there is a change in cash flow sign, from positive to negative or vice versa, calculation by the IRR method produces an additional solution. Bromwich (1976, p. 103) provides an example whose series of cash flows are: − £1,000; £2,550; − £1,575. Two IRR solutions are possible, 5 per cent and 50 per cent. Therefore, where multiple rates of return exist there would appear to be no mathematical or economic grounds for preferring one rate to another.

In summary, therefore, different solutions are more likely to arise between the NPV and IRR methods when one or more of the following conditions exist:

1 There is a significant difference between the initial investments required by each project.
2 There is a significant difference between the pattern of the cash flows system of the various projects (e.g. one project has high cash flow in early years and low cash flows in latter years: while another project has low cash flows in early years and high cash flows in latter years).
3 The projects have unequal lives.

When estimating the cash flows of a proposed capital investment project, the relevant 'opportunity' or 'differential' costs, and not just the direct outlay costs, must be taken into consideration. Costs that are not relevant to the appraisal are ignored. These include all sunk costs. An opportunity cost can be defined as the cost of the next best opportunity forgone. Two examples should illustrate what we mean by relevant costs. First, consider a firm which has a machine which originally cost £10,000 but has recently been surplus to requirements. Two alternatives are possible, either to sell the machine now for £4,200 or use it in a new project that is currently under evaluation. The original cost is an historical cost and is therefore an irrelevant sunk cost. The cost of using the machine in the project is equal to the worth of the best (and in this case, only) alternative forgone; that is, its current sales price of £4,200. Second, consider a project that uses a particular material. This material was bought a year ago for £750 but is now obsolete and would therefore only fetch a scrap price of £50. However, if not used in this project it could be used in another project as substitute for another material which would cost £225. Using the opportunity cost concept, we consider the alternative. As in the previous example, the historical cost is irrelevant. Two choices exist, either to sell the material for scrap or use it as a substitute. Since the latter represents the greater sacrifice it is therefore the relevant cost if the original project is undertaken.

The rationale behind the use of the NPV approach in the private sector is accepted by government as being exactly analogous to the public sector. This is because, to quote HM Treasury (1984, p. 14), 'jam today is worth jam tomorrow' because, just as in the private sector, 'more weight is given to earlier than to later costs and benefits'. The contentious issues in the public sector are what is the appropriate discount rate to be used and what account should be taken of costs and benefits which cannot be measured directly in money terms.

The Value of the Discount Rate

The calculation of the opportunity cost of capital is a complex topic. We begin this section by providing a brief introduction to its calculation in the private sector, as this complements our discussion in the previous section and is a useful preface to considering what is an appropriate rate for public sector investment opportunities.

In the private sector we will assume, for simplicity, that there are only two sources of funds: equity finance and debt finance. The suppliers of debt finance receive their return by way of fixed interest payments, while those that supply equity funds have claims over the residual funds which remain after all other payments (including interest payments) have been made. Typically equity investors receive annual dividends and they can also sell their shares should they wish to liquidate their investment; the market price of these shares is a reflection of their expected future earnings. The supply of debt finance is less risky than supplying equity finance and so investors will demand a lower rate of return on a firm's debt securities than on its equity securities. Additionally, the cost of debt finance is made even cheaper because debt interest payments are a tax-deductible expense. The overall cost of capital for a firm is the weighted average cost of these two sources of finance and is calculated as follows:

$$k_o = k_e. (E/V) + k_d. (1 - t_c). (D/V) \tag{1}$$

where:

k_o = the firm's overall cost of capital
k_o = the required rate of return on the firm's equity finance
k_d = the required rate of return on the firm's debt finance
t_c = the corporate tax rate
E = the market value of the firm's equity securities
D = the market value of the firm's debt securities
$V = E + D$ = the total market value of the firm.

The cost of each source of funds is a function of three components:

1 *The time preference rate:* this is the rate of return investors would require from a riskless investment when no changes in future prices are expected. Economists would describe this rate as that required in order to forgo current consumption.
2 *The expected rate of inflation:* the higher the rate of inflation, the lower is the real value of the expected future returns and hence the higher the rate of return investors will require.
3 *The riskiness of the investment:* investors are assumed to be risk-averse and therefore the required rate of return they require will increase with the perceived riskiness of an investment.

The appropriate values of the cost of equity and debt finance are the current required returns from these securities as they represent the opportunity cost of utilizing such funds. The current overall return, or weighted average cost of capital, is equal to the discount rate used in the evaluation of the firm's projects.

The cost of debt funds (k_d) can be calculated as follows:

$$D_o = \sum_{t=1}^{n} \frac{I_t}{(1 + k_d)} + \frac{P_n}{(1 + k_d)^n} \tag{2}$$

where:

D_o = current market value of the firm's debt securities
I_t = total interest payments in period t
P_n = total principal repayment in period n
n   = number of periods to the maturity of the debt securities.

As previously stated, the sole returns to the equity investors are dividend payments (unless otherwise sold in the market), as these securities are assumed to have an infinite life and so have no maturity value. Dividend payments are not fixed, and they are much more difficult to estimate as they depend on the overall performance of the firm. The cost of equity finance (k_e) can be calculated as follows:

$$E_o = \sum_{t=1}^{\infty} \frac{DIV_t}{(1 + k_e)} \tag{3}$$

where:

E_o = current market value of the firm's equities
DIV_t = total dividend payments in period t.

There are numerous assumptions that can be made about the pattern of expected future dividends. Perhaps the most quoted model (Gordon, 1959) is one that assumes that dividends will grow in the future at a constant annual rate, g. Given this assumption, the cost of equity finance can be calculated as follows:

$$k_e = \frac{DIV_1}{E_o} + g \tag{4}$$

To illustrate the use of the above formula, consider the position of a private sector firm financed solely by debentures and equity shares. The debentures have a face value of £1.5 million, an annual interest rate of 10 per cent, mature in five years' time and are currently selling at their face value. Using equation (2), the cost of debt finance can be calculated as follows:

$$£1.5m = \frac{£150,000}{(1+k_d)} + \frac{£150,000}{(1+k_d)^2} + \frac{£150,000}{(1+k_d)^3} + \frac{£150,000}{(1+k_d)^4} + \frac{£1,650,000}{(1+k_d)^5}$$

k_d = 10 per cent.

The current market value of the firm's equity finance is £1 million and the firm is expected to pay a perpetual dividend of £120,000 each year (that is, g = 0). This information can be used in equation (3) to calculate the cost of equity finance:

$$\text{£1 million} = \frac{\text{£120,000}}{k_e}, \text{ therefore } k_e = \frac{\text{£120,000}}{\text{£1 million}} = 12 \text{ per cent}$$

Assuming a corporation tax rate of 40 per cent, we now have all the information to use equation (1) to calculate the firm's cost of capital:

$$k_o = 12.\,(1/2.5) + 10.\,(1.0 - 0.40).\,(1.5/2.5) = 8.4 \text{ per cent}$$

This is the appropriate cost of capital for this firm providing that it is only considering further investments that have the same risk characteristics as those previously evaluated, and that its gearing (that is, the ratio of debt to equity) is not expected to change in the foreseeable future. Where these conditions are not met, the calculation of the cost of capital becomes much more difficult. For a detailed discussion on the impact of project evaluation see Collier, Cooke and Glynn (1987).

Although the operational framework may differ, the opportunity cost of capital is equally relevant to investment decisions in the public sector. The discount rate for use in the public sector is commonly referred to as the test discount rate (TDR). The basic rate for public sector expenditure has been assessed at 5 per cent per year in 'real' terms (see HM Treasury, 1984, p. 14). The background to current government policy in this area is provided by two 1978 publications: a white paper *The Nationalised Industries* (Cmnd. 7131) and a Treasury Working Paper *The Test Discount Rate and the Required Rate of Return on Investment* (Treasury Working Paper No. 9).

The TDR was introduced in the early 1960s as a means of promoting consistent investment appraisal by nationalized industries. Its use subsequently spread to other public sector analyses involving a comparison of costs and benefits over time. The rate is expressed in 'real' terms; that is, it is used to discount costs and benefits expressed in terms of constant prices. Initially the TDR was set at 8 per cent in the mid–1960s and raised to 10 per cent in 1969 The rate was reviewed in 1972 but not changed. In 1978, as stated in the previous paragraph, the TDR was fixed at 5 per cent in real terms (Cmnd. 7131, paragraphs 58–65). As Treasury Working Paper No. 9 states (p. 4):

> The view taken was that in order to get the best allocation of investible resources between public and private industries, the discount rate used in the public sector should be similar to the return which private firms would consider acceptable on new investment. . . it seemed sensible to set a rate for public

enterprises which corresponds broadly with that sought by large private firms of good standing engaged in low-risk business.

Ever since this system was introduced there has been much criticism of the validity of basing the TDR on the profitability of the private sector, especially when used for non-commercial public sector evaluations. Bird, McDonald and McHugh (1982, p. 485) provide a useful summary of the three most commonly suggested discount rates. These are:

1 *The long-term government bond rate*   This is the rate paid by the government in order to acquire finance from sources other than taxation. However, this rate is more a reflection of overall government macroeconomic policy and bears little relationship to the opportunity cost of particular projects.

2 *The social opportunity cost rate*   This is the rate whereby government projects should generate a return at least equal to the private sector projects displayed by the government applying the funds to public sector investment. The argument is that funds should not be diverted to the government sector if they can be put to a more productive use in the private sector. It is this view which is currently accepted by government.

3 *The social time preference rate*   This rate reflects the rate of return required by the community to forgo current consumption for future consumption. It stresses that government projects should only be undertaken which produce a favourable trade, in the collective judgment of the community, of current for future expenditure.

In the absence of market imperfections, approaches (2) and (3) would be equal. However, the existence of market imperfections results in the social opportunity rate exceeding the social time preference rate. This has led authors to suggest that a rate somewhere between these two rates should be utilized – a synthetic rate. Baumol (1965) has suggested that the choice between these two rates is 'indeterminate' in the sense that the institutional barriers and the existence of risk will perpetually inhibit any tendency for the two rates to come into equilibrium. For further discussion on this complex issue see Layard (1972), particularly Part Three. Since the publication of Cmnd. 7131 the discount rates to be used by nationalized industries have not been specified centrally. Each industry, in consultation with its sponsor department, has determined its own discount rate for appraisal purposes, choosing a rate believed to be consistent with earning a 5 per cent required rate of return (RRR) on its investment programme as a whole.

Cost-Benefit Analysis

Just as there is some academic debate as to what discount rate should be used for public sector investment appraisal, there is also much discussion as to what constitute the relevant costs and benefits for certain of these projects. Essentially, this debate concerns those projects which are undertaken by other than the trading organizations within the public sector and which involve broader considerations than simply, for example, the replacement of worn out equipment. As stated in the introduction, while the replacement of a fleet of buses by a transport authority is relatively straightforward, the choice of a new motorway scheme by the Department of Transport is far harder to evaluate. In the former illustration it is assumed that the replacement vehicles will simply provide a similar service to those vehicles presently operated. The need is to consider the economic life cycle of each alternative in order to determine the optimal replacement. It is a consideration that can be limited to the purchase cost of each vehicle together with its pattern of operating costs (see Cooke and Glynn, 1981). In the latter illustration consideration has also to be taken of social costs and benefits. Similar considerations would also be required when attempting to consider the competing demands for investment between government departments, such as between state education and the National Health Service or between public sector housing and defence. The technique that has evolved to assist government in making such decisions is costbenefit analysis (CBA).

Under CBA the decision criterion is that a project should be undertaken providing that the discounted value of the social benefits attributed to the project exceeds the discounted value of the social costs attributed to the project. Social benefits are not solely restricted to cash returns but include any favourable effects that may affect members of the community at large; for example, the time saved in travelling because a hospital is sited at a particular location. Equally, social costs are not restricted to the cash outlays of a project but also include any other undesirable side effects; for example, the siting of a dam will displace land that would otherwise be available to farmers, wildlife, country ramblers and so on. The accountant engaged in a CBA of a project is not, in essence then, asking a different sort of question from that being asked by the accountant of a private firm. Rather, the same sort of question is being asked about a wider group of people – who constitute society – and is being asked more searchingly. Instead of asking whether the owners of the enterprise will become better off as the result of the firm's undertaking productive opportunities, the accountant asks whether society as a whole will become better off by undertaking this project rather than not undertaking it, or by undertaking instead any of a number of alternative projects.

Broadly speaking, for the more precise concept of revenue in the private sector firm the accountant substitutes the less precise, but more meaningful, concept of social opportunity cost – the social value forgone when the resources in question are moved away from alternative economic activities into the specific project. For the profit of the firm, the accountant substitutes the excess benefit over cost, or some related concept used in an investment criterion. Social benefits amount to a potential Pareto improvement. The project under review, to be economically feasible, must be capable of producing an excess of benefits such that everyone in society could, by a costless redistribution of the gains, be made better off.

While the scope and nature of projects submitted to CBA may be clear, complications can arise. Such complications (be they direct or indirect) can be on the supply side or the demand side. As Prest and Turvey (1965, p. 688) state: 'Construction of a fast motorway, which itself speeds up traffic and reduces accidents, may lead to more congestion or more accidents on feeder roads if they are left unimproved.' When considering costs and benefits, therefore, particular attention must be paid to 'externalities' and 'secondary benefits'. Externalities cover a wide range of costs and benefits which accrue to organizations and individuals other than those responsible for sponsoring a particular project. The question that arises is: how far should the project sponsor take these costs and benefits into account? Prest and Turvey (1965) suggest that a distinction could be made between technological and pecuniary spillovers. Promoters of public investment projects should take into account the external effects of their actions in so far as they alter the physical production possibilities of other producers or the satisfaction that consumers get from given resources. They should not take account of sideeffects if the sole effect is via the prices of products or factors. Two examples illustrate these points. First, when the construction of a reservoir upstream necessitates more dredging downstream then this should be included. Second, the greater profitability of restaurants and garages along an upgraded road should not be included, as this is simply a reflection of more journeys undertaken along this route and represents only a transfer of business from other establishments on less popular routes.

With regard to secondary benefits, we need worry about secondary benefits or costs only to the extent that market prices fail to reflect marginal costs and benefits. For example, if an irrigation scheme increases farm production we should only include the costs of the water itself and not take account of any value that arises from increased farm output in terms of costs alone. The reason is that a properly functioning price mechanism performs the function of inputting these values for us. Suppose that only one farm product, potatoes, is produced. The market demand for potatoes is a derived demand, and so reflects the value of additional supplies and the marginal costs of collection, grading and distribution.

A typical CBA might produce the (summarized) results shown in table 5.4.

Table 5.4   Barchester City Council Introduction of a mini-bus service

	Annual costs (£m)
Annual net operating loss	(2.00)
Benefits	
Traffic diverted to new service	
1 Existing buses:	
time	0.60
comfort/convenience	0.80
2 Private motor vehicles:	
time	0.40
cost	0.75
3 Pedestrians:	
time	0.20
Net annual benefit	£0.75

If we assume that these vehicles have an operational life of five years, and that 10 per cent is an agreed discount rate, then this scheme should produce benefits in net present value terms of approximately £2.8 million.

In the illustration in table 5.4 three values have been placed on time spent travelling, a frequent element in many CBA analyses. The project leader has to consider how units of travelling time can be converted into equivalent units of money. One line of approach could be to seek out situations where individuals have to choose between spending money and spending time and then study the choices that they make. Such situations often occur when people make a particular journey between two places by more than one mode of transport. Other things being equal, commuters prefer lower money costs and faster travel. Suppose that, in the illustration above, the new minibus scheme provides a service that on average is one-third faster (previous average journey times being approximately 15 minutes) but costs 10 per cent more (with the present average fare being 30 pence). Anyone who switches from the existing bus service to the new service must therefore value time saved by at least 36 pence per hour saved. By collecting and analysing a large number of observations it is possible to deduce the average value of time savings to people with particular characteristics making particular types of journey.

The valuation of time is a good example of a benefit that can be valued, albeit with some difficulty. However, there are a range of other goods for which no meaningful valuation can be provided. Typically these are pure public goods which can jointly benefit many people and where it is difficult to exclude people from the benefits. Examples include street lighting and pollution control. In some instances the application of CBA becomes impossible. As Layard (1972, p. 29) states:

> since the benefits cannot be valued, it is still useful to compare the costs of providing the same benefit in different ways. This is called *cost effectiveness analysis* and is regularly used in defence, public health and other fields. Apart from not valuing benefits, the procedures are exactly the same as in costbenefit analysis.

Conclusion

Even though expenditure in a particular year may be limited by a cash limit or capital expenditure ceiling, such constraints do not reduce the importance of appraisal. On the contrary, it enhances the importance and technical difficulty of choosing those uses of limited funds which will provide the greatest benefits. In the space of one chapter it is impossible to cover all the detailed aspects of investment appraisal.

Instead the main principles of appraisal have been introduced. In addition to the references already cited readers should refer to Mishan (1971a, b), Sugden and Williams (1978), and Pearce and Nash (1981). All three references provide detailed analysis of the principles of CBA.

Since the 1960s government's major preoccupation has primarily been with the practices of investment appraisal adopted by its trading organizations, principally the nationalized industries. As Lapsley (1986, p. 136) points out:

> This is the most evident from the continuing guidance issued to these industries over many years by the principal government department responsible for financial and related matters, H. M. Treasury. This attracted criticism, on the grounds that investment appraisal should also be undertaken by nontrading organizations.

More recently some of these criticisms have been redressed. The Department of Health, formerly the Department of Health and Social Security (DHSS, 1981, 1982) have, for instance, issued detailed instructions regarding the management of its capital programme, which entails the advocacy of current HM Treasury guidance. Even though various initiatives have been undertaken by way of the provision of guidance, there has been little knowledge of the actual practices employed within the nontrading segments of the public sector. The recent work of Lapsley (1985, 1986) provides as clear an indication as is possible.

Lapsley's (1985, 1986) research involved sending questionnaires to all ten UK water authorities, to 88 local authorities and 68 health authorities. The local authorities surveyed had outstanding debt in excess of £100 million (as a proxy for capital intensity) and the health authorities were those that had (then) recently undertaken major capital projects. Overall, usable responses were received from all the water authorities (100 per cent), 41 local authorities (47 per cent) and 46 health authorities (67 per cent). This provided an overall response rate of 58 per cent. The techniques of investment appraisal adopted by these bodies are summarized in table 5.5 This shows there is increased use of discounting techniques and attempts at CBA. However, it also reveals that there is evidence that some analysts are still using less justifiable approaches such as the accounting rate of return and payback. There is therefore still room for improvement.

Table 5.5   Techniques of options appraisal utilized by non-trading oganizations

| | | No. Respondents[a] | |
| | | --- | --- | --- |
		Water[c] authorities 10	Local authorities 33	Health authorities 31
1	Accounting measures[b]	2	28	7
2	Payback	7	9	9
3	Discounted cash flow	10	19	22
4	Cost-benefit analysis	4	3	12
5	No formal techniques	–	5	6

[a] The number of respondents relates to those replies that were able to reply to this section of the questionnaire. Also note that most respondents gave more than one technique.

[b] This includes revenue account analysis, accountant's rate of return.

[c] Since privatized.

Source: Lapsey (1986), p. 145

Appendix 5.1
Present value table
Present value of 1, i.e. $(1 + r)^{-t}$
where r = discount rate
t = number of perods until payment

Periods	Discount rate (r)									
(t)	*1%*	*2%*	*3%*	*4%*	*5%*	*6%*	*7%*	*8%*	*9%*	*10%*
1	0.990	0.980	0.971	0.962	0.952	0.943	0.935	0.917	0.917	0.909	1
2	0.980	0.961	0.943	0.925	0.907	0.890	0.873	0.857	0.842	0.826	2
3	0.971	0.942	0.915	0.889	0.864	0.840	0.816	0.794	0.772	0.751	3
4	0.961	0.924	0.888	0.855	0.823	0.792	0.763	0.735	0.708	0.683	4
5	0.951	0.906	0.863	0.822	0.784	0.713	0.713	0.681	0.650	0.621	5
6	0.942	0.888	0.837	0.790	0.746	0.705	0.666	0.630	0.596	0.564	6
7	0.933	0.871	0.813	0.760	0.711	0.665	0.623	0.583	0.547	0.513	7
8	0.923	0.853	0.789	0.731	0.677	0.627	0.582	0.540	0.502	0.467	8
9	0.914	0.837	0.766	0.703	0.645	0.592	0.544	0.500	0.460	0.424	9
10	0.905	0.820	0.744	0.676	0.614	0.558	0.508	0.463	0.422	0.386	10
11	0.896	0.804	0.722	0.650	0.585	0.527	0.475	0.429	0.388	0.350	11
12	0.887	0.788	0.701	0.625	0.557	0.497	0.444	0.397	0.356	0.319	12
13	0.879	0.773	0.681	0.601	0.530	0.469	0.415	0.368	0.326	0.290	13
14	0.870	0.758	0.661	0.577	0.505	0.442	0.388	0.340	0.299	0.263	14
15	0.861	0.743	0.642	0.555	0.481	0.417	0.362	0.315	0.275	0.239	15

Appendix 5.1 Continued

Periods					Discount rate (r)					
(t)	11%	12%	13%	14%	15%	16%	17%	18%	19%	20%
1	0.901	0.893	0.855	0.877	0.870	0.862	0.855	0.847	0.840	0.833
2	0.812	0.797	0.783	0.769	0.756	0.743	0.731	0.718	0.706	0.694
3	0.731	0.712	0.693	0.675	0.658	0.641	0.642	0.609	0.593	0.579
4	0.659	0.636	0.613	0.592	0.572	0.552	0.534	0.516	0.499	0.482
5	0.593	0.567	0.543	0.519	0.497	0.456	0.437	0.437	0.419	0.402
6	0.535	0.507	0.480	0.456	0.432	0.410	0.390	0.370	0.352	0.335
7	0.482	0.452	0.425	0.400	0.376	0.354	0.333	0.314	0.295	0.279
8	0.434	0.404	0.376	0.351	0.327	0.305	0.285	0.266	0.249	0.233
9	0.391	0.361	0.333	0.308	0.284	0.263	0.243	0.225	0.209	0.194
10	0.352	0.322	0.295	0.370	0.247	0.227	0.208	0.191	0.176	0.162
11	0.317	0.287	0.261	0.237	0.215	0.195	0.178	0.162	0.148	0.135
12	0.286	0.257	0.231	0.208	0.187	0.168	0.152	0.137	0.124	0.112
13	0.258	0.229	0.204	0.182	0.163	0.145	0.130	0.116	0.104	0.093
14	0.232	0.205	0.181	0.160	0.141	0.125	0.111	0.099	0.088	0.078
15	0.209	0.183	0.160	0.140	0.123	0.108	0.095	0.084	0.074	0.065

6

Auditing

Introduction

This chapter principally discusses the role of external audit in the
public sector. Audit, in this context, is an ex-post activity that is
designed to cover dual roles: fiscal/regulatory and value for money
(VFM) auditing. The former role, fiscal auditing, is the more
traditional responsibility. It involves auditors in ensuring that funds
have been expended in accordance with the terms by which such
monies were appropriated, and that accounts have been properly
prepared. The latter role has received growing attention in recent
years, with a trend towards extending the scope of public sector
auditing to include an assessment as to whether departments and
agencies manage their operations efficiently and whether their programmes are effective in terms of the objectives by which they were
initiated. The public sector auditors' mandate therefore extends
beyond that of their private sector counterparts who generally confine
their energies to the attest/fiscal compliance role.

The first part of this chapter discusses the statutory basis of auditing
under the headings: central government, local government, the
National Health Service, and the nationalized industries. The second
part considers the more recent development of VFM auditing. The
concluding section considers the relationship between the external and
internal auditor. It is not the intention of this chapter to provide
general guidance on detailed auditing techniques, for this readers
should refer to specialist text books. This chapter correlates with the
theme of accountability introduced in chapter 2 . This link is usefully
provided by the Australian Audit Office (1986, p. 1):

Accountability in its simplest terms means the obligation to
answer for a responsibility that has been conferred. It presumes

the existence of at least two parties, one who allocates responsibility and one who accepts it with the undertaking to report upon the manner in which responsibility has been discharged.

Audit is a process that is superimposed on an accountability relationship. It is carried out to investigate and report on the responsibility assumed, and to establish that a report on the discharge of the responsibility is a correct or fair one. The audit is usually performed by a third party, primarily serving the interests of the party who delegated the responsibility.

Audit, as shown in figure 6.1, provides the independent link in the management cycle between programme and budget choices, and the use of funds and the results achieved.

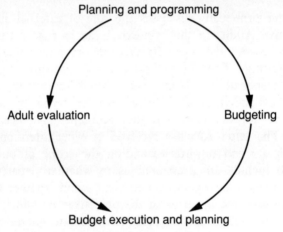

Figure 6.1   The financial management process

The Statutory Basis of Auditing

Central government

The present Comptroller and Auditor General (C & AG) is the fifteenth appointed since 1866 He is the head of the National Audit Office (NAO), which was established on 1 January 1984 to replace and continue the work of the former Exchequer and Audit Department (E & AD). The establishment of the NAO followed the passing of the National Audit Act of the previous year, 1983 This Act, and the other developments discussed in this section, arose because of a general feeling that reform was long overdue. As Normanton (1980, p. 176) states:

The Exchequer and Audit Departments Act of 1866 (as slightly amended in 1921) created the office of the Comptroller and Auditor General and charged him to identify and report upon the public accounts and to ensure that expenditures were authorised by Parliament and supported by the Treasury. In the financial year 1866–7 the cost of the United Kingdom supply services was £39 million.

In theory, though not always in practice, the 1866 Act required a 100 per cent audit of all transactions. The 1921 Act revoked this unworkable requirement and so condoned the concept of test auditing and, in more recent times, the adoption of a systemsbased audit. Because the expenditure of many departments runs into hundreds of millions of pounds it is therefore a major audit task to check that the accounting and financial control systems underlying reported expenditure are both efficient and accurate. The C & AG's audit responsibilities are summarized in table 6.1 The NAO performs both financial and VFM audits. In 1989–90 45 per cent of NAO direct costs were devoted to financial audit and 53 per cent to VFM audit work.

In 1989–90 the NAO audited expenditure and revenue totalling over £300 billion. Most of the expenditure was incurred by government departments and recorded in annual accounts submitted to Parliament. Over 60 per cent of public expenditure flows through these accounts, as well as grants to local government and funds for the National Health Service, nationalized industries and public corporations. The accounts were audited by the NAO and the C & AG gave his opinion on – or certified – each one. Most of the revenue was collected by Customs and Excise and the Inland Revenue. In 1989–90 the C & AG qualified his opinion on some 20 separate accounts. He also reported on eight occasions where departments had spent more than the sums authorised by Parliament and had incurred excess votes. Some 1,400 financial issues were raised in 'management letters' sent to departments and other bodies.

The C & AG's VFM reports attract widespread interest as the following four newspaper comments illustrate:

The National Audit Office is planning to intensify its scrutiny of public spending next year with further investigations into the Government's privatisation programme, green policies, homelessness, housing and inner city strategies. (*The Times*, December 1989)

Table 6.1   The audit responsibilities of the Comptroller and Auditor General

The C & AG has certain *duties* laid on him by statute, principally concerned with his annual examination of accounts. In addition he has *discretionary powers* to carry out other examinations and report the results. There are also some limitations in the scope and nature of his work.

He must	He may	He does not
Audit and certify the appropriation accounts of all government departments	Audit and certify other accounts by agreement	Formally disallow expenditure, not himself give judgements or rulings on questions of legality
Audit the revenue accounts	Have right of access to a wide range of bodies where he is not appointed auditor, but which are largely financed by public funds	Audit or have access to the accounts of nationalized industries or local authorities
Examine departmental store accounts	Examine the economy, efficiency and effectiveness of expenditure and the use of resources by bodies where he is appointed auditor or has rights of access, either under statute or by agreement	Have a general power to 'follow public money wherever to goes', with rights of access to companies organizations or individuals receiving grants, subsidies or other assistance from public funds

Table 6.1 cont.

He must	He may	He does not
Audit and certify other accounts as laid down by the exchequer and Audit Departments Acts and other statutes	Report to Parliament on the results of these examinations	Questions the merits of policy objectives when carrying out examinations of economy, efficiency and effectiveness
Report as necessary to Parliament on the results of these audits		Examine questions of maladministration by departments affecting individual members of the public (this is the field of the Parliamentary Commissioner for Administration)
		Report other than to Parliament (except on audits of the international organizations, where he reports to governing bodies)

More than 200 university lecturers who were made redundant with golden handshakes averaging £80,000 have been re-hired. The blunder was uncovered by the National Audit Office . . . (*Daily Express*, December 1989)

Britain's £750 million-a-year maternity services need better planning and more resources to tackle unacceptably high levels of perinatal deaths amongst the babies of the poor and deprived, the National Audit Office, Parliament's financial watchdog, said in a report published yesterday. (*The Guardian*, March 1990)

Last week's National Audit Report on the 'Quality of Road and Bridge Construction' pulls few punches in its look at the work of the Department of Transport, the Welsh Office and the Scottish Development Office. It is a document that refreshingly refuses to accept bland excuses and smokescreens for the state of Britain's road system. (*Construction News*, December 1989)

One hundred and fourteen years after the passing of the 1866 Act the Government issued a green paper (Cmnd. 7845, March 1980) on the role of the C & AG. This was followed by the Public Accounts Committee's first special report, session 1980– , and the government's response to that report (Cmnd. 8323). These two documents provided, for the first time in over a century, a summary of the various arguments on the subject of a national audit office.

Paragraph 64 of the green paper welcomed views from the parliamentary committees and other interested bodies and individuals on the government's views, which are summarized as follows:

(a) The role of the C & AG should be:
   (i) to provide a basic financial and regulating audit of departmental accounts;
   (ii) to undertake an examination of the economy and efficiency with which public funds are spent;
   (iii) *in appropriate cases*, to investigate the effectiveness of prog-rammes and projects in meeting established goals.

(b) The effective working relationship between the C & AG and the PAC should be preserved.

(c) In the case of nondepartmental bodies an important objective of the C & AG's examination should be to review the effectiveness of the arrangements under which ministers monitor and control the payment of public funds to such bodies.

(d) Decisions whether to provide for C & AG audit or inspection of such bodies need to be taken case. The C & AG *should not* cover the nationalized industries.

(e) Certain powers or direction available to the Treasury in the E & AD Acts are obsolete and should be removed in any new legislation.

(f) The government are prepared to consider alternative arrangements for controlling the budget of the C & AG, but the implications for the staff of the E & AD would need to be considered.

(g) The independence of the C & AG of both the Executive and Parliament should be reaffirmed and there should be no change in his status as an office holder under the Crown.

The PAC's response to the green paper/discussion document came in the form of a three volume report in February 1981: *The Role of the Comptroller and Auditor General* (HC 115). While agreeing with the general views expressed in paragraph 64 (a) above, the PAC proposed more radical changes. Paragraph 8.1 stated:

the present legislation is out of date and does not reflect the nature of the audit at present carried out by the C & AG. More importantly, it is essential to make statutory provision for a framework of public audit in this country sufficient to ensure accountability to Parliament for the wider range of public expenditure now and in the future.

The specific proposals of the PAC were set out in paragraph 8.10 to 8.16. In summary they proposed that: the C & AG should have the right to audit the accounts of all bodies that were substantially supported from public monies, including nationalized industries and private sector companies; that, for England and Wales, the (then) district audit service should be transferred from the Department of the Environment to the C & AG, with similar arrangements for Scotland; and that the audit of health authorities should likewise be transferred to the C & AG. A national audit office, headed by the C & AG, was proposed to centralize and coordinate public sector audits. The costs of this office, it was proposed, would be borne by a separate vote of the House of Commons, who would establish a public accounts commission to oversee its administrative functions. In many aspects the PAC's proposals accorded with the present practice adopted by New Zealand (see Glynn, 1985, p. 127).

The government's response to the PAC's proposals came in July 1981 (Cmnd. 8323). It was not in favour of giving the C & AG such an extended and comprehensive remit. Paragraph 6 stated:

It remains the Government's view that it would be useful to introduce legislation to provide an uptodate prescription of the C & AG's functions. *But this is not a pressing need.* Experience of the past two years suggests that the existing legislation need not in fact inhibit further desirable changes in the work of the C & AG and the PAC.

There the debate rested until Norman St John Stevas MP brought a private member's bill to the House of Commons. After a stormy passage, and much pruning, this bill emerged as the National Audit Act, 1983. The Act, which is in three parts, only partially meets the proposals of the PAC. Part I of the Act provides that the C & AG shall be an officer of the House of Commons. This move had been opposed by the Government (Cmnd. 8323, paragraph 26). The Public Accounts Commission was also established to oversee the provisions of this Act. The composition of the Commission is as follows:

1 the member of the House of Commons who is for the time being the Chairman of the Committee of Public Accounts;
2 the Leader of the House of Commons; and
3 seven other members of the House of Commons appointed by the House, none of whom shall be a Minister of the Crown.

Each year the C & AG must present to the House of Commons the operating costs of his department. Paragraph 4(2) states:

The Comptroller and Auditor General shall for the financial year ending 31st March 1984 and for each subsequent financial year prepare an estimate of the expenses of the National Audit Office; and the Commission shall examine that estimate and lay it before the House of Commons with such modifications, if any, as the Commission see fit.

Part II of the Act is devoted to economy, efficiency and effectiveness examinations. Specifically excluded from these provisions were over

20 nationalized industries and other public bodies (many of these have since become candidates for privatization). They are listed in Schedule 4 of the Act. Part III of the Act is entitled Miscellaneous and Supplementary. Paragraphs 11 and 12 remove the previous power of the Treasury to give, in certain circumstances, directives to the C & AG. Though there is no record of this power being exercised, this is an important amendment of principle.

In 1989–90 the NAO submitted 42 VFM reports and memorandums to the Public Accounts Committee. Following on from his previous annual report, the C & AG again noted that there remained five main obstacles to the achievement of good value for money in the public sector:

1 poorly articulated aims and objectives, making measurement of performance difficult;
2 failure to apply a businesslike approach in measuring revenues or in achieving reasonable levels of return on investment;
3 poor management and maintenance of assets;
4 weakness in project management – in the development of equipment, in implementing information technology, in construction and in many other areas;
5 inefficient control and monitoring, often because of inadequate management information systems.

One 1989–90 report, which will be referred to again in chapter 10, concerned the sale of the Rover Group. In this report the NAO raised questions about the proceeds. All the land and other assets had not been valued and there had been no consideration of a clawback provision should the company profit from subsequent disposals.

VFM studies are designed to bring Parliament's attention to any area of potential improvement, including staffing, control and assessment procedures. Some studies have pointed to the possibility of savings in public expenditure: £75 million on improved Health Service purchasing (economy); possible savings of £1.5 billion in Royal Air Force equipment maintenance (efficiency). Other studies deal with the effectiveness of programmes: for example, weaknesses in the roads programme. Sometimes the NAO's VFM reports indicate that it is too late to take remedial action, though lessons can be learnt in the future.

Local government

Local government audit has a long history. Jones (1985, p. 1) refers to the earliest known reference in English legal records. Dated at approximately 1430 it concerns a writ, 'Commission ad computa collectorem denorionum pro clausura villae', which may be translated as a 'Commission for the hearing of the accounts of the collectors of money for the walling of a town'. This was an adaptation, evolved by the courts, of the writ of account which from the thirteenth century had been available against bailiffs, factors and receivers. Commencing in the sixteenth century, the intervention of successive parliaments has led to the present-day role of the district audit. Some seven Poor Law Acts culminated in the Poor Law Amendment Act 1844, Section 32 of which provided the auditor with 'full powers to examine, audit, allow, or disallow of accounts, and of items therein'. Over the next 138 years several Acts of Parliament enhanced the role of the district audit service, the most recent legislation for England and Wales being provided by the Local Government Finance Act 1982.

Much of the impetus for the 1982 Act arose out of the 1976 report of the Committee on Local Government Finance (chaired by Sir Frank Layfield). This report pointed out that there existed no clear accountability for the expenditure of public money on local services and called for an audit service independent of both central and local government. The Local Government Finance Act 1982 (Section 11) established the Audit Commission for Local Authorities in England and Wales (the Commission).

The Commission came into being on 1 April 1983. It has two main responsibilities:

1 To secure continued integrity of local government, so that confidence in the institutions of government is not eroded by concerns over fraud and corruption.
2 To help authorities improve the returns on the £25 billion + as required by Section 15, viz:

> An auditor shall by examination of the accounts and other wise satisfy himself. . . that the body whose accounts are being audited has proper arrangements for securing economy, efficiency and effectiveness in the use of its resources.

The Commission has a chairman and up to 20 members, who represent the interests of community charge payers, local authorities, health authorities (see below), employees and accountants. The day-to-day operation of the Commission rests with its Controller. At present the majority of audit appointments remain with the district audit service, whose statutory responsibilities were transferred from the Department of the Environment to the Commission. However, an increasing proportion of audit appointments have been made to private sector accounting firms, the intention being to ultimately provide for a 50/50 split of appointments between the Commission's own staff and the private sector.

All local authority auditors are expected to review aspects of value for money as part of their annual audit programme. The Commission provides guidance on certain of the services or costs they wish reviewed; for example, in introducing a higher proportion of civilians into the police force or boarding out a higher proportion of children in care. In the former case, by employing civilian clerical staff a greater proportion of funds can be allocated for direct policing policies. In the latter case, it is considerably cheaper to board children with foster parents, and social workers would argue that in practice this is also often in the children's best interest. Like the reports of the NAO, the reports of the Commission receive wide attention and are often referred to in the media. The Commission sees itself as motivating authorities to make improvements by helping them to help themselves. Specifically the Commission (Audit Commission, 1983, p. 9) sees its mission as being to:

1 identify, in the course of the annual audit effort, specific local opportunities to improve value for money by reference to other steps that have already been taken successfully in other authorities facing similar problems;
2 promote good management practice by documenting achievements and training auditors to spot potential improvements, and publishing the results of special reports;
3 encourage – even promote – action, though (auditors') reports to officers and members, management letters to the authority and (if necessary) reports in the public interest;
4 monitor implementation performance during annual audits, drawing attention as required to any shortfall;
5 co-ordinate the efforts of related organizations.

The Commission does not believe that it would be fruitful simply to gauge individual local authorities' spending levels against aggregate spending levels (1983, p. 17):

> . . . the Commission will not be judging its performance against local authority spending levels since this would be incompatible with its stated mission of helping authorities to improve *returns* on their annual investment and, in any case, any cost reductions will not be achieved by the Commission but by members and officers of authorities demonstrating the 'will to manage'.

Henley et al (1989, p. 275) consider that the 'broad ambit' of the local government audit service is nowadays similar to that of the NAO. They do, however, highlight some important differences due to the structure of local authority accounts and the system of reporting. First, members of the public, as local government electors, have the right to inspect, question and object to the accounts and to question and take issue with the auditor on matters arising in his or her report. No such rights exist with respect to the accounts of central government. Second, either as a result of his or her independent actions, or acting as a result of an objection by a member of the public, the auditor can seek redress in the courts when an item of account is contrary to the law, or where money has not been brought to account or loss has been incurred through wilful misconduct. In such circumstances councillors and officials can be sanctioned and made personally liable for misappropriated funds. Councillors can also be barred from local government office. Third, more recently, local government auditors have been given powers of early intervention when a local authority has taken a decision which would involve unlawful expenditure or a course of action which would lead to unlawful loss. The powers were given in The Local Government Act 1988, which enables the auditor to issue a prohibition order which, subject to a right of appeal to the courts, precludes the authority from implementing such a decision. The Act also grants the auditor the power to call for a judicial review of an authority's decision.

Under Section 26 of the Local Government Finance Act 1982, the Commission has a duty to undertake comparative and other studies to enable it to make recommendations for improving VFM. Under Section 27 the Commission must report on the impact of statutory provisions or any ministerial directions or guidance on such VFM. In practice, the study of a service is likely to reveal issues for attention by both local government and central government. Both types of report may therefore emerge from a single study. Comparative studies carried out in 1991–2 included: Social Services Management; Housing – The Changing Role; and Community Charge. Table 6.2 provides a summary of the cost of VFM studies and the value improvements achieved from 1983–4 to 1989–90.

In Scotland, the local authorities' auditors duties are contained in the Local Government (Scotland) Act 1983 All auditors of local authority accounts for periods commencing after 31 March 1983 are expected to observe the *Standards for the External Audit of Scottish Local Authorities* published by the Accounts Commission (a similar

Table 6.2 Cost of VFM studies and value improvements achieved from 1983–84 to 1989–90

	1983–84 £m	1984–85 £m	1985–86 £m	1986–87 £m	1987–88 £m	1988–89 £m	1989–90 £m
Total Audit Commission fees charged to local authorities	15	20	22	24	25	28	32
Fees charged for VFM work (estimate)	5	6	7	7	8	8	10
Achieved value improvements (cash terms) (cash terms) annual, cumulative		128	247	359	461	516	532

Source: Audit Commission, *Report and Accounts* year ended 31 March 1990

body to the Audit Commission for England and Wales). This publication (at p. 29) gives the auditor the same mandate as that provided by Section 15 of the 1982 Act (see above).

Current Labour Party policy would like to see the establishment of a Quality Commission which would incorporate some of the present duties of the Audit Commission in England and Wales and the Accounts Commission in Scotland. Such a body would have a statutory duty to promote the quality of local government services – whether provided internally, by the private sector, or voluntary organizations. This proposal to establish a broad range of quality assurance standards for different services reflects the Labour Party's concern that current VFM investigations concentrate overly on cost-cutting. For the foreseeable future, the notion of a Quality Commission remains only of academic interest.

National Health Service

Up until October 1990 the various National Health Service (NHS) Acts prescribed that the Secretaries of State should employ auditors to audit the accounts of all health authorities. For health authorities in England, these auditors were civil servants on the staff of the DHS; for health authorities in Scotland, civil servants in the Scottish Office, and so on. With the passing of the National Health Service and Community Care Act 1990, the 1982 Act was amended to allow the Audit Commission to become responsible for the appointment of auditors to health service bodies. Those staff employed by the Department of Health as auditors were transferred to the district audit service of the Audit Commission. The NHS as a whole will remain subject to audit by the NAO. Under the NHS Acts the C & AG is required to examine, certify and report on the annual summarized accounts of NHS expenditure and he is permitted to examine the accounts, records and audit reports of the health authorities. Rigden (1983, p. 173) likens the functions and responsibilities of the C & AG 'to those of a primary auditor of group accounts. He is entitled to take account of the work of the statutory auditors (now the Audit Commission) in deciding what further work he needs to undertake'. Pursuant to the provisions of the NHS Act 1977 and other enabling powers, the respective Secretary of State regulates on all aspects of financial control of health authorities.

While traditionally little NHS audit work has been awarded to private sector firms, eight pilot contracts were awarded in 1983 These trial contracts for the audit of district health authorities required these firms to spend 40 per cent of their time on value for money work. In January 1983 the *Report of the DHSS/NHS Audit Working Group* was published (DHSS 1983b). It laid great emphasis on value for money auditing and recommended that all health authorities establish value for money teams whose role would be to effect annual savings which could be used for improving services. Paragraph 6.28 recommended an increase in 'the rate of efficiency savings from the present target of 0.5 per cent year over year, to say 1.0 per cent'. Other issues raised in this report included the pooling of the internal audit service of some authorities and the establishment of audit committees. Lapsley and Prowle (1978) carried out comprehensive surveys that lent considerable weight to the reforms suggested in the working group's report. However, progress was slow, hence the recent changes embodied in the 1990 Act, which clearly recognizes the success of the Audit Commission in local government. Time alone will tell if the Commission is to be equally successful in the field of health care. A Health Studies Directorate, charged with developing health VFM topics, has been established. The first three-year programme of health studies was as follows:

1989–90	*1990–91*	*1991–92*
Energy management *	Day Surgery	Acute bed management
Sterile services*	Pathology Laboratory services	Nursing management
	Estate management	Integration of health services in the community

* Department of Health responsibility with support and guidance from the Audit Commission.
Source: Audit Commission, *Report and Accounts* year ended 31 March 1990

The Directorate includes medical staff and is liaising closely with appropriate professional bodies, including Royal Colleges. The Director of Management Practice is developing health profiles, similar to the Commission's work with local authority profiles, which will compare costs between health authorities. These are based on existing sources of information but presented in a different way.

Nationalized industries

The relevant Secretary of State of each nationalized industry appoints a firm of private sector auditors to carry out financial/regulating audit. For example, under the provisions of the Transport Act 1962, the secretary of State for Transport appoints the external auditors of the accounts of the British Railways Board (the auditors must, incidentally, be members of one of the professional accountancy bodies recognized as qualified to undertake the audit of limited liability companies). Each year, the audited accounts and accompanying audit report are sent to the Secretary of State who, in turn, presents them to Parliament. This brief report combines three elements, common to all the audit reports of nationalized industries:

1 basis of appointment; for example, Section 24 (2) of the Transport Act 1962.
2 reference to the fact that accounts have been prepared in accordance with approved Auditing Standards and the accounts represent a 'true and fair view of the state of the Board's affairs'.
3 reference to the fact that accounts also comply with the requirements of the relevant Act of Incorporation and any directions received from the Secretary of State.

The audit reports of nationalized industries merely mirror the reports of private sector limited companies. Over the years there has been much debate as to whether or not this state of affairs is really acceptable even given the fact that these industries are highly independent bodies. The present situation had not been envisaged by early British socialist thinkers (see Normanton, 1980, p. 181). Even in more recent times there have been calls to make nationalized industries, through their audit reports, more accountable to Parliament. Paragraph 8.10 (c) of the PAC's 1981 report, *The Role of the Comptroller and Auditor General*, stated that the present arrangements for the financial audit of nationalized industries should continue but that the C & AG should have access to the books and records of these bodies in order to enable him to report to the House of Commons (paragraph 4.16 – 4.19). However, as referred to above, Schedule 4 of the National Audit Act 1983 specifically excluded from its provisions over 20 nationalized industries and other public bodies.

In relation to other areas of the public sector, it seems somewhat inequitable that the C & AG has no right of access to the records of nationalized industries, given that government can regulate certain of their activities; for example, pricing policy, funding restrictions and trading restrictions. Such regulations can have a material impact on the performance of these industries and it surely cannot be accepted that audit reports be presented to the Secretary of State of a government that has imposed them. The principle in all other areas of the public sector is that there is an armslength relationship between the audited body and the auditor. Without even criticizing the valuable work done by the private sector audit firms it should be a matter of principle that their reports should be presented to the C & AG rather than to the respective Secretary of State. Indeed, in many respects, such an arrangement would strengthen the independence of the auditor, not only in relation to an industry's sponsoring department but also with respect to the potential pressures of overbearing industry chairmen. In turn the C & AG would have a right of overview and could instigate value for money investigations by his own staff or, perhaps more effectively, by the private sector auditors. This would be preferable to the *ad hoc* provisions available under Section 11 of the Competition Act 1980, whereby the Secretary of State for Trade can direct the Monopolies and Mergers Commission to investigate efficiency, costs, the level of quality of the service provided and possible misuse of monopoly power within nationalized industries. Glynn (1985, p. 13) points out that the results of such investigations are often not followed up. If the principle is accepted that the Audit Commission appoints private sector auditors of health and local authorities, why should not the C & AG appoint the auditors of the nationalized industries and other public bodies? This view would be supported by many individual consumer councils. For example, Report No. 24 of the Post Office User National Council (POUNC) (1984) states:

Government sets financial targets for the nationalized industries. But customers at present have difficulty in knowing whether they are getting value for money. It is necessary to relate financial requirements, operational performance and quality of service. The Post Office and its unions have entered into agreements which are designed to improve productivity. Customers are entitled to know how they will benefit.

Value for Money Auditing

Value for money (VFM) audits have developed in recent years as a way of expanding the more traditional role of the auditor away from the more straightforward examination of the fairness of the financial statements of an organization. With the exception of nationalized industries, all areas of the public sector now undergo VFM audits. VFM auditing is not new, and in many ways Britain is now only explicitly upon a path that other countries have already followed. In Canada, for example, the Auditor General Act of 1977 requires the Auditor General to report to the House of Commons when: 'money has been expended without due regard to economy or efficiency, or satisfactory procedures have not been established to measure and report the effectiveness of programs, where such procedures could appropriately and reasonably be implemented'. This Act was quickly passed following comments made by the Auditor General in his report for the fiscal year ended 31 March 1976 In that report the Auditor General had declared that (p. 9):

> I am deeply concerned that Parliament – and indeed the Government – has lost, or is close to losing, effective control of the public purse. . . *Based on the study of the systems of departments, agencies and Crown Corporations audited by the Auditor General, financial management and control in the Government of Canada is grossly inadequate.*

These were strong words. The emphasis in that statement (shown in italics) was contained in the original report at the request of the Auditor General.

Accountability in the public sector occurs when politicians and the public at large are assured that public funds are being spent efficiently, economically and on programmes that are effective. VFM auditing assists this process by reporting upon management's performance at both central and devolved government levels.

Value for money can be thought of as consisting of three elements: *economy, efficiency and effectiveness.* The first two of these elements are fairly uncontroversial but the third element, effectiveness, is both hard to define and difficult to measure. These three elements were previously discussed in chapter 3 (see also figure 3.2).

VFM auditing provides regular systematic feedback to those responsible for the initial formulation of objectives. This review operation is one that is well suited to the diagnostic and interpretive skills of the auditor, particularly since there are financial implications, which always have a bearing on overall financial strategy, in all government activities.

How is VFM auditing different from traditional auditing or management consultancy? A conventional audit of financial statements is designed to provide independent, objective opinion that financial information prepared by management has been presented fairly. As part of the process the auditor may include an examination of accounting and information systems, and may make recommendations to management to improve these systems. Generally, audit reports are predictable and short because the auditor is guided by generally accepted accounting and audit principles and standards. Management consulting assignments generally require solutions to perceived problems and experience at implementing solutions. They may frequently involve advice on specialized management decisions or implementing specialized management systems. The range of situations, solutions and systems is very diverse. There is no predictable form of reporting, and there are no 'generally accepted' standards for decision-making or systems to guide the consultant.

VFM auditing is a blend of both conventional auditing and management consulting. It benefits from the independence, objectivity, and reporting skills of auditors, complemented by the specialized analytical systems and implementation skills that may be available from management consultants. The report should be attention directing rather than providing detailed solutions.

In adapting to this expanded role the auditor faces many difficulties. There will be an increasing need for specialist staff who will have to work with departmental management in determining whether or not they and their staff have been successful in producing the level and quantity of service required by those who formulate policy. The role of the auditor should be to support management by assisting in pointing out deficiencies and advising on possible courses of action. The auditor is not concerned with policy, but with its effects and whether such effects correspond with the intentions of the policy. This is a monitoring function, a comparison of the situation that exists with that which might have been expected. For each part of the organization it is then necessary to identify activities undertaken, and their purpose. An examination should be made of those outputs that are measurable and the costs involved: this information is needed to assess efficiency and effectiveness. The VFM auditor is concerned to see that planned activities have been achieved, and should not be involved in the setting of targets.

As previously stated, the phrase 'value for money' has a wide and ambiguous meaning. Many current government programmes reflect major attempts to improve social and economic conditions in an increasingly complex society. As government expenditures have grown, the objectives and results of such programmes have come under increased public scrutiny. Holtham and Stewart (1981, p. 3) state:

> We see the new concern as arising in an era of restraint, but see that the case for value for money stands apart from the political stance taken – whether it is for or against cuts in local government expenditure. Value for money is justified whatever level of expenditure is aimed at. Questions of value for money are about political judgment – the judgment of what is value for money. Value for money does not remove political judgment – it may well increase the emphasis on it. We argue, however, that

the process of search for value for money is politically neutral, even though what is decided in that process will not be.

The last sentence of this quotation draws an important distinction. The auditor is not concerned with policy, which is the responsibility of elected politicians and public servants who administer their directions. The auditor is concerned with investigating the outcomes of policy and whether such effects correspond with the intentions of the policy. As we have said, this is a monitoring function. To say that a particular department (or programme) provides value for money means that those who strive to provide the service do so as best they can, given the resources that are available and the environment within which they operate. It is impossible to provide an absolute measure of value for money. The auditor must examine whether resources could be put to alternative uses, whether objectives could be achieved by an alternative strategy and (if practicable) compare the operations of one particular department with another.

The auditor must determine the reasonableness of these individual judgments and it may be that specialist (non-accounting) assistance will need to be sought. For example, in considering the efficiency and effectiveness of a regional airport it may be that a specialist transport economist could assist the auditor in assessing the effectiveness of the airport's operations.

Efficiency refers to the productive use of resources. In order to produce efficiency measures it is important to identify and measure programme outputs and inputs in order to establish how well resources are being used. Efficiency measures are only possible when outputs can be separated from each other and possess uniform characteristics. As we said in chapter 3, a repetitive process meets these criteria. As we also said in chapter 3, there are instances when efficiency measures are either not practicable or not possible. The example we gave there was a community police programme. Though tasks may be clearly stated (school visiting, crime prevention enquiries, contact with ethnic minorities, etc.) outputs, not being tangible, cannot be measured. Figure 6.2 provides a useful Canadian overview of the efficiency element of a VFM audit.

Politicians and administrators should clearly be interested in the effectiveness of the programmes with which they are most directly concerned. Many of the comments made by these two group, on the impact of particular programmes are based on neither reliable nor valid information. Indeed the public seem to expect those committed to a particular service to extol its virtues. Statements to the effect that a

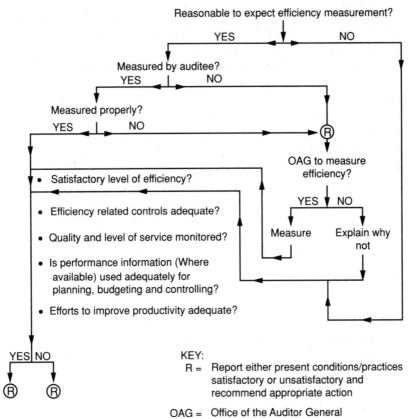

Figure 6.2   Schematic overview of an efficiency audit
Source: Glynn (1985), p. 19.

particular programme has had an increase in funding do not say anything about the quality of the service offered. Neither does a statement such as 'there will be no increase in postal charges in the next six months'.

The public, as clients, equally base their attitudes to the quality of the services they receive on subjective assessments that are more than a little conditioned by their individual social attitudes. What one might term 'topical' programmes, such as the general quality of health care, the price of electricity, the level of defence expenditure, and so on, receive wide publicity. By contrast, little attention is given to lesser funded 'acute' programmes such as those for the mentally ill, drug addiction and the provision of overseas aid. Whoever the commentator is, the opinions expressed are often only beliefs based on sketchy information that is only indirectly relevant.

Programme evaluation, through effectiveness auditing, is measuring the extent to which goals have been attained. The goals are the aims or outcomes that a programme purports to pursue, and for which it can be held accountable (where measurable). Programme evaluation is more than an examination of the manner in which a programme is implemented. It should also review the results achieved. The aim of the auditor should be to link programme processes; for example, the number of children receiving a particular immunization vaccination should be linked to the outcome, here possibly expressed in terms of a decrease in a particular illness or infirmity. Such an analysis can provide useful and constructive information which can guide politicians and administrators in making programme improvements as well as provide a reasonably objective assessment on behalf of the public at large. In some instances it may be possible to produce quantitative data to support recommendations; in other instances it may be provided by the perceived value of a service based on a consumer survey.

Every investigation has inevitably to be tailored to local operating conditions. There can be an overall standard approach. The auditors' role is to direct the attention of those responsible for devising and initiating policy. Auditors are not directly concerned with the solution of problems; if they were; they would become responsible for those solutions and thereby lose their objectivity and status to provide an independent examination and appraisal of a service. It is management that have to address themselves to the solutions, either by using internal resources or by engaging outside consultants.

The most critical requirement of an effectiveness audit is a clear statement of the programme objectives for which the level of achievement is to be measured. The client should identify those objectives as a matter of course in the relevant engagement documentation. Indeed, such documentation should make reference to the source of these objectives; for example, enabling legislation or ministerial direction. The importance of this requirement can be appreciated from the following passage taken from the United States General Accounting Office's *Exposure Draft: Comprehensive Approach for Planning and Conducting A Program Results Review* (1978, p. 21):

The lack of an objective set of standards or principles to govern effectiveness measurement systems creates the potential for two unique problems that may affect the conduct of a program results review assignment. Although these problems may never surface, they should be anticipated and the methods for resolving the potential problems should be clarified before beginning the review. These potential problems involve:

- Irreconcilable differences between the review staff and program management over the appropriateness of the system used to measure effectiveness.
- Contingent work responsibilities that are not readily identifiable before preparing the work or bid proposal.

The subjective nature of measuring program effective–ness may lead to irreconcilable differences between the review staff and program management. The appropriateness of specific performance indicators, data sources and performance standards is determined primarily by their relationship to program goals although this is not always precise. In the absence of such precision, reasonable approximations may be considered. Reasonableness, however is a subjective judgment, which in turn can lead to differences of opinion.

On this last point three solutions are possible: (1) the conflict is passed to a higher authority; (2) the auditor, as the independent assessor, is granted the authority to assent and defend whatever position he or she believes appropriate; or (3) no further work is done and the VFM audit is restricted to only two elements – economy and efficiency. Whatever the solution, it should be resolved prior to the commencement of the review.

Assessing the effectiveness of a programme in achieving a desired level of results is the newest and most difficult area of work that the auditor has to adapt to. Figure 6.3 illustrates the approach to be adopted when considering the effectiveness component of a VFM audit.

Given the fact that many other countries have formally adopted VFM in advance of Britain it is useful to review developments in some of these other countries. As Hopwood states (1982, p. 43): 'Familiarity with experience elsewhere should instil a greater realization of the differences between what should be done and what is said to be done, and what is done and what might be done.'

In the USA there has been a wide concern with the efficiency of government programmes for more than four decades. Initially such reviews were separate from the financial compliance audits. In the 1970s there were developments that integrated compliance and value for money auditing. More recently there have been criticisms of the balance between these two areas and, on occasions, the GAO has been accused of neglecting its more traditional audit responsibilities in the

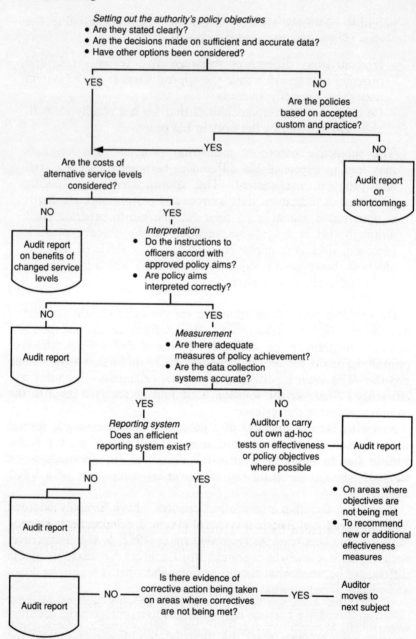

Figure 6.3   Approach to effectiveness auditing
Source: Butt and Palmer (1985), figure 6.3.

area of financial compliance and regularity. The approaches developed in the USA can be characterized by their diversity. Most publications provide, in the main, for *ad hoc* multidisciplinary reviews of an agency's effectiveness. In contrast to the UK, where value for money reviews are perceived as an enhancement to the role of existing auditors, half of the professional staff of the GAO are nonaccountants. One reason for the nonstandard approach in the USA is that much of the investigatory work undertaken by the GAO is done at the request of the Congress.

The introduction of value for money auditing in Canada was accompanied by a number of other institutional innovations, all of which were designed to increase the accountability of public sector organizations. While the role in respect of economy and efficiency was a direct one, that in respect of effectiveness was an indirect one. So as to avoid any political consideration of policies, the auditor's brief is to monitor and report upon agencies' and departments' approaches for monitoring and reviewing their own effectiveness. Despite considerable progress over the years, the Auditor General's Department consider that there is still much progress to be made. Their emphasis is on ensuring that the adoption of standard routines for management practice will result in the realization of greater efficiency and effectiveness.

In Australia legislative changes in 1979 permitted the Auditor-General to carry out efficiency audits. The legislation said nothing about effectiveness and did not define the term efficiency, thereby providing a source of some confusion and debate (Glynn, 1987). The (then) Auditor General endeavoured to clarify the debate on the extent of his authority in various publications, beginning with his 19845 Annual Report. This report stated, *inter alia*, that efficiency auditing 'involves an evaluation of the effectiveness of administrative actions and decisions taken by management in achieving program objectives within the policy guidelines and legislative framework provided by government'. New Zealand's auditing approach also closely follows that of Canada.

Sweden has experimented with both budget and auditing reforms. Even so there have been no easy solutions to monitoring the country's public expenditure. Currently much effort is being directed at understanding the organizational processes of questioning and debate which such audits should stimulate rather than seeing the problem in terms of administrative techniques alone. In the EC there has been only a limited introduction of expanded audit mandates by individual member countries. There remains a strong legal bias to the audit process, one that places considerable reliance on examining the probity of state institutions.

To date, despite a wealth of experience, there has been no standard approach that adequately covers all the varied aspects of value for money auditing. Further research is needed, for example into developing output measures for both efficiency and effectiveness. In the UK, attempts to gain greater value for money have been related more to the present depressed economic climate than any need to provide for the wider accountability of government expenditure. Typically, the emphasis has been upon the problem of monitoring output/standards while reducing financial inputs in real terms.

The phrase 'value for money' is now part of the vocabulary of many governments. The increase in audit mandate of the six countries discussed has arisen largely because government agencies tend to exercise greater restraint. As both politicians and the public become more economically orientated there is a knockon effect such that organizations are required to place a far greater emphasis on controlling costs and on the provision of relevant financial information. Private sector auditing emerged following the great economic collapses of the latter part of the nineteenth century and, more recently, that of the 1930s. Similarly, continued economic restraint in the public sector is now enabling auditors to, at least in part, contribute to demands for greater public accountability.

The auditors of many of the recent VFM reports of the National Audit Office (NAO) are to be congratulated for tackling some rather contentious issues and presenting their findings in such an informative manner. The report on the Department of the Environment's operation of the (then) rate support grant (RSG) system, published in April 1985, is a case in point. The report is in four parts. The approach of the NAO was to examine the effectiveness of the system in pursuing the objectives of central government and the consequent impact of the system on the activities of local authorities. Part 4 assesses the effectiveness of the system under four headings:

1 constraint on total spending;
2 influence on distribution of expenditure between services;
3 equalization;
4 impact on local authorities and local accountability.

A glossary of terms and four appendices are also provided.

Far from meeting its objectives, the NAO reported that (paragraph 37):

The original purposes of the RSG system introduced in 1981–82 were to provide a fairer and more objective method of grant distribution and to eliminate previous incentives to high spending. The general structure of this unitary grant system was well designed to achieve these purposes, but the detailed arrangements incorporated a number of elements which either detracted somewhat from the equity of the system or added to its complexity.

Relationship between External and Internal Auditors

The duties performed by the internal auditor should be seen to be complementary to the work performed by the external auditor. This applies to both financial and VFM audits. The external auditor should review the work of the internal audit staff to determine their effectiveness in assisting management to improve the quality of information that is necessary if they are to monitor satisfactorily the efficiency and effectiveness of the programmes under their charge.

The role and objectives of internal audit may vary between different parts of the public sector, depending on attitudes, statutory requirements, size, etc. The CIPFA statements on internal audit practice in the public sector define internal audit as:

an independent appraisal function within an organization for the review of activities as a service to all levels of management. It is a control which measures, evaluates and reports upon the effectiveness of internal controls, financial and other, as a contribution to the efficient use of resources within an organization.

It is the responsibility of internal audit to review, appraise and report upon the following matters:

1 The soundness, adequacy and application of internal controls. Internal control can be said to comprise the whole system of controls established by management, in order to:

(a) safeguard its assets;
(b) ensure reliability of records;
(c) promote operational efficiency; and
(d) monitor adherence to policies and directives.

The establishment of internal controls is the responsibility of management, not of internal audit, but as a service to management it is part of the latter's role to review, appraise and report on the soundness and adequacy of these controls.

2 The extent to which the organization's assets and interests are accounted for and safeguarded from losses of all kinds. Proper arrangements for the control and custody of the organization's assets should be built into the organization structure. The role of internal audit is to ensure that these arrangements are implemented and that they remain satisfactory.

3 The suitability and reliability of financial and other management data developed within the organization.

For internal audit to carry out these responsibilities it is essential that it operates with adequate independence. It is also recognized that at the same time there is a need for close cooperation with the other departments and sections of the organization and with the statutorily appointed external auditor, particularly with regard to the exchange of information and to making the best overall use of audit resources. The chief internal auditor must be assisted by sufficient staff of the right quality and quantity. Conditions vary from organization to organization and across different parts of the public sector, some organizations being noted for having a history of indifference to internal audit.

Internal audit is an integral part of internal control. The extent to which the external auditor can dispense with detailed work depends in no small part on the effectiveness of the system of internal control. This is all the more important with the introduction of VFM audits. However, the standard of internal audit in the public sector is not generally very good. It has often been seen as a necessary evil for ensuring that the conduct of those responsible for operating the organization remains within prescribed rules, regulations and legislation. One would have hoped that, with the various developments to improve managerial performance throughout the public sector, departments and agencies would have upgraded their internal audit function. Government should review the present low standard of internal audit within all levels of public sector administration, especially at the central government level. One must presently conclude that management does not view the current internal audit function as a significant service – thus, on occasions, questioning its very *raison d'être*.

In other countries there has been a trend to expand the roles of internal audit to meet the growing public concern that the administration of government be subject to review and control. For example, the

Commonwealth Government of Australia has, in recent years, devoted much attention to the quality of service from its internal audit staff. Criticisms contained in various Auditor-General's reports could be just as easily directed at the British public sector. The reports have noted in particular (Connolly, 1980, p. 14):

- diversion of internal audit staff to other duties, reducing effectiveness of the internal audit function;
- arrears of work resulting in inadequate coverage by internal audit;
- audit methodology not geared to a systemsbased approach;
- emphasis on error detection rather than on evaluating the adequacy of control systems, resulting in fragmentation and inadequate coverage of operations;
- working papers not providing adequate documentation on the scope and quality of the audits in a manner necessary for audit management and;
- inadequate knowledge of ADP for auditing computerized systems effectively.

De Paula and Attwood (1982, p. 73) stress that while the independent auditor and the internal auditor have some common objectives there are fundamental differences. Two of areas of difference they highlight are particularly relevant to the public sector – scope and responsibility. Whereas the extent of the work undertaken by the independent external auditor arises from the responsibilities placed on him or her by statute, that of the internal audit is determined by the management. Further, the internal auditor, being an employee of the organization, does not have the independence or status which the external auditor possesses.

One way that communication between the organization, the external auditor and the internal auditor can be improved is through the establishment of an audit committee. Though there is no general statutory requirement in the UK for the creation of audit committees some have nevertheless been established. Even as far back as 1978 the white paper on the nationalized industries welcomed the development of audit committees and the contribution they could make to improved efficiency. Because the structure, constitution and objectives of public sector organizations vary so much, it would be impracticable to suggest a standard role for audit committees but such committees might usefully embrace the following:

1 discussing with external auditors the scope and purpose of their audit before its commencement;

2 agreeing the responsibilities and scope of internal audit and reviewing its findings;
3 reviewing with the external auditors their evaluation of internal audit and discussing their recommendations;
4 reviewing financial statements and accounts before publication;
5 identifying and considering potential VFM investigations.

Conclusion

At present the auditing profession cannot fully deliver on its VFM audit mandates. This is partially due to the fact that the auditor's role is evolving in response to changing public needs and expectations. He or she is a third party intermediary in a broadly defined accountability relationship between, on the one hand, government and management, and on the other hand, politicians and the public at large. Issues which the profession needs currently to address centre upon training and fundamental research into what constitute acceptable efficiency and effectiveness measures. The profession's efforts will also need to be channelled into guiding management in developing sound information systems. The major inhibiting factor, referred to elsewhere in this text, is the lack of political will to reform the general framework of financial management, and to define more clearly the scope of programme objectives. Both of the factors are outside the auditor's influence, thereby demonstrating that the value of their work is limited.

7

Central Government

Introduction

This chapter is in three parts. First, an outline of the way central government departments request funds is provided – the 'supply procedure'. Second, a brief summary is given of the efforts currently being introduced to reform the structure and form of central government reports. Government financial reporting and control is an evolving area. The concluding part of the chapter reviews the recent history of management reform.

The Supply Procedure

Statutory authority for the supply of funds to meet expenditure is provided by means of annual Consolidated Funds Acts and by an annual Appropriation Act. Funds made available under the Acts relate to a specified financial year. Any money not required to meet chargeable expenditure in that year cannot be carried forward to the next financial year; it must be surrendered to the Consolidated Fund. This fund is the government's account at the Bank of England into which tax revenue and other receipts are paid, and from which the majority of the government's sterling expenditure is financed.

Supply estimates are then prepared and form the basis on which a supply resolution(s) is normally passed before the end of July. A subsequent Consolidated Fund (Appropriation) Bill is then brought before the House of Commons and passed before the summer recess. The resulting Act provides the government with the final authority to spend up to the amounts requested in the supply estimates. It is known as the Appropriation Act because it not only grants approval for the total sums requested, but also prescribes how the overall sum is to be apportioned to particular votes in order to finance specified services.

Occasionally, revised estimates may be presented before the Act is passed. This generally, occurs because it has been decided to reduce the provisions sought in an estimate, or because it is necessary to take account of the consequences of transferring the functions of one department to another.

Because the new financial year is starting when the estimates are first submitted to the House, and final approval is (then) some months off, statutory authority for issues out of the Consolidated Fund to meet expenditure during this period is provided by a system of lump-sum votes on account. These are normally presented to Parliament in the previous December, along with the winter supplementary estimates for the previous year. In general they seek provision for the forthcoming financial year.

Authority for the issue of an amount equal to the total of the votes on account, pending passage of the Appropriation Act, is given in the Consolidated Fund Act passed during the winter, usually December.

There are therefore three Acts during the year that cover the granting of funds by Parliament to the government. The Appropriation Act, normally in July, authorizes the issue out of the Consolidated Fund of monies sought in the main estimates and summer supplementaries. It also appropriates this amount to individual votes, and performs the same function for the lump sums authorized by the preceding winter and spring Consolidated Fund Acts in respect of the previous year, and for excess votes in respect of the year before that. The winter Consolidated Fund Act authorizes the issue out of the Consolidated Fund of the total sum required by the winter supplementaries for the current year and for the vote on account for the following year. Finally, the spring Consolidated Fund Act authorizes the issue of the amount required in the spring supplementaries for the current year and also the total sum required to meet any excess votes in the prior year.

Supply estimates are based on a cash accounting system for payments and receipts. The provision for expenditure reflects the amounts expected to be paid during the financial year. No provision is made in votes for commitments entered into but not yet matured, nor for supporting services for which the receiving department is not required to make a cash payment.

In addition to this year on year process of requesting Parliament to sanction public expenditure, there are also the on-going series of public expenditure surveys which predict the level of public expenditure over the medium term. These forecasts, which are made by Treasury economists, are published twice a year, under Schedule 5 of the 1975 Industry Act. One is usually published with the Budget in the *Financial Statement and Budget Report* (FSBR or 'Red Book'). The other is contained in what has become known as the 'autumn statement'. 1982 saw the first publication of the autumn statement, which can be taken to refer to both the publication and the Chancellor's oral statement (see *Economic Progress Report* 153, HM Treasury, January 1983). The Chancellor of the Exchequer's Budget speech (confusingly titled, since it is primarily concerned with the raising of revenue) has become a much more important occasion in recent years. Whereas Budget speeches once consisted mainly of a very detailed and technical discussion of taxation and borrowing, they now also contain a review of the progress of the British economy against the world economic background and a description of government economic policies. They also introduce new measures for which the government seeks Parliament's approval. Many, though, might still agree with Mr Harold Macmillan, who said in his 1956 Budget speech: 'To tell the truth, I have often thought of Budget Day rather like a school speech day – a bit of a bore, but there it is.'[1]

The annual survey system for planning public expenditure over the medium term has now been in use for 30 years. Its basis followed on from the Plowden Committee's recommendation (Cmnd. 1432, 1961) that: 'Regular surveys should be made of public expenditure as a whole, over a period of years ahead, and in relation to prospective resources; decisions involving substantial future expenditure should be taken in light of these surveys.'

Following the Chancellor's Budget statement in March 1981, the government changed the basis of planning public expenditure from 'volume' to 'cash'. Previously estimates and surveys had been conducted in constant prices, rather loosely described as 'volume'. The use of constant prices enabled an appreciation of the physical inputs since changes in an amount signified a change in volume. While this system may have been satisfactory when inflation was negligible, it has been seen as more of a disadvantage in recent years. It is the government's view that the actual *cash spent* must be considered in relation to, and made consistent with, the government's objectives for taxation, the borrowing requirements and the money supply.

The advantages of cash planning, as set out in *Economic Progress Report 139*, November 1981, are said to be as follows:

1 Ministers discuss the cash that will actually be spent, and therefore what will have to be financed by taxation or borrowing, instead of talking about 'funny money' – the numbers which could be misleadingly different from the resultant cash spent.

2 Expenditure figures can be related more readily to the revenue projections, so that 'finance [can] determine expenditure and not expenditure finance'.

3 Changes in public sector costs are brought into the discussion. The previous constant price system did not bring out the effect of, for example, the rapid relative rise in public service pay in 1979−80 resulting from the Clegg Commission and other comparability awards. Nor, conversely, did it enable the planning figures to reflect the government's stance on public service pay since then.

4 Previously, the 'volume' plans − that is, plans at constant prices − were regarded by spending managers as entitlements, carried forward from year to year regardless of what was happening to costs. This meant that programme managers had little incentive to adapt their expenditures in response to increasing relative costs, except in short term response to the annual cash limits. For example, if a programme successfully absorbed a cash limit squeeze in one year by increased efficiency, this expenditure saving was not carried forward into future plans. The presumption now shifts in favour of maintaining planned cash expenditure, rather than a given 'volume' of provision regardless of cost.

5 The decisions in the annual survey, as they relate to the year ahead, can be translated directly into the cash limits and estimates presented to Parliament, without revaluation from one price basis to another.

While allowances are provided for inflation (a percentage for pay and a percentage for others costs), the change to cash planning was expected to motivate spending managers to think more about what level of service they can provide with only a given amount of money. As noted in chapter 4, this has not transpired; instead the Treasury plays the dominant role in budget provision.

Having described the control procedures of public expenditure, we ought also to mention briefly the roles played by the Comptroller and Auditor General (C & AG) and the various Select Committees of the House of Commons. The C & AG's role is more properly understood if his full title is given: 'The Comptroller General of the Receipt and Issue of Her Majesty's Exchequer and Auditor General of Public Accounts'. He is not a civil servant but is a direct Crown appointee who can only be removed from office by an address from both Houses of Parliament. As his title suggests, he has two functions. As Comptroller General he is charged with authorizing the amounts paid out to spending departments by the Paymaster General, in accordance with the votes specified in the Appropriation Act. As Auditor General he audits, on behalf of the House of Commons, accounts of the transactions of the Consolidated Fund, National Loans Fund and every Appropriation Account. He submits reports on these and other accounts to Parliament. His more general role was discussed in chapter 6.

The (all-party) Public Accounts Committee considers the accounts of each government department and the reports on them by the C & AG. The committee has become a powerful instrument for the exposure of waste and inefficiency. It submits to Parliament reports which carry considerable weight, and its recommendations are taken very seriously by the departments and organizations that it examines. The government's formal reply to these reports is presented to Parliament by the Treasury in the form of a Treasury minute, and the reports and minutes are debated annually in the House. There is, though, quite a time lag before the Public Accounts Committee reports on the Appropriation Accounts. These accounts are usually prepared by the Permanent Secretary of each department, who is designated the 'Accounting Officer', by the November following the year end. The committee usually makes an interim report to the House in the following July. The final report therefore appears 15 months after the financial year end.

Public expenditure is also examined by Select Committees of the House of Commons, which study in detail the activities of government departments and require the attendance of ministers and officials for cross-examination. The system of Select Committees was reformed in 1979 in line with the recommendations of the 1978 Report of the Select Committee on Procedure. The 14 Select Committees are as follows:

Agriculture	Home Affairs
Defence	Industry and Trade
Education, Science and the	Scottish Affairs
Arts	Transport
Employment	Treasury and Civil Service
Energy	Welsh Affairs
Environment	
Foreign Affairs	

Source: Steel and Stanyer (1980), p. 400

This then is the basic framework for controlling public expenditure at the central government level. It is one that presents very summarized information on a cash accounting basis and relies heavily on the investigatory abilities of both the staff of the C & AG and the various Select Committees. This area is one that also attracts the interest of political scientists. Heclo and Wildavsky (1981) provide a useful insight into the political intrigue that underlies the operations of this bureaucratic machine. In their words (p. 6): 'the political administrative culture of British Central Government is a shadowy realm usually left to the chance observations of politicians' memoirs and civil servants' valedictions'.

Central Government Financial Reporting

Financial information on the government's activities and plans follows an annual cycle of five major documents:

1   Financial statement and budget report (March/April)
2   The Autumn statement (November)
3   Departmental reports (January/February)
4   Supply estimates (March)
5   Appropriation accounts (Autumn following previous year end).

The purpose and content of each document is as follows:

Financial Statement and Budget Report (DSBR)

This document is issued by the Treasury on Budget day, typically in March/April each year. the document is also known as the 'Red Book' and suppements the Chancellor's speech in the House of Commons, providing much more detailed background information. It is a document in which the government sets out the Budget, the short-term economic forecast and the medium-term financial strategy, which provides the financial framework for economic policy.

Autumn statement

The Autumn statement is normally published in November each year. it includes a short-term forecast of the UK economy and the announcement of National Insurance contribution rates and thresholds for the year beginning the following April. It sets out the Treasury's latest economic forecast and the planning totals for the next three years, and provides the broad departmental allocation of expenditure which have been agreed during the public expenditure survey (PES). In recent years the autumn statement publication has been considerably expanded to incorporate the most important details of programme expenditure which were formerly incorporated in the public expenditure white paper (PEWP).

Departmental reports

From 1991, the PEWP was replaced by a series of departmental reports published in the early part of each year. These describe in some detail each department's spending plans, its aims and objectives and various output measures against which performance is assessed.

Although these reports do not have to follow a common style and content each contain information in a common format. Cm.918, *Financial Reporting to Parliament*, which was published in January 1990, outlines those components which must have a standard format and/or location within the report (see below).

Supply Estimates

These represent the government's formal request to Parliament for cash to finance the major part of central government's expenditure. The main estimates are presented to the House of Commons in March. Other supplementary estimates are presented during the course of the year, as extra funds are needed.

Appropriate accounts

These are audited by the Comptroller and Auditor General (C & AG) and published in the autumn following the end of the financial year. They record how voted monies have been spent and include reports by the C & AG where appropriate.

This series of publications follows reforms introduced by two white papers, both entitled *Financial Reporting to Parliament* (Cm.375 published in May 1988 and Cm.918 published in January 1990). These reforms followed much discussion in the 1980s on the structure and form of government expenditure reports. See, for example, Likierman and Vass (1984) and the C & AG's Report (HC 576, Session 1985–6).

As we have said the main reforms instituted by these two white papers led to the replacement of the annual public expenditure white paper (PEWP) (previously published in January each year) by an extended autumn statement and, since 1991, by the introduction of annual departmental reports. These changes followed from recommendations set out by the Public Accounts Committee (PAC) in its Eighth Report of 1986–7 (HC 98) Members said that they wanted documents tailored more specifically to Parliament's needs in its consideration of departments' expenditure proposals and put forward three proposals (Cm.375). These were that:

1 The autumn statement should include as much as practicable of the material from Chapter 1 of the PEWP.
2 Volume II of the PEWP, which provided information on individual departments' plans, should be split into separate departmental reports.
3 The remaining material in Volume 1 – the so-called 'additional analyses' – which included detailed information about departmental subprogrammes and the English, Scottish and Welsh components should take more time to produce and be made available in alternative ways, as technical releases, in the spring.

The Treasury and Civil Service Select Committee broadly welcomed the proposals in Cm.375 in their Sixth Report for 1987–8 (HC 614). After consulting with other departmental Select Committees, however, the Public Accounts Committee (PAC) said in its Eighteenth Report for 1988–9 (HC 354) that they did not consider deferral of the publication of departmental reports to March (spring) to be a satisfactory way of bringing the reports alongside the estimates and urged the Treasury to examine the possibility of bringing forward the publication of both documents to January. Cm.918 sought to address this issue by committing the government to see if these reports could be made available a couple of months earlier. Indeed, following on from the government's Next Steps agencies (see below), for many government executive operations outturn information in departmental reports will, in future, be supplemented by individual agencies' annual reports to Parliament. These reports will normally be made in the early months of each financial year, allowing the inclusion of outturn information relating to the financial year just ended. Agencies' reports will thus provide information on both the financial and operational performance of the activities they cover at an earlier stage than is possible in departmental reports.

It is government's intention that departmental reports need not follow a standardized format, or 'housestyle', but that they must include certain common core components. The reports should therefore incorporate the following components (based on Cm.918):

1 **Components which must have a standard format and/or location within each report**

   (a) *Cash plans* that will, as previously, cover a nine-year period, spanning five outturn years, the current year, and three plan years, and show the following information:

   (i) central government's own expenditure (distinguishing between voted and other expenditure);
   (ii) central government grants to local authorities (identifying most specific grants and EC current grants as separate items);
   (iii) other elements of central government support to local authorities as appropriate;
   (iv) financing requirements of public corporations (distinguishing between voted and other items).

   (b) A *brief statement of the department's overall aims and objectives*, giving ordered priorities and listings where appropriate.

   (c) Establishment costs (i.e. *running costs* and *manpower*). The tabular presentation of running costs and manpower information should follow the layout as presented in the 1989 Public Expenditure White Paper.

   (d) *Local authority expenditure.* For those departments where it is relevant, a table should be included showing local authority expenditure for the five outturn years and the current year. This table should also, as a minimum, provide a separate functional breakdown for current and capital expenditure.

2 **Essential features of the report as a whole**

   (a) *Evaluation, output and performance information.* Each report should, as far as is practicable, provide information on the achievement of efficiency and effectiveness programme targets, together with targets for future years.

   (b) *Major initiatives to secure better value for money.* The objectives of each initiative should be clearly described, along with information on what has been achieved to date, and what is planned to be achieved.

   (c) *Next Steps Agencies.* For each agency, departments should provide information on gross and net cash provision, and manpower and other establishment costs, along with a description of its aims, objectives and efforts to provide value for money.

(d) *Information on public corporations.* Apart from the provision of their financing requirements, additional information should also include:

   (i) objectives set by the government and by the industry itself;

   (ii) performance against external financial limits (EFLs);

   (iii) outturn and plans for internal resources and external finance, including government grants; revenue forecasts and forecasts and factors determining revenue and costs; and comparisons of planned expenditure with outturn;

   (iv) investment plans;

   (v) current outlook; and, where relevant, progress to privatization.

(e) *Information on non-departmental public bodies.* At least an 'equivalent' level of detail should be provided as under the previous arrangements.

(f) *Expenditure on publicity and advertising.* The Treasury and Civil Service Committee (Second Report, 1987–8) recommendation that departmental reports should give information about the costs of major publicity and advertising is to apply for departments who spend £1\2 million or more a year on paid UK publicity.

(g) *Explanations of changes in plans from previous white papers.*

(h) A *cross-reference to the relevant estimates booklets.*

(i) A *bibliography.*

(j) An explanation of recent significant (undefined) changes in *classification* or allocation of expenditure.

(k) Reference to any significant *receipts from the EC* in respect of the department's programmes.

(l) Description where relevant of the *split of responsibility* and expenditure between the department and territorial departments.

(m) With respect to the territorial departments, a description of the *block* arrangements.

At the time of writing only reports for 1991 and 1992 have been published and it is too early to evaluate the input that these new reporting arrangements will have. Clearly Select Committees will have an important role to play in further developing the presentation of these reports to ensure that they provide greater accountability. It is believed that all but two committees have carried out some form of investigation based on information provided in the 1991 series of reports. However, the approach to such investigations was not systematic.

Management reform

Chapter 4 briefly reviewed various management techniques that have been tried and then abandoned by government. These included planning, programming, budgeting (PPB) and programme analysis and review (PAR). This section brings discussion on the process of central government management reform up to date by reviewing developments since 1980. We commence by reviewing the work of the Efficiency Unit, established in 1979, and then move on to consider the Financial Management initiative, launched in May 1982, and the Next Steps initiative, launched in February 1988.

The political emphasis for these and other initiatives has been crucial to a Conservative government set on a course of action that can best be described by the phrase 'small is beautiful'. Efficiency and effectiveness have become the buzz words that have been used to eliminate waste and reduce the level of public sector manpower.

The Efficiency Unit

One of Margaret Thatcher's first appointments when she became Prime Minister was that of Lord (then Sir) Derek Rayner as a part-time adviser on improving efficiency and eliminating waste in government. Rayner, a Marks and Spencer executive, had the support of five or six fulltime civil servants – the Efficiency Unit – which since July 1983 has formed part of the Cabinet Office. The main plank of Rayner's approach to improving efficiency was the establishment of a programme of scrutinies which were designed to examine not the merits of policies but rather their implementation. There have been well over 300 scrutinies carried out since 1979 The scrutiny approach involves selecting targets for examination, typically over a 90-day time-scale. The examining officer in a scrutiny is a member of the department in which it is to take place, not a member of the central unit, and is normally appointed from within the department. The key elements in scrutinies are as follows:

The aim is greater value for money by improving the efficiency and effectiveness with which departments deliver policies, programmes and service.

The focus is priorities for improvements.

The Permanent Secretary supervises the process in association with the mininster.

The scrutiny takes nothing for granted but looks directly at what actually happens at all levels of the area under study.

The examining officer comes from within the department but not from the area to be reviewed.

The examining officer is independent and reports direct to the minister and Permanent Secretary.

The scrutiny process as a tight schedule and is in four parts: investigation; action plan; implementation; implementation report.

The action manager converts the report into results and delivers a report on what has been achieved within two years of the start of the process.

The Efficiency Unit will be involved throughout the process.

Source: Efficiency Unit, (1988).

Table 7.1 outlines the five stages involved in a scrutiny.

In the words of one commentary, looking back over five years, (PM, 1984, p. 13):

The scrutiny approach therefore encouraged the intensive application of a fresh mind to an activity. The emphasis is on questioning and on finding facts out for oneself, rather than relying on conventional wisdom or paper. Officers are expected to go out and talk to the people who do the work rather than confine their questioning to top people in headquarters.

Stage three is the crucial stage of any scrutiny. The action document is expected to be produced within three months of the completion of the scrutiny report and to contain for each recommendation:

1 Minister's response;
2 suggested modification (where applicable);
3 consultations required;
4 legislative action required;
5 administrative action required;
6 target date(s) for implementation;
7 the expected savings (in money and in manpower) and by when;
8 the names of the officials responsible for carrying through the actions.

Table 7.1   Stages in a scrutiny

---

1   Setting up a scrutiny

The Minister	Approves subject for scrutiny
Permanent Secretary	Identifies the action manager
	Chooses the examining officer
	Issues the specification
Scrutiny liaison officer	Informs the relevant staff and the trade union side
	Co-ordinates the starting brief

2   Doing the investigation

Study plan	Plans the scrutiny
Examining officer with support advice from the Efficiency Unit	Approves the team
	Drafts the study plan
	Consults those concerned including trade unions
	Circulates the study plan within 15 working days of starting the scrutiny
Minister and Permanent Secretary	Review the study plan with the scrutiny team
Fieldwork	Collects evidence
Examining officer with support and advice from the Efficiency Unit	Organizes team
Action manager	Assists the examining officer
Synopsis	
Examining officer with support and advice from Efficiency Unit	Prepares the synopsis after 60 working days
	Discuss the synopsis with the Permanent Secretary
	Consults the trade union side on emerging findings affecting staff
Permanent Secretary	Reviews the synopsis with the scrutiny team
Report	Drafts report
Examining officer with support and advice from the Efficiency Unit	Informally consults interested managers
	Issues report to the minister and Permanent Secretary

Table 7.1   Stages in a scrutiny (*cont.*)

Permanent Secretary	Discusses the report with the scrutiny team
Efficiency Unit	Comments on the report
Minister	Accepts the report
3 Action Plan	
Action manager	Prepares the action plan
	Consults trade unions and other interested bodies
Minister and Permanent Secretary	Decide on recommendations
	Decide whether and how to public
	Approve the action plan
Efficiency Unit	Comments on the action plan
4 Implementation	
Permanent Secretary	Responsible for implementation
Action manager	Ensures approved recommendations are implemented
Scrutiny liaison officer	Acts as Permanent Secretary's agent
5 Implementation Report	
Action manager	Prepares final implementation report within two years
Permanent Secretary	Ensures that implementation report is accurate and implementation is achieved
Efficiency Unit	Comments to the minister on results achieved
Minister	Accepts implementation report

Source: Efficiency Unit

One of the by-products of the scrutiny programme was the establishment of the MINIS system in, initially, the Department of the Environment. The MINIS system was introduced in 1980 and is a management information system designed to identify resources consumed on specified activities by organizational units. These organizational units typically represent undersecretary commands. MINIS derives its name from the phrase 'Management Information for

Ministers'. Other departments have installed similar systems, complete with acronym. These include MINIM and MAIS for the systems installed in the Ministry of Agriculture, Fisheries and Food, MAISY for the Cabinet Office, ARM in Trade and Industry and FMIS for the Department of Education and Science.

The Financial Management initiative

The Financial Management initiative (FMI) was launched by the Prime Minister in May 1982 as part of her government's reply to the Treasury and Civil Service Select Committee's third report (HC 236, Session 1981–2), published three months earlier. This report, entitled *Efficiency and Effectiveness in the Civil Service*, called for (paragraph 94):

1 A common framework of analysis. . . for the proper management and evaluation of programmes and assessment of efficiency and effectiveness. . .
2 . . . Ministers should not be able to escape accountability by not declaring objectives and targets. Ministers may choose to delegate the carrying out of particular tasks to their subordinates, especially their permanent secretaries but, because they are answerable to Parliament, they will need to satisfy themselves that the delegated tasks are being performed satisfactorily. Ministers should realize that ability to manage their Departments is as important to the country as their performance on the floor of either House or in Committees.

Other recommendations included:

1 improvements to the information provided in the annual public expenditure white paper;
2 the adoption of MINIS, or its equivalent, by all departments (and, as appropriate, other public sector bodies);
3 the provision of greater responsibility to line management.

The government's reply was contained in a white paper – Cmnd. 8616: *Efficiency and Effectiveness in the Civil Service*. Paragraph 13 spelt out three clear principles for management reform:

The aim of the financial management initiative is to promote in each department an organization and system in which managers at all levels have:

(a) a clear view of their objectives and means to assess and, wherever possible, measure outputs or performance in relation to their objectives;

(b) welldefined responsibility for making the best use of resources, including a critical scrutiny of output and value for money; and

(c) the information (particulary about costs), the training and the access to expert advice that they need to exercise their responsibilities effectively.

These three principles were originally spelt out in the working document with which this initiative was launched (reproduced in Cmnd. 8616 as appendix 3) Each department was required to develop and define a plan which on completion was to be sent to the Treasury and the Management and Personnel Office (MPO). The MPO forms part of the Prime Minister's Cabinet Office. The plans produced by departments were summarized in another white paper (Cmnd. 9058, September 1983). The scale of the proposals meant that the implementation would take several years to complete. Cmnd. 9058 estimated that the cost of implementation over the first two years would be some £35 million, which would cover staff costs, computer hardware and software, and consultancy.

The central task of the FMI was to alter the way in which decisions are made about public expenditure, particularly through the creation of line management responsibility. In many ways one could argue that there was nothing new in the FMI; it was simply that many of these changes were almost two decades late in being recommended since they closely resemble many of the proposals contained in the Fulton Commitee Report of 1968 (Cmnd. 3638). In one review (PM 1986, p. 8) it was stated that:

> The story is still very much one of departments making steady progress in establishing information systems, trying to acquire the relevant basic financial skills, feeling their way towards some rudimentary output and performance measures and deciding on the best approach to reorganising departmental structures and responsibilities.

The Financial Management Unit was established to assist central government departments with implementation of the FMI. Later it was redesignated the Joint Management Unit and, even more recently, absorbed within the Treasury's Management Policy and Running Costs group.

Paragraph 19 of *Progress in Financial Management in Government* (Cmnd. 9297, July 1984) considered that there was a 'concerted effort to push forward improvements in management'. This momentum was being monitored by:

1 *The Treasury*, with its provision of guidance to departments on the development and application of output measures and performance indicators.
2 *The Cabinet Office (Management and Personnel Office)* leading in major areas of training and personnel management.
3 *The Financial Management Unit* set up by the Treasury and MPO in order to disseminate useful lessons and good practice, and to bring common problems to the attention of the central departments.
4 *The Efficiency Unit* in its main aim of encouraging and assisting individual departments to make their top management systems effective.

Gray and Jenkins (1986) conclude that while the FMI has enhanced the status and operation of certain aspects of financial management, notably those relating to the management of costs, this has tended to be at the expense of the integration of strategic management and even of accountability itself. They note that the FMI represents a particular view of what accountable management (and even management accounting) is about. Whereas in the 1970s efficiency meant the maximization of outputs for given levels of input, the language of the FMI, and for that matter other associated developments, indicates that the code of accountable management now in use emphasizes a responsibility (and accountability) for reducing inputs regardless of output. Little is heard about policy effects or outcomes.

The hallmark of a good management information system is that it should be politically neutral; that is, it should address the economic consequences of government policy regardless of their ideological viewpoint.

In a more recent study, Gray and Jenkins et al. (1991, p. 49) note that:

Although many in central government speak of the FMI as if it were a homogeneous concept and practice, there are conceptually and operationally many FMIs. This is true both between and within departments as well as in the Treasury. Some conceive the FMI simply as a limited, if useful, instrument for controlling *costs*. Others regard it as a more substantial system for planning, allocating and controlling *resources*. For a few it is, more significantly, a general philosophy and regime of departmental *management*.

Despite the original aim of integrating operational and resource responsibilities, almost everyone in Whitehall confirms that in practice FMI has concentrated on the management of resources.

The Next Steps initiative

The Next Steps initiative was recommended by the Efficiency Unit in its report, *Improving Management in Government: The Next Steps Agencies* (Cm. 1261). They suggested that many civil service managers wanted to see further changes to give more room and flexibility for the exercise of personal responsibility. The report went on to recommend that 'to the greatest extent practicable' the executive functions of government, as distinct from policy advice, should be carried out by 'units clearly designated within departments' – agencies. The day-to-day responsibility for each agency lies with a chief executive. This person is responsible for management leadership within a framework of policy objectives and resources set by the responsible minister, in consultation with the Treasury. These new agencies will generally be within the civil service, and their staff will continue to be civil servants. To co-ordinate this development, a Next Steps project manager has been appointed. Located in the Cabinet Office, he reports directly to the Prime Minister.

By November 1991 (Cm. 1761 – *The Next Steps Initiative*) there were 56 agencies plus 30 executive units in the Customs and Excise. These new bodies took over the management of some 200,000 civil servants and 8,000 armed forces personnel – around 40 per cent of the civil service. By April 1992 it is projected that the number of agencies will have risen to 70 and that around 50 per cent of the civil service will be organized on Next Steps principles.

In a review by the Next Steps project manager (Kemp, 1990, p. 26) three beneficiaries of this initiative were identified:

1 The taxpayer: The financial targets set for each agency are designed to be demanding, 'so that the taxpayer can be certain that the money that is provided for these services is used in the most efficient way'.
2 Customers: 'Each agency has quality service targets. Many take the form of cutting turnround times.'
3 Staff: 'The Agencies are putting considerable efforts into seeing what skills are needed and putting into effect the appropriate

development programmes to ensure that their existing staff can meet them . . . There have also been financial rewards for staff.'

In the early days of this initiative there are examples of improved service to customers. Companies House, for example, which was established as an agency in October 1988, had by April 1991 reduced from 25 days to 12 days the time it takes to process documents, against a target reduction to 18 days. Companies House also sends out registration forms which are already preprinted with the details they have on record so that companies only need make alterations. Targets are reviewed year on year. The targets for Companies House for the two years to April 1991 were as follows (Cm.1261):

1 A 10 per cent reduction in the proportion of companies which have not filed all accounts and annual returns required by the Companies Act, so that by June 1991 the compliance rate will be increased to 83 per cent.
2 A 20 per cent reduction in the time taken to process documents so that by April 1991 documents are on average available to the public within 18 working days of being delivered to Companies House.
3 A 12 per cent increase in output per member of staff.
4 A 7 per cent decrease in unit costs in real terms.

In the event, for target (1) 78 per cent was achieved; for target (2) 7 days was achieved; for target (3) 17 per cent was achieved; and for target (4) 2 per cent was achieved. Each annual review now reports the actual improvements achieved together with the revised targets for the coming year.

Despite obvious successes Kemp (1990, p. 27) does note that many staff have been fearful of the Next Steps initiative:

It would be foolish to deny that there has been great suspicion that when we talk about freedoms and flexibilities what we are actually talking about is worsening existing terms and conditions. I can state categorically that this is not the case.

Conclusion

The Conservative government is now in its fourth consecutive term of office. In the early years of the Thatcher administration we had the Efficiency Unit. Now we have the Next Steps initiative and the Citizen's Charter Unit. Indeed, members of parliament will be able to ask questions directly about the Citizen's Charter. Mr William

Waldergrave, the minister in charge of this initiative, faces questions from MPs every three weeks. Allied to the Citizens' Charter, Cm. 1730, *Competing for Quality* (November 1991), seeks to subject government programmes to market testing. This white paper proposes four changes:

1 providing incentives to managers to pursue competition;
2 promoting competition through the establishment of targets and by the dissemination of best practice;
3 ensuring fair competition by removing the obstacles and disincentives to contracting out;
4 encouraging the private sector to identify further opportunities for providing public services under contract.

These reforms are to be coordinated by a newly created Public Competition and Purchasing Unit in the Treasury.

Time alone will tell whether these initiatives will significantly add to the drive towards improved VFM in central government, or, as so often in the past, will in the end have little effect.

Notes

1 From 1993 there is to be a change from spring to end-of-year budgets. The change will lead to a slight timing revision of some of the government's financial reports.

8

Local Government

Introduction

While the basic origins of our present structure of local government can be traced back to Anglo-Saxon times, the last two decades of the nineteenth century saw the establishment of local government in the UK as we know it today.[1] The most recent reorganization of local government started in 1965 in London with the widening of the boundaries of the metropolis. Local government in Northern Ireland was next to be reorganized in 1973.[2] The following year witnessed the disappearance of the county boroughs in England and Wales and the introduction of a two-tier system of counties and districts (introduced by the Local Government Act 1972). This reform also included the introduction of metropolitan counties and metropolitan districts with different functions to their non-metropolitan counterparts. The 1972 Act also established the Local Government Boundary Commission. Its initial task was to recommend the boundaries for the 1974 reorganization but since then it has undertaken regular reviews of boundaries and electoral arrangements in all tiers of government. Changes in Scotland, in 1975, were broadly similar to those introduced in England and Wales. They do, however, operate under a different legislative framework and legal system.

The 1980s witnessed another round of changes. The Local Government Act 1985 led, in April 1986, to the abolition of the Greater London Council and the six metropolitan county councils. The six metropolitan counties were Greater Manchester, Merseyside, South Yorkshire, Tyne and Wear, West Midlands and West Yorkshire. The functions and responsibilities of these authorities were transferred to constituent borough and district councils or joint authorities made up of elected members from the lower tier authorities. The government's proposals for the abolition of these authorities were originally introduced by the Department of the Environment in October 1983 (Cmnd. 9063, *Streamlining the Cities*.) In the government's view these seven authorities had consistently exceeded their expenditure targets. Paragraph 1.8 of Cmnd. 9063 pointed out that whereas shire county councils were responsible for 87 per cent of total expenditure on local services in their areas, the Greater London Council and the metropolitan county councils were responsible for 16 and 26 per cent respectively. According to Richards (1985), the government estimated savings of approximately £100 million per annum by the removal of this tier of government. Transitional costs, composed mainly of staff compensation and redundancy, were estimated at £40 million for 1986–7, while staff numbers were forecast to be reduced by some 8,000. By contrast, Coopers and Lybrand estimated that abolishing the Greater London Council alone would cost the government six to eight times more than it had bargained for. Their report, which was commissioned by the Greater London Council, claimed that many of the savings proposed could just as well be made without the expensive and managerially disruptive reform of local government. Most recently the government (DOE, April 1991) has reiterated that estimated savings were in the order of £100 but that the number of posts saved was revised downwards at 6,500. London is unique in Europe as a capital city that does not have one unitary level of local government to manage its affairs.

Local government reform looks likely to continue into the 1990s. In April 1991 the Department of the Environment issued a consultation paper entitled *The Structure of Local Government in England*. This paper states that the government believes that there should be a move towards unitary authorities where these do not already exist. The government hopes that the first new unitary authorities can be set up by April 1994. The Department issued a second consultation paper a few months later in July 1991 entitled *The Internal Management of Local Authorities in England*. In this paper the government introduced a wide range of alternative options to the way local government is currently managed. Options include the introduction of a cabinet system at the local government level and directly elected mayors. The annex to this paper reviews a number of models of executive management of local authorities in other countries. This latest discussion paper (DOE, July 1991, para. 4) summarizes the government's view that:

. . . local authorities' role in the provision of services should be to assess the needs of their area, plan the provision of services and ensure the delivery of those services. There are also fields in functions and providing roles. But councils should be looking to contract out work to whoever can deliver services most efficiently and effectively, thus enabling the authority to be more responsive to the wishes of their electorate.

Since the Second World War local authorities have lost many of their functions to central government. Some, such as the Poor Law (1934, 1947), most civil airports (1945), electricity (1947), gas (1948) and most recently water (1974) have been transferred to public corporations (see chapter 10). Other, such as trunk roads (1946), hospitals (1947) and most remaining local health services (1974), have been transferred to central government. Polytechnics are now centrally funded and from 1992 colleges of further education also ceased to be a local authority responsibility. More recently local authorities have gained responsibility for care in the community and special responsibility for young people at risk. Local authorities are currently having to cope with changes in a number of major service areas for which they remain responsible, such as education, social services and refuse collection and disposal. Table 8.1 summarizes, as at 1990, the main functions carried out by local authorities in England and Wales. Holtham (1989) provides a more detailed analysis of the structure and functions of local authorities in Britain.

With this brief introduction, the remainder of this chapter is in five parts and considers: local authority income and expenditure, local taxation, capital expenditure control, external reporting and a case study on one local authority's efforts to reform its structure of financial management.

Since the introduction of the Public Expenditure Survey Committee (PESC) system in the early 1960s successive governments have taken the view that all local government expenditure, not merely the grant aided element, should form part of the public expenditure planning process. The UK trend is more and more geared towards central control of local authority spending, with the unfortunate effect that management often become discouraged from long-term planning. This approach can be contrasted to that adopted in the United States and a number of European countries, where there is no detailed control of local government spending. With this trend towards greater national planning, one wonders how much longer local decision-making can continue in any meaningful sense. While recent Department of the Environment discussion papers offer the view that the proposed changes, as outlined above, will promote more effective, speedy and business-like decision-making, elected councillors and management

Table 8.1   Main functions of local authorities as at 1 April 1990

Function	Metropolitan		England and Wales non-metropolitan		London		Scotland	
	Joint	District	County	District	Joint	Borough	Region	District
Community charge collection		X		X		X		X
Consumer protection		X	X			X	X	
Education		X	X			X	X	
Environmental health		X		X		X		X
Fire service	X		X		X		X	
Housing		X		X		X		X
Industrial development		X	X	X		X	X	X
Libraries		X	X			X		X
Passenger transport	X		X				X	
Planning								
Strategic plans		X	X		X		X	
Development control		X		X		X		X
Police	X		X		(Central Government)		X	
Recreation		X		X		X		X
Refuse disposal		X	X			X		X
Social services		X	X			X	X	
Transport and highways								
Policy and principal roads		X	X			X	X	
Non-principal roads		X	X	X		X	X	
Water							X	

Source: Holtham (1989)

have to live with the fact that well over 80 per cent of their income comes direct from central government.

Local Authority Income and Expenditure

All local authority spending has to be authorized by statute or subordinate legislation. Such legislation can be divided into two broad categories: that which imposes an obligation on local authorities to do something (mandatory legislation) and that which permits local authorities to provide certain additional services at their own discretion (permissive legislation). Annex 12 of the Layfield Committee Report (Cmnd. 6453, 1976) usefully illustrates the classification of services into these two categories. The only exception to this principle is provided under Part III of the Local Government and Housing Act 1989 whereby authorities may undertake limited discretionary spending up to the limit of £2.50 per head of 'relevant population'. Such funds can be spent by a local authority on purposes 'in the interests of their area or any part of it to all or some of its inhabitants' (Local Government Act 1972, Section 137).

Local authorities account for around one quarter of central government expenditure. Total current and capital spending (which includes debt interest) by local authorities in 1990–1 is estimated to be £57.3 billion (Cm. 1520, *Public Expenditure Analyses to 1993–94*, HM Treasury, 1991). England accounts for around 85 per cent of expenditure, Scotland around 10 per cent and Wales around 5 per cent. Most equivalent spending in Northern Ireland is central government spending carried out by Northern Ireland departments. Education spending has been over 40 per cent of the local authority total in recent years. Most of the rest goes on law and order, housing and other environmental services, personal social services and transport expenditure. Although in theory each local authority can make its own decisions about the level of service it provides, such decisions are heavily influenced by the control that central government exercises over funding. This has been demonstrated in recent years with the introduction of so-called 'rate-capping' (introduced by the Rates Act, 1984) and more recently 'capping' revenue expenditure associated with the introduction of the community charge (often referred to as the poll tax). In the first year of operation (1984–5) 18 English authorities, which together accounted for about three-quarters of the overspending in England, were selected for rate limitation in 1985–6 under the provisions of the 1984 Act. They were set expenditure levels requiring in most cases a cash standstill on 1984–5 adjusted budgets. The government's view is that it is unwilling to have local authorities consuming an ever-increasing share of real national resources because this leaves less available for other sectors of the community.

Under a changed definition of the planning total, introduced in 1989, the government no longer makes provision for total local authority expenditure. However, as Cm. 1520 (para. 5.21) points out:

> a projection of local authority self-financed expenditure for the forward years has to be made in order to provide a path for general government expenditure. The projection has been made by deducting planned central government support for local authorities from projections of total local authority expenditure net of capital receipts.

Table 8.2 (Cm. 1920, table 5.11) provides outturns and projections of local authority expenditure over the period 1986–7 to 1994–9. Projections in this table have been prepared on an aggregate basis; that is, for current expenditure, net capital and debt interest taken as a whole. The actual levels of current and capital expenditure are for individual local authorities to determine in the light of central government support made available and the financial and community charge implications. Table 8.3 (Cm. 1920, table 5.8) shows the service distribution of current expenditure in the years 1986–7 to 1991–2 and Table 8.4 (Cm. 1920, table 5.9) shows capital expenditure on the same basis.

The Local Government Finance Act 1988 provided for major changes in the system of local authority current finance in England and Wales from 1 April 1990. Similar changes were introduced in Scotland in 1989. The changes introduced were threefold. Cm. 1021 (para 4.6) summarizes these changes:

- The system for distributing the new *Revenue Support Grant* (RSG) will be different from that for the previous Rate Support Grant. The new grant will be the main block of support from the taxpayer for local authority services, and will be the means of compensating for differences in the Government's assessment of the amount authorities have to spend to provide a standard level of service.
- The Community Charge, payable by all adults (with certain limited exceptions).
- Locally set business rates will be by a *National Non-Domestic*

Rate (NNDR), set by central government at a uniform poundage (or multiplier) for England and (separately) for Wales. Increases in the NNDR poundage will be limited to no more than the increase in the retail prices index in the year to the previous September. The proceeds of the NNDR in England and (separately) Wales will be pooled and distributed to local authorities as a common amount per chargepayer. In Scotland, from April 1990, the Secretary of State will prescribe the non-domestic rate income for individual authorities, in line with the Government's policy of harmonising non-domestic rates in Scotland and England over time.

Under this system, central government intends to establish the amount of local authority support before the start of the financial year. At the margin, therefore, local authorities' spending decisions will be reflected fully in the community charge. This system is designed to reflect what the Conservative government believes to be a central objective, that of imposing accountability between elected local councillors and their electorates.

While government might well state that actual levels of expenditure are for individual local authorities to decide, such a discretion is in fact tightly controlled from Whitehall. As the Environment Secretary announced on 31 October 1990, government is prepared to make full use of its powers to 'cap' authorities' revenue budgets if necessary. Cm. 1311 (para 1.73), *Autumn Statement 1990*, indicates that the government considers:

> year on year increases of 9, 7 or 5 per cent as excessive, depending on how far the resulting budget exceeds an authority's Standard Spending Assessment (SSA). Any budget more than 12 per cent above the SSA would be considered excessive.

Local authorities have four main sources of finance for capital expenditure. These are:

1 Credit approvals: central government permissions to borrow, or enter into other credit arrangements for capital spending;

2 Capital grants: provided by government to finance specified proportions of expenditures on particular programmes;

Table 8.2   Local authority expenditure in the United Kingdom

	1986–87 outturn	1987–88 outturn	1988–89 outturn	1989–90 outturn	1990–91 outturn	1991–92 estimated outturn	1992–93 projections	1993–94 projections	£million 1994–95 projections
Total local authority expenditure	42,107	44,992	47,249	53,637	57,374	63,800	76,000	70,500	73,000
less central government support	33,393	35,792	36,621	38,363	42,521	53,300	58,500	61,100	63,900
equals local authority self-financed expenditure	8,713	9,200	10,627	15,274	14,853	10,500	8,500	9,000	9,000

(1) *The estimated outturn figures for 1991–92 are rounded to the nearest £100 million, as are the new plans for central government support. The projections of total local authority expenditure and local authority self-financed expenditure are rounded to the nearest £500 million.*

Source: Cm. 1920, Table 5.11

Table 8.3 Local authority current expenditure in Great Britain by territory and function

	1986–87 outturn	1987–88 outturn	1988–89 outturn	1989–90 outturn	1990–91 outturn	£million 1991–92 estimated outturn
England						
Agriculture, fisheries, food and forestry	154	163	171	96	54	60
Trade, industry, energy and employment	176	186	204	212	250	276
Roads and transport	1,792	1,806	1,790	1,926	2,288	2,383
Housing	609	704	672	671	314	344
Other environmental services	2,376	2,558	2,696	3,028	3,898	4,197
Law, order and protective services	3,890	4,250	4,681	5,284	5,901	6,595
Education	13,228	14,506	15,572	16,242	17,813	19,947
Arts and libraries	437	467	498	551	614	659
Personal social services	2,631	2,968	3,301	3,717	4,178	4,587
Social security	2,979	3,085	3,279	3,747	4,265	4,925
Total current expenditure in England	**28,272**	**30,692**	**32,864**	**35,474**	**39,575**	**43,974**
Scotland						
Agriculture, fisheries, food and forestry	4	4	3	3	3	4
Trade, industry, energy and employment	13	14	20	19	24	26
Roads and transport	289	304	318	339	348	394
Housing	79	44	29	11	9	7
Other environmental services	387	403	434	460	518	575
Law, order and protective services	375	416	444	502	559	607

Table 8.3 cont.

	1986–87 outturn	1987–88 outturn	1988–89 outturn	1989–90 outturn	1990–91 outturn	£million 1991–92 estimated outturn
Education	1,650	1,805	1,959	2,161	2,348	2,534
Arts and libraries	56	60	65	73	86	94
Personal social services	350	393	440	499	566	633
Social security	349	404	422	497	539	693
Total current expenditure in Scotland	**3,552**	**3,846**	**4,135**	**4,565**	**5,000**	**5,567**
Wales						
Agriculture, fisheries, food and forestry	10	10	10	12	12	13
Trade, industry, energy and employment	12	13	14	17	17	20
Roads and transport	111	122	128	139	151	160
Housing	10	11	13	14	14	17
Other environmental services	194	203	223	253	308	353
Law, order and protective services	204	225	246	2079	307	342
Education	796	856	941	1,025	1,134	1,276
Arts and libraries	20	21	24	26	29	32
Personal social services	135	149	176	200	237	274
Social security	190	192	209	228	257	299
Total current expenditure in Wales	**1,681**	**1,802**	**1,983**	**2,193**	**2,466**	**2,787**
Total current expenditure in Great Britain	**33,505**	**36,339**	**38,982**	**42,232**	**47,041**	**52,328**

Source: Cm. 1920, Table 5.8

Table 8.4 Local authority gross capital expenditure in Great Britain by territory, cash block and service[1]

	1986–87 outturn	1987–88 outturn	1988–89 outturn	1989–90 outturn	1990–91 outturn	£million 1991–92 estimated outturn
England						
ELAB[2]						
Housing	2,874	3,124	3,402	4,784	2,843	2,673
Transport	695	755	961	1,138	918	1,037
Education	728	758	975	1,237	1,150	1,003
Personal Social Services	113	144	171	218	163	159
Home Office	49	53	60	69	50	50
Ministry of Agriculture, Fisheries and Food[3]	29	29	41	49	34	47
Other Services						
Environment	846	884	1,126	1,582	916	982
Other departments[4]	61	60	76	111	76	71
Total Other Services	907	943	1,201	1,693	992	1,053
Housing Association						
Grant	120	122	169	314	278	298
ELAB[2]	**5,515**	**5,928**	**6,980**	**9,501**	**6,427**	**6,320**

Table 8.4 contd.

	1986–87 outturn	1987–88 outturn	1988–89 outturn	1989–90 outturn	1990–91 outturn	£million 1991–92 estimated outturn
Law and Order Services (Home Office)						
England	149	169	197	242	220	270
Wales	8	10	13	16	7	14
Total Law and Order Services	**158**	**179**	**210**	**258**	**227**	**284**
Urban Programme						
Other environmental services	295	318	306	276	301	
Other departments	25	29	30	30	17	16
Total Urban Programme	**319**	**347**	**335**	**339**	**293**	**317**
Memo item: not in cash blocks[5]	8	88	6	5	3	2
England – Total	**5,991**	**6,452**	**7,518**	**10,087**	**6,944**	**6,909**
Scotland						
SO/LA1 – non housing	466	493	544	616	521	593
SO/LA2 – housing	440	596	616	635	612	610
Memo items: not in cash blocks[6]	2	2	1	1	1	1
Scotland-Total	**909**	**1,090**	**1,161**	**1,252**	**1,134**	**1,203**
Wales						
WOLAB[2]						
Transport						
Employment						

Table 8.4 cont.

	1986–87 outturn	1987–88 outturn	1988–89 outturn	1989–90 outturn	1990–91 outturn	£million 1991–92 estimated outturn
Home Office	3	4	2	3	5	
Welsh Office	438	513	518	639	572	606
Total WOLAB[2]	**442**	**517**	**520**	**642**	**577**	**606**
Wales-Total	**450**	**526**	**533**	**658**	**584**	**620**
Local authority gross capital expenditure in Great Britain	**7,350**	**8,068**	**9,213**	**11,997**	**8,661**	**8,733**

(1) The blocks reflects the arrangements for distributing central government support for local authority capital expenditure and for monitoring this expenditure.

(2) ELAB is English Local Authorities Block and WOLAB is Welsh Office Local Authorities Block.

(3) Expenditure on flood and coast protection and harbour improvements. Other expenditure on agriculture, fisheries and food is included in "Other Services".

(4) Includes employment, trade and industry arts and libraries and agriculture, fisheries and agriculture, fisheries and food (other than flood and coast protection and harbour improvements)

(5) Expenditure by internal drainage boards.

(6) Expenditure on ports, airports and Training Agency projects which is not the responsibility of the Secretary of State for Scotland.

Source: Cm. 1920, Table 5.9

3 Revenue contribu   which are subject to the accountability of the
tions to capital outlay: community charge;
4 Capital receipts: the ability to redeploy proportions of capital
                           receipts from the sale of land, houses and
                           other assets.

With respect to the redeployment of capital receipts, Cm. 1021 (para
4.11) points out that local authorities are required to set aside 75 per
cent of their council house capital receipts and 50 per cent of most
other receipts to redeem their debts.

In concluding this section, brief reference must also be made to local
authority investment powers. The 1980s have witnessed much debate
concerning local authority powers to borrow and lend funds for
purposes other than traditional needs – the Hammersmith & Fulham
case, for example. Local authorities lend day-today cash surpluses in
the money market as part of prudent day-to-day cash management.
Additionally, substantial cash surpluses have been generated by the
disposal of assets and there has been a need to invest these funds over
the short, medium and long term. More worryingly, some local
authorities have been playing the money markets by, for example,
borrowing money earlier than needed, or even if not needed at all, in
order to make a profit by lending it on at a better rate of interest. While
the first two activities are deemed within the power of local authorities,
the latter, which amounts to market speculation, is not permissible.

The main powers that allow local authorities to borrow and lend are
now contained in Part IV of the Local Government and Housing Act
1989 (previously covered by paragraphs 1–12 of Schedule 13 of the
Local Government Act 1972) and a number of Treasury controls.
Section 111 of the 1972 Act also empowers local authorities to do
anything whether or not involving borrowing 'which is calculated to
facilitate or is conducive to, the discharge of any of their functions'.
However, legal opinion states that market speculation is not covered
by Section 111 since local authorities have statutory functions to
perform and cannot therefore diversify into other ventures.

Local Taxation

April 1990 saw the replacement of domestic rates in England and
Wales by the community charge (often popularly referred to as the poll
tax). Scotland had introduced the community charge in 1989. This

change has proven to be fraught with political and financial setbacks for the government, who now intend to introduce a council tax, effective from April 1993.

Rates are a tax on property. A rate, expressed as pence in the £, is charged on the rateable value of property. In theory the rateable value of a property should reflect the annual rent obtainable on the open market, net of the cost of any repairs. The taxation of property by means of rates can be traced back to the Poor Relief Act, 1601. Chapter 10 of the Layfield Committee Report (Cmnd. 6453) provides a concise overview of the arguments for and against this type of property tax. Arguments in favour of the rating system include:

1 the ease with which its yield could be attributed to the smallest unit of local government;
2 the form of tax is relatively simple to understand, even though the underlying details may be difficult to comprehend;
3 property is visible and easily identifiable;
4 the yield is predictable and certain;
5 evasion is extremely difficult;
6 collection costs, in proportion to yield, are not high;
7 there are no problems of confidentiality of the taxpayer's personal income and circumstances (except when rebates are claimed).[3]

Criticisms of the rating system can be divided between its impact on domestic and non-domestic ratepayers. As far as domestic ratepayers are concerned, two of the major criticisms concern the ability to pay and the variation between rateable value and income. As regards the ability to pay, there are four elements to this complaint. First, rates take a proportionally large share of the income of poorer households. Second, rates are arbitrary because assessments vary widely for what is apparently the same type of house. Third, rates paid by individual households bear no relationship to their income. Fourth, there is a related complaint that there are extra wage earners in some households who enjoy local services but do not pay local taxes. At least part of this variation arises from the difference in the level of rateable values between areas. Prior to its replacement, the rateable value of similar houses was over twice as high in some parts of the country as in others.

For businesses, as non-domestic ratepayers, there is no direct accountability between themselves and the local authorities since they have no vote. (It is, of course, equally true that all eligible individuals can vote in local elections regardless of whether or not they pay locally levied taxes.) Business rates bear no relation to an ability to pay since they are in no way related to the profitability of the business. Business rates must be paid even when a business is making no profits and their allowability as an expense is of little benefit when no corporation tax is paid. Birdseye and Webb (1984) point out that rates are the biggest form of tax paid by UK businesses. They noted that the Confederation of British Industry estimated that close to £6 billion were paid in rates by UK businesses in 1984–5. This could be compared with the Treasury estimate of £4 billion paid by businesses in mainstream corporation tax and £1.7 billion paid by the employers' national income surcharge.

The Layfield Committee, in reviewing the rating system, also considered alternative sources of local revenue and concluded that only a local income tax was a feasible alternative. However, while a local income tax would be equitable between individuals, fairness between different areas would still have to be achieved by some centrally administered grant. The main disadvantage of a local income tax was felt to be that it would complicate and possibly frustrate central government's use of income tax as a major tool of demand management.

Successive governments over the decades since the Layfield Report declined to consider reform of local taxation. However, an internal departmental review in 1984 led two years later to the green paper *Paying for Local Government* (Cmnd. 9714). The theme of this paper was the need for increased local government accountability. It was the government's view that:

> Effective local accountability must be the cornerstone of success-ful local government. All too often this accountability is blurred and weakened by the complexities of the national grant system and by the fact that differences arise amongst those who vote for, those who pay for and those who receive local government services.

> The present local government financial system does not streng-then local accountability. Local authorities' main income sources are non-domestic rates, domestic rates and Exchequer grant. All of them are unsatisfactory.

> – Non-domestic rates are paid by businesses and public institu-tions to whom local authorities are not directly answerable.
> – Domestic rates are paid by a minority of local electors, and vary in a way that now has little regard to the use made of local authority services. The burden of rates is carried on too few shoulders.

– Central government grants are calculated in a very complicated way that conceals the real cost of services from the local electorate.

With respect to the last of these concerns, the National Audit Office reviewed the operation of the rate support grant in 1985. This report provides a useful overview of the operation of the rate support grant system and considered the effectiveness of the system under four headings. A summary of findings is as follows:

1 Constraint on total spending

Figures presented in paragraph 4.4 of the report indicated that while authorities continued, as a group, to overspend there were some improvements in performance since 1981–2. Prospective overspending for 1984–5 was estimated at just over 4 per cent. The NOA point out that, as it became apparent each year that targets were not going to be met, the government has progressively increased its previously planned levels of local authority spending for subsequent years to allow the overspending authorities more time to moderate their expenditure. The system of targets and penalites has, so far, fallen some way short of producing the results intended by government. It is for this reason that the government has taken powers under the Rates Act 1984 to impose direct limits on the rates or precepts which might be levied by selected authorities, and so on their total spending (the aforementioned rate-capping provisions).

Paragraphs 4.13 to 4.17 point out that many authorities have been guilty of 'creative accounting' in order to maximize grant entitlement and minimize penalties. Expenditure can, for example, be artifically increased by making additional contributions to special funds or capital outlay, and by accelerating the repayment of borrowings; it can be artificially reduced by meeting normal current expenditure from special funds, reducing or reversing budget contribution to other funds or capital outlay, and by deferring the repayment of borrowings.

2 Influence on distribution of expenditure between services

Specific grants only meet about 10 per cent of authorities' expenditure but the NAO thought that the distribution of expenditure between services, was effective in securing delivery of services at least to the minimum standards implied by the government's expenditure plans.

Whether this pattern can continue in the future as tighter expenditure controls are introduced remains open to question.

3 Equalization

The report illustrates (paragraphs 4.38 to 4.40) that the primary use of the grant system has been to constrain spending, and that efforts to enable authorities to finance similar standards of services, by levying similar rate poundages, have yet to be realized.

4 Impact on local authorities and local accountability

The NAO reported the results of a survey carried out by the Audit Commission which indicated that 69 per cent of local authorities did not plan their current expenditure for more than one year ahead. However, this practice seemed to pre-date the introduction of the present rate support grant. The Commission also concluded that local authorities had responded to uncertainties of the grant system by building up additional financial reserves. The NAO concluded that this amounted to deliberate padding (paragraph 4.58) and that it must at least be open to question whether these authorities could prudently have set their rate poundages at generally lower levels. There was also evidence that many officers and members of local authorities found the operation of the rate support system too complex, yet one principal aim of government had originally been to make the system less complex.

The Green Paper recommended, from April 1990, the introduction of a community charge in place of domestic rates. Three types of community charge were introduced:

1 Personal   –falling on virtually all adults;
2 Collective –for people living in multiple occupation rented accommodation and institutions;
3 Standard   –for second home owners, up to a maximum of two
individual charges.

With the community charge came the community charge register. All adults were expected to pay at least 20 per cent of the community charge, including those in receipt of social security benefits. Government would retain the right to cap the community charge of individual councils. A uniform business rate (UBR) was to replace non-domestic rates. The UBR would be set by central government, applied nationally and the monies raised reallocated to councils pro rata to population. During the passage of the legislation through Parliament the UBR became the national non-domestic rate (NNDR).

Despite heavy opposition (see Hale, 1988) the community charge and the revenue support grant, which replaced the rate support grant, took effect from April 1990 following the passing of the Local Government Finance Act 1988.

The implementation of this tax has caused considerable administrative and budgetary strain on local government and has proved to be a very unpopular move. Local/central government relationships have become strained, even in Conservative local administrations. The government published targets for the initial level of tax averaging £265 per adult, but the levels budgeted by local authorities came to one third more on average, at £354. Nearly all local authorities, Conservative and Labour alike, were over target. The major reason for this discrepancy was that local authorities budgeted for around £2.5 billion more expenditure than the government had assumed. For 1991–2, government announced the capping system in advance of budget-making, and in so doing revealed a growing reliance on this device for curtailing local government expenditure. *Local Government Chronicle* (9 November 1990) reported that this move would involve more than half of the shire counties having to cut their expenditure below the rate of inflation in order to avoid being capped.

Year two of this scheme saw the government working on a target level of poll tax for 19912 of around £380 per adult, while local authority and independent forecasts were in the region of £400–430 per adult (see *Local Government Chronicle* 5 August 1990, 21 September 1990 and 2 November 1990). When Michael Heseltine MP launched his challenge for the Conservative leadership in Autumn 1990 he made reform of the community charge a major issue in his campaign. The Conservative leadership crisis saw John Major become Prime Minister in November 1990 and Heseltine return to government as Secretary of State for the Environment with the task of reviewing implementation of the community charge.

When interviewed in the *Conservative Councillor Magazine* (Summer, 1991) Heseltine stated that 'local government is going through a period of profound change that is unavoidable and unstoppable'. In April 1991 the Department of the Environment issued two consultation papers: *The Structure of Local Government in England* and *A New Tax for Local Government*. In the first of these two documents the government states that there should be a move towards unitary authorities where these do not already exist. The second document outlined plans for the abolition of the community charge and its replacement by a council tax. By September 1991 the Conservative Party journal *Politics Today* admitted that the community charge had 'failed to secure general support and acceptance which every type of taxation must have'.

The Queen's Speech reopening Parliament on 31 October 1991 included reference to a new Local Government Finance Bill which would pave the way for the introduction of the council tax. The main features of this new tax are:

1 Its rates, to be set by each council, will reflect the capital value of property distributed within eight bands. The lowest band is to be set at £40,000 and the highest at £320,000.
2 Scotland and Wales will have a separate banding structure, but no regional variations will be introduced in England.
3 There will be a 25 per cent discount for single-person households.
4 Poorer people will be protected by discounts, with no minimum contribution; that is, up to 100 per cent relief.
5 Second homes will receive a 50 per cent discount.
6 There will be a single bill for each household.
7 Capping of the permitted expenditure of councils deemed by the government to be overspending will continue.
8 The business property rate will continue to be set and collected nationally.

With respect to point 2 above, no regional variation will mean that householders in some parts of the country will be at a significant disadvantage to householders in other parts of the country. As we have said, properties will be valued and allocated to one of eight bands, ranging from Band A for properties with a value of up to £40,000 to Band H for properties valued at £320,000 or more. Current projections would indicate a bill of £267 (£200 for a single-person household) for Band A property owners and a bill of £802 (£600 for a single-person household) for Band H property holders. A property owner in Manchester, for example, with a property valued at £60,000 would be at a significant advantage to somebody in London with a similar property but whose value is around £100,000.

The Labour Party has favoured a return to the rating system. The then shadow secretary of state, David Blunkett, speaking in favour of rates, has stated that (*Public Finance and Accountancy*, 15 February 1991):

With graduated capital values as the new base for bills, and an improved benefits system, this solution would be difficult to evade, easier to administer and cheap to collect.

Capital Expenditure Controls

Since the Local Government Planning and Land Act 1980, stricter controls have been imposed on the ability of local authorities to raise capital expenditure. These provisions were initially detailed in a Department of the Environment circular issued in 1983, now replaced by a 1991 circular under the Local Government and Housing Act 1989, and reflect central government's desire to restrict what it deemed to be hitherto excessive levels of expenditure. The government sought to impose a national cash limit on total local authority capital expenditure. This new process of allocating capital resources to local authorities had as its central feature the designation of six service blocks – housing, education, transport, social services, urban aid and 'other services'. As Holtham (1986, p. 75 states):

> The government's aim was that authorities could aggregate the allocations given in each of these [then] five blocks and spend the total as they see fit – the allocations were not limited to the service blocks on which they were given. Though this flexibility works at the margin, there are powerful pressures against authorities making fullest use of it. Each block falls under the purview of a different central government department and they can feel that it is necessary to 'protect their block'. It is certainly not unknown for the representative of one particular central government department to warn authorities that if they transfer allocations out of 'their' block the authorities will lose allocations in the following year.

Under this procedure individual local authorities make a bid for funds to the relevant central government department. The 'other services' block is allocated on the basis of recommendations made by local authority associations.

This system for central government control of local authority expenditure was reviewed by the Audit Commission in 1985. In its report, *Capital Expenditure Controls in Local Government in England*, the Commission identified three problems. Lack of control arose because the criteria used by government to measure the target for capital spending nationally are significantly different from the criteria used to monitor each individual authority. Local inefficiency arose because of waste, delays in undertaking projects, rushed appraisals and under-utilized assets. The Commission also found that there was a large backlog of capital work arising from the failure of many authorities to maintain their housing stock, schools and roads in sound condition.

The Commission offered six suggestions for a new approach to improve capital controls:

1 a three to five year planning horizon for capital;
2 adequate provision for depreciation and replenishment of fixed assets in accounting treatment and spending totals;
3 encourage councils to rely less on borrowing;
4 minimal central involvement in the details of local programmes and projects;
5 incentives to dispose of under-utilized assets;
6 simplification of the system, particularly to avoid the need to distinguish between revenue and capital expenditure for control purposes.

In relation to relying less on borrowing, the Commission advocated savings via value for money reviews, increased charges, particularly council house rents, and further disposal of under-utilized assets. The recommendations on accounting and planning for the depreciation and replacement of fixed assets requires the accountancy profession to quickly develop a new form of capital accounting. The Commission further recommended that the (now former) public expenditure White Paper target should only reflect local authority spending met by borrowing. On such a basis it is suggested that councils will never overspend and will usually come close to spending at target. Allied to this proposal were two related recommendations. The first was that there should be no funding controls over projects being aggregated into a new 'efficiency' block. Audit would determine, ex-post, whether such savings were actually achieved. The second was that the revenue funding consequences of new capital schemes should be disregarded from total expenditure for the purpose of calculating block grant penalties. The 1980 controls which were supposed to put an end to the stop-go cycle in capital spending prevalent in the 1970s ended up, in practice, having the same effects, if not worse.

The 1986 green paper, *Paying for Local Government*, accepted that problems existed and suggested two alternative approaches:

1 a net external borrowing limit, for both revenue and capital expenditure;
2 control over gross expenditure, including allowance for capital receipts, and with contributions to capital as a limited supplement to the allocations.

Following further discussion, the Department of the Environment issued a consultation paper, *Capital Expenditure Controls*, in 1988. This document proposed a new scheme whereby there would be three sources of finance for capital commitments:

1 borrowing/credit arrangements;
2 grants from government or contributions from third parties;
3 local authority funds, specifically revenue contributions and capital receipts not used to redeem debt or meet future commitments.

The Local Government and Housing Act 1989, which came into force in April 1990, dealt with the controversial issue of capital receipts. Capital receipts are monies received from the disposal of any interest in an asset, typically arising from the sale of land and buildings. At the time when a capital receipt is received a part of that receipt must be set aside to reduce the level of that local authority's debt. In the case of Home Office services, 75 per cent of the gross receipt must be set aside. For all other receipts, 50 per cent must be set aside. The balance can be used to finance capital expenditure or finance leases. The Act also provides for a minimum amount of a local authority's principal debt to be repaid from revenue each year. This amount may be altered by regulation but is currently 4 per cent.

External Reporting

The most recent legislation relating to local authority accounts is the Local Government Finance Act 1982. Part III of this Act provides for the establishment of the Audit Commission (see chapter 6) and contains some additional provisions that, together with other legislation referred to in succeeding paragraphs, forms the legal framework for local authority accounting. The relevant sections of the 1982 Act are summarized in table 8.5. In the main, the provisions of the 1982 Act provide local electors with the right of access to financial information, and the Secretary of State for the Environment with rather wide powers of regulation with respect to the keeping of accounts, and their form, preparation and publication. Until February

1986 these provisions were contained in the DOE's *Draft Accounts and Audit Regulations* (see below).

Table 8.5   Accounting provisions of the Local Government Finance Act 1982

Section	Provision
12 (1)	All accounts to which this section applies shall be made up yearly at 31st March or such other date as the Secretary of State may generally or in any special case direct . . .
15 (1)(a)	. . . that the accounts are prepared in accordance with regulations made under section 23 below and comply with the requirements of all other statutory provisions applicable to the accounts;
17 (1)	. . . any persons interested may inspect the accounts to be audited and all books, deeds, contracts, bills, vouchers and receipts relating to them and make copies of all or any part of the accounts and those other documents.
23 (1)	The Secretary of State may by regulations applying to bodies whose accounts are required to be audited in accordance with this Act make provisions with respect to:-
	(a) the keeping of accounts;
	(b) the forms, preparation and certification of accounts and of statements of accounts;
	(c) the deposit of the accounts of any body at the offices of the body or at any other place;
	(d) the publication of information relating to accounts and the publication of statements of accounts;
	(e) the exercise of any rights of inspection or objection conferred by section 17 above or section 24 below and the steps to be taken by any body for informing local government elections for the area of that body of those rights.
24 (1)	Any local government elector for the area of a body whose accounts are required to be audited in accordance with this Part of this Act shall be entitled:-
	(a) to inspect and make copies of any statement of accounts prepared by the body pursuant to regulations under section 23 above and any report made to the body by an auditor; and
	(b) to require copies of any such statement or report to be delivered to him on payment of a reasonable sum for each copy.

Since the early 1970s there has been a renewed interest in improving the uniformity of local authority external reports and in bringing them more in line with private sector conventions. This is not necessarily a new theme. Jones and Pendlebury (1982) provide a brief summary of the more important professional and governmental regulations concerning English local authority accounts since the end of the nineteenth century. In more recent times, *The Form of Published Accounts*, first published in 1955, has remained one of the more important self-regulating documents referred to by local authority accountants. Since revised and rewritten, this document has attempted to provide for the uniform classification and presentation of accounts while allowing authorities a wide range of discretion. For example, local authorities are not restricted as to the basis on which events are recognized in their accounts, though the majority adopt some form of income and expenditure accounting.

Income and expenditure accounting is analogous to a profit and loss account, and provides a classified summary of transactions during a given period prepared under the accruals accounting convention. That is, income and costs are recognized as they are earned and incurred, not as money is received or paid. A 1981 survey, carried out by the Chartered Institute of Public Finance and Accountancy, revealed that 29 per cent of the sample survey used income and expenditure as the base for its revenue. This survey also revealed that 46 per cent of the authorities used the 'income and converted payments' base, while 20 per cent of the authorities used the 'converted receipts and payments' base. These latter two approaches are both modified forms of the accruals accounting convention.

Under the income and converted payments method all revenues are accrued when they are earned, but the payments made throughout the year are not accrued. At the year end all invoices that have been received but have yet to be paid are added together and a single total entry is put through the books of account accruing all payments due to be made. At the beginning of the next financial year this entry is reversed so that as payments are subsequently made in respect of these accrued accounts, individual expense accounts are debited thereby making the net effect zero in the new year. The advantage claimed for this system is that there is no need to incur the expense of maintaining suppliers' accounts since they will soon make it known when money is overdue. One wonders, though, whether any finance officer would ever allow such a state of affairs.

The converted receipts and payments approach applies the reasoning outlined in the previous paragraph to receipts as well as payments.

Although it is fairly commonly used, its rationale is far less easy to conceptualize since all authorities require debtors accounts in order to keep track of who owes them money and by what amount. Neither of these two approaches allows for interim position statements on anything other than a receipts and payments basis.

Local authorities also adopt the principle of fund accounting. Simply expressed, a fund is represented by a set of self-balancing accounts that segregate specific activities in accordance with special regulations, restrictions or limitations. For each separate fund the local authority must produce a separate revenue account and a balance sheet. In addition to reporting upon the separate funds, most local authorities also provide a summary revenue account and a consolidated balance sheet; some also provide a statement of source and application of funds.

Probably the most confusing aspect of local authority accounting to accountants not familiar with this area of the public sector is the novel approach adopted with respect to capital accounting. The reasons for this approach are twofold:

1 Under Section 2 of the General Rate Act 1967, local authorities are not allowed, in law, to budget for an operating deficit.
2 Schedule 13, paragraph 7(i) of the Local Government Act 1972 requires that where expenditure has been met by borrowing, a sum equivalent to an instalment and interest should be debited to the relevant operating statement in order that the loan be repaid within a specific period.

The two provisions thus direct that the principal repayments of loans are taken off the balance sheet and passed through the revenue account. The normal convention with private sector companies and the nationalized industries is to charge the interest on the loan and an allocation representing the depreciation of the asset(s) to the revenue (profit and loss) account. The law, as it relates to local authorities, states that provision must be made on an annual basis for the repayment of debt. The practice for local authorities, therefore, is that principal repayments replace the provision for depreciation. Fixed assets in the balance sheet therefore appear net of capital discharged rather than net of depreciation. The asset remains on the balance sheet, at acquisition cost, even when the loan that financed its acquisition has been repaid. Only when it is sold or transferred is it written out of the balance sheet. Fixed assets are usually classified as either 'capital outlay' or other 'long-term outlay'. The former term relates to identifiable and saleable assets, such as buildings or vehicles, and the latter term is used to identify assets which cannot be physically disposed of but can only be improved or upgraded, such as roads. A Department of Environment circular (DOE 14/81) stipulates the maximum period over which loans, for given categories of assets, must be repaid.

The failure of local authorities to depreciate their assets runs counter to one of the cornerstones of accounting – the matching principle, which states that the accounts should only be charged with those costs that contribute to the service provided in the period of account. While in many cases the principal repayments may approximate a charge for depreciation, the effect of historical depreciation on balance sheet information is not achieved unless the asset's value is correspondingly reduced. Current proposals for capital accounting may well change this. Readers may wish to recall the earlier discussion on depreciation from chapter 1.

Local authorities have, since 1980, been expected to comply with the Statements of Standard Accounting Practice (SSAPs) issued by the Accounting Standards Committee. As noted in chapter 2, the Accounting Standards Board has, since the passing of the Companies Act 1989, taken over the development and publication of accounting standards. While standards are developed primarily for commercial entities, a panel of local authority specialists advised the Committee on their applicability to local authorities. Two main standards have caused difficulty. SSAP 12 deals with depreciation and, for the reasons outlined above, it is presently not adopted by local authorities. SSAP 16, recently withdrawn, dealt with current cost accounting. The Local Government Planning and Land Act 1980 required 'direct labour organizations' a to compute their required rates of return on a current cost accounting basis. The direct labour organizations employ local authority staff in preference to private sector contractors for the maintenance of assets. A Department of the Environment circular (DOE 10/81) outlines in some detail the provisions of the 1980 Act. Basically, direct labour organizations must earn a positive rate of return on capital employed as the Secretary of State may direct. The Secretary of State has the power to close down any direct labour organization if it operates at a deficit for three consecutive years.

Jones and Pendlebury (1982) reported the results of an empirical survey of the published reports of 60 English local authorities. They rather pessimistically state that their results show (p. 133): 'that current local authority accounting practices do not conform to the professional and statutory requirements', and that 'local authority accounts simply are not comparable'.

In an effort to address such criticisms a draft Code of Practice on local authority accounting was published towards the end of 1986. It is the work of a joint CIPFA/Audit Commission working party which was set up after the shelving in February 1986 of the DOE's *Draft Accounts and Audit Regulations*. The working party adopted two central principles to their work: that local authority accounts should be readable and intelligible; and that a format should be achieved to reduce the variety in accounting treatment between authorities.

Appendix 8.1 provides a commentary on a set of local authority accounts which illustrate many of the points raised in preceding paragraphs. This appendix also illustrates statistical and other financial data that complement the financial information published in the annual report. The local authority concerned is Kent County Council, who also provide the case study for the next section of this chapter.

Local Authority Financial Management – The Experience of Kent County Council

Changes outlined in the Education Reform Act 1988 and the Local Government Act 1988 have meant that local authorities are having to prepare schemes that allow for financial delegation to all service-providing departments. Perhaps the most explicit area where this has occurred is in the field of education, where the Education Reform Act 1988 requires local authorities to prepare schemes for financial delegation to schools. Throughout the 1980s there has been a growing trend towards decentralized resource management. Given that it is central government's view that local authorities must institute management arrangements to 'promote more effective, speedy and business-like decision-making' (*DOE, Internal Management of Local Authorities in England*, 1991) it is clear that more and more local authorities are having to adopt a more devolved management style.

In this section we review the efforts of one authority, Kent County Council (KCC), to develop a devolved management structure, particularly with respect to the finance function. In many respects KCC can be regarded as an exemplar of financial management reform. In the words of its chief executive (Sabin, 1989):

Devolved management is about:

Creating an organization where control over resources and accountability for delivery of services are held in the same place. . . . removing the frustration of the manager about the remoteness of these controls;

Making jobs more interesting and challenging, and providing greater opportunities for developing professional and managerial skills . . . and more rounded people . . . people who feel more satisfied in doing their job because they control more of the things involved;

People are thinking about what they are delivering to their customers . . . and how they can effect it . . . and because they are controlling resources, having a greater pride in the job.

In KCC, devolution is taken to mean a management style which allows those nearest the point of service delivery the maximum control of the functions which impinge on them, and the services required to operate within a specified organizational framework where accountabilities and limits of authority are clearly understood. The main objective of this reform is to improve the efficiency and effectiveness of service delivery. KCC has more than 50,000 employees, an annual turnover of £1 billion and over 1,500,000 customers. Local management in Kent's 750+ schools was introduced well inside central government's timetable. In social services the latest legislation on community care introduced an approach pioneered by KCC.

The role of the finance director in Kent can now be summed up in three primary functions:

1 corporate financial adviser;
2 statutory officer, responsible under S.151 of the Local Government Act 1972 for the proper financial administration of the authority;
3 head of profession for the finance function.

Before the finance function at KCC was reorganized, the finance director controlled a department of about 580 staff. Following reorganization about 350 staff have been relocated within the major service departments. Now only the staff of the corporate finance division, about 30 in number, and the staff of the finance services division, about 200, report directly to the finance director. The corporate finance division has three main areas of responsibility:

1 Securing the financial input to the corporate management process. This includes the preparation, co-ordination and monitoring of the medium-term plan and the overall KCC budget.
2 Developing, implementing and maintaining the corporate financial framework. This includes the setting of standards, ensuring their adoption and monitoring compliance throughout the council.

3 Technical advice to the client side of KCC regarding financial management legislative requirements. This includes, for example, determining the requirements for compulsory competitive tendering.

The financial services division, likewise, has three main areas of responsibility:

1 Delivery of a range of financial support services which can more effectively be provided from the centre. Such services are to be provided on a commercial basis. For example, some services are sold to service departments or to specialist clients, such as the Superannuation Fund, or to external agencies, such as the South East England Tourist Board.
2 Linking with corporate finance to contribute to the formulation of financial policy in appropriate areas.
3 Operational links with the devolved financial activities. For example, financial services control the payroll system and deal with aggregate responsibilities such as PAYE.

Devolved finance activities, within departments such as education and social services, operate within a framework established by corporate finance and have certain operational relationships with financial services. The devolved finance resources, within client-focused departments, provide a full range of financial support which includes the preparation of budgets and accounts, the development of financial information systems, payroll input, payments and income. The relationship between the finance director and devolved finance staff is based on the head of profession role.

As head of profession, the finance director has overall responsibility for the quality assurance for financial management within the council. This responsibility includes developing the skills and competencies of all finance staff, both central and devolved to service departments. Senior finance managers are expected to exercise head of profession responsibilities, delegated from the finance director, within their own spheres responsibility; that is, heads of corporate finance and financial services, and heads of finance in the major service departments. As responsibility for managing finance activities becomes more and more devolved, the finance director's responsibility will increasingly be fulfilled through the head of profession role.

The reorganization of the KCC finance function is critical to the overall restructuring of management within the authority. By devolving two-thirds of the finance staff into service departments the necessary support is in place and managers are more accountable for the quality of service they offer their customers. Devolution also fosters greater financial awareness at the point of service delivery. Financial advice, particularly with respect to achieving greater economy and efficiency, is also closer to the customer. Finally, by devolving so many finance staff, there is the ability to provide improved financial information, 'tailored' when necessary to provide much more relevant local information.

While central finance services are developing FMIS, a new computer financial management information systems package, local finance support will enable information to be 'owned' at a more local level and provide departments with the ability to vary the ways in which their data is displayed and analysed. Three versions of the system exist: for education, social services and 'the rest', the latter group covering 28 different departments and units. Some 500 managers have on-screen access to FMIS, while the rest of the county's 2,500 budget managers have a paper information and interrogation link into the system.

Just as the finance department has been involved in a devolved management structure, so too have other departments. In addition to the personnel department, a number of other central support departments have also embraced this change in corporate culture, including, where appropriate, the adoption of a head of profession role. At the local area level, devolved services such as accounting and finance are having to negotiate the quality of the services that they provide. For example, social services operates from five area offices, each of which has an area finance/information manager who has to negotiate service level agreements (SLAs) with all operational units as to the level, quality and charges associated with the services provided. Failure of an area finance function to achieve negotiated SLAs could mean that this service could be contracted in from outside or negotiated from elsewhere in the county, most probably from another area finance office.

Conclusion

The main issue underlying much of the discussion in the first half of this chapter is constitutional. Local/central government policies severely restrict the rights of local authorities to manage their own affairs. Since 1984 the courts have become increasingly embroiled with disputes between local authorities and the Secretary of State. Certainly one former Chancellor, Nigel Lawson, has argued that all local taxation should end (*Local Government Chronicle*, 5 April 1991). Such remarks may not be welcomed by local authorities, who feel that it is becoming more and more difficult to decide the priorities of spending within the restraints of the law. A report by the PA Consulting Group to the DOE on compulsory competitive tendering (CCT) suggests that financial services, engineering, legal services, architects, information technology, trading standards and licences should be subject to CCT. This extension of CCT was one of the principal strands of Prime Minister John Major's Citizen's Charter. Support for the extension of CCT is also proposed by the Audit Commission. In its report *Competitive Councils* (December 1991) the Commission states that councils should take steps to ensure there is a clear split between the provision of legal advice and legal services. The latter should be set up on a practice account basis as in the private sector, and effectiveness should be regularly monitored against private firms. While conceding that hourly rates in the private sector are usually higher, the Commission maintains that the cost of contracting out can be lower than maintaining an inefficient in-house service. At present councils spend around £200 million annually on legal services, of which about £19 million is spent on the private sector. Some authorities, such as Kent reviewed above, have anticipated the expansion of CCT. The reorganization of their various support services has been designed, in part, to facilitate the introduction of CCT.

In a consultation paper, *The Structure of Local Government in England* (April 1991), the DOE states that 'government believes that there should be a move towards unitary authorities in the shire counties where these do not already exist'. It is the department's view that having a single tier, instead of the present district/shire relationship, should reduce bureaucracy, improve the co-ordination of services, increase the quality of services and reduce costs. In another consultation paper, *The Internal Management of Local Authorities in England* (July 1991), the DOE outlines a wide variety of options to change local authority management arrangements. These range from a cabinet system, as in the management of central government, to directly elected mayors – a very different type of arrangement.

All the signs are that the 1990s will see further changes in the management of local government together with much more devolved resource and financial accountability.

Notes

1 Sidney and Beatrice Webb (1963) provide an interesting history of English local government for those readers interested in the source of such everyday terms as 'shire' counties and Justices of the Peace.
2 The current circumstances under which Northen Ireland is administered precludes its further discussion in this chapter.

3 Under the General Rate Act 1987 domestic ratepayers could pay by instalments and a system of rate rebates was introduced, the latter being revised by the Local Government Act 1974. The amount of relief which domestic ratepayers could obtain varied, depending upon their income, their family circumstances and the amount of rates which they paid. Local authorities received a grant of 90 per cent towards the costs of the rebate granted, although the whole cost of administering the scheme fell upon the local authority itself.

Appendix 8.1 Kent County Council Financial Report 1989–90

This appendix briefly reveiws the reports and accounts of Kent County Council 1989–90. It illustrates the authority's attempts to provide factual and readable information on its financial performance. In the original report, the tables presented in Section 1 were presented as bar charts.

Section 1 Financial Summary

In the financial year, which ended 31 March 1990, Kent County Council spent in excess of £960 million on the provision and maintenance of essential services for the people of Kent. Expenditure at this level makes Kent one of the largest local authorities in the country.

Revenue expenditure by type	£m
Employees	524.6
Agency	118.4
Materials and equipment	88.9
Premises	51.0
Debt charges	36.8
Student grants and other costs	35.7
Transport	35.3

Revenue expenditure by service	£m
Education	465.6
Police	108.8
Social Services	103.2
Highways	95.5
Other	91.0
Fire	26.6

The weekly cost of these services to the average domestic ratepayer with a rateable value of £190 was £7.05p.

Education	£4.24p
Social Services	90p
Highways	67p
Police	49p
Other	48p
Fire	27p

The range of services provided is vast but includes:

- *Education* – in addition to the visible core of the system, namely schools and colleges, it provides activities ranging from the Careers Service and Adult Education to Recreation, Social and Physical Training.
- *Road System* – here KCC maintains and enhances the road system and provides streetlighting.
- *Public Protection* – an umbrella heading covering our Police Force, Fire Brigade and the work of Trading Standards and Emergency Planning.
- *Care* – the provision of care for children, handicapped and elderly people and families with problems. These are key aspects of the work of the Social Services.
- *Environment* – Kent County Council is committed to ensuring a clear and pleasant environment to the benefit of both the individual and the business community.
- *Economic Support* – help and support of country-wide initiatives for job creation and the improvement of the prospects for people and businesses in the county.

KCC aims to provide all its services in an efficient and responsive manner which meets the needs of the users of the services, including those who pay for them and in doing so takes full advantage of new technology and the latest management initiatives.

In managing efficiently the resource of this diverse and complex organisation, KCC managers adopt the principles, criteria and best practice of the private sector.

Where did the money come from?

The revenue expenditure of £890 million was met from five main sources.

Source of revenue expenditure	£m
Rate income	438.3
Rate Support Grant	221.2
Other income	113.4
Other government grants	65.9
Sales, fees and charges	52.0

The two main sources were:

- *Rate Support Grant* – This is the general grant paid for the last time in 1989–90 to local authorities by central government. In 1983/4 it financed 47% of the County Council's expenditure as opposed to 25% in 1989–90. In effect the Council has lost about £198 million in revenue from Rate Support Grant.
- *Rates* – Despite the loss of grant, the County Council's precept of 209.35p in 1989–90 was the third lowest of the 39 English shire counties. In fact the impact of the continued reduction in government grant has been to encourage us to use locally generated resources more efficiently and thus strengthen our accountability to the local rate-payer.

Capital expenditure by type	£m
Infrastructure	33.5
Land and buildings	21.0
Plant and machinery	9.7
Vehicles	0.1

Capital expenditure by service	£m
Highways	32.5
Education	18.0
Property, supplies and services	5.2
Social Services	2.9
Police	2.6
Other	1.8
Fire and Public Protection	1.3

How was capital expenditure financed?

Capital expenditure in 1989–90 of £64.3 million was financed from three main source as shown.

Sources of capital expenditure	£m
Loan	30.8
Capital receipts	28.2
Other	5.3

A considerable proportion of capital expenditure has been met by the sale of surplus land and buildings. The more of these capital receipts generated, the less we have to borrow, which reduces interest payments and helps to keep rates down.

What are the Rates?

This is the last Annual Report dealing with rates as a property based local tax levied by County and District Councils.

The amount of rates you paid was based on the following two elements:

Rateable Value

The rateable value of a property was fixed by the government's valuation officer. In the case of a house this was based on the property's notional rent value.

The Rate in the £

This was determined as follows:

- The Council calculated through the budgetary process the cost of providing all of its services for the following year.
- From this total it deducted the amount of government grant and income from fees and charges which it expected to receive.
- The sum remaining was the amount which needed to be collected from ratepayers. This was divided by the total rateable value of all properties in the country to give the rate in the £.

The amount of rates you then paid was calculated by multiplying the rateable value of your property by the rate in the £.

The 14 District Councils in Kent calculated their rate in the same way. The District Council rate was added to the County rate (called the precept) to produce the rate bill for the year.

Individual rate bills were set out by the Districts who were responsible for collection. After deducting their share of the rates they transferred the remainder to the County Council.

Who pays the rates?

The total rateable values upon which the amount of rates paid are based were distributed as follows in Kent.

Total Rateable Value at April 1989 –   £210.3m comprising:
Domestic (e.g. Houses)   113.8
Commercial (e.g. shops, Offices)   43.2
Other Undertakings (e.g. Electricity)   19.3
Industrial (e.g. Factories)   17.4
Miscellaneous (e.g. Hospitals)   8.3
Education/Cultural (e.g. Schools)   6.4
Entertainment (e.g. Cinemas)   1.9

Rates and the Community Charge

Major changes in the methods of financing local authority services came into operation in April 1990 and will be reflected in the next Annual Report. Domestic rates were abolished and replaced by a system of flat-rate Community Charges, payable by most adults. Other properties had their rateable values reassessed and are subject to the uniform National Non-Domestic Rate. The existing Rate Support Grant from the Government has been abolished and replaced by a new Revenue Support Grant.

Section 2   Financial Report

1 This section of the Annual Report gives details of expenditure and income for the year and includes the Council's Accounts set out on pages 190 to 210. They consist of:

- Statement of Revenue Expenditure and Income covering all services
- The Consolidated Balance Sheet – which sets out the financial position of the County Council at 31 March 1990
- The Consolidated Statement of Revenue and Capital Movements– which summarises the total movement of the Council's funds
- The Superannuation Fund Accounts – an extract from the more detailed published statement
- The summary accounts of the various in-house contractors which show the operation of the work undertaken on highways maintenance and construction, vehicle maintenance, grounds maintenance and catering.

These accounts are supported by the Statement of Accounting Policies and various notes to the accounts.

2 The foreword sets out the main features of the Council's financial position in 1989–90. A brief explanation of the financial aspects of

the Council's activities is set out earlier in the Kent Reports.
3 The Council's final expenditure in 1989–90 exceeded income by £10 million (1.2%). The additional expenditure related to:

- the response to Child Abuse
- emergency spending relating to weather condition and policing requirements
- national pay awards in excess of the budgeted contingency
- reduced interest receipts

It was therefore necessary to find £10 million from internal resources and this was achieved partly by using Transport Supplementary Grant (TSG) to finance revenue expenditure rather then capital (£4 million) and partly by using £6 million of the County Council's working balance.

Auditor's Opinion

We certify that we have completed the audit of the accounts of Kent County Council for the year ended 31 March 1990 in accordance with Part III of the Local Government Finance Act 1982 and the Code of Audit Practice.

In our opinion the statement of accounts presents fairly in accordance with the policies set out below the financial position of the authority at 31 March 1990 and its income and expenditure for the year then ended.

Accounting Policies

The accounts of the County Council have been compiled in accordance with the Code of Practice on Local Authority Accounting issued in July 1987 by the Chartered Institute of Public Finance and Accountancy, and are also consistent with the guidance notes issued by the Institute on the application of Statements of Standard Accounting Practice (SSAP) to local authority accounts.

With the exception of the In-house contractors accounts (page 210 which are shown on a current cost accounting basis all other accounts are maintained on a historical cost basis.

Separate accounts are maintained for capital and non-capital transactions, the latter designated as revenue transactions.

Basis on which debtors and creditors at year end are included in accounts

For revenue transactions the County Council's accounts are kept on the basis of income and expenditure.

In order to account for income and expenditure attributable to the financial year, sums paid after 31 March 1990 for goods received or services rendered during the financial year 1989–90 have been included in the accounts. Similarly, sums known to be due to the Council during the year are entered in the accounts. Where actual amounts are not known, estimated sums have been included.

Nature of substantial reserves and provisions

Under the provisions of paragraph 16 of Schedule 13 of the Local Government Act 1972 (as amended by the Local Government (Miscellaneous Provisons) Act 1976), the County Council maintains the following funds:

* *Provisions*
  Insurance Fund
  Renewal and Repairs fund
* *Reserves*
  Special Fund
  General County Fund
  Information Technology Fund

The available balances on all funds are on temporary loan to the Consolidated Loans Fund.

Basis of provision for redemption of debt

The County Council administers a Consolidated Loans Fund under the powers contained in Schedule 13 of the Local Government Act 1972, as amended. In accordance with those powers, all loans raised by the Authority are paid into the Consolidated Loans Fund and are pooled. The revenue accounts of the Authority are charged with annual instalments of principal for the loan advances made from the Fund. Interest charges paid by the Fund are recharged to the revenue accounts at an average pooled rate calculated on the basis of advances outstanding at 1 April, with advances during the year being proportion converted to a yearly basis.

Basis on which capital works are recorded in the balance sheet

Capital expenditure is included in the accounts on a cash basis which is in line with accepted practices but is contrary to the accruals concept of SSAP 2.

Capital expenditure on highways, street lighting and on plant and vehicles, which is met from loan, is written down each year by the amount of the loan repaid during the year.

Other capital works and expenses are retained in the balance sheet at their original cost. Any contributions received towards that cost from other sources, such as capital grants, are included in the balance sheet under capital discharged.

Basis of renewal provisions

Annual contributions from revenue accounts are made to the Renewal and Repairs Fund for the replacement of vehicles and plant at the end of their working life, such contributions being enhanced to cover any increases in replacement costs. Replacement of vehicles and plant is made through the Renewal and Repairs Fund. Where assets are acquired under finance leases, the leasing rentals are charged to revenue or the Renewal and Repairs Fund.

The cost of the leased assets relating to the Renewal Repairs Fund are not shown in the balance sheet. The liability for future rentals payable are disclosed as a note on page 61.

Basis of Valuation of Real Property and investments

Real Property has been included in the accounts at cost price. All investments are shown at the original cost including brokerage and stamp duty.

Allocation of central administration expenses

There is a complete allocation of central administration and office expenses to all services. The cost of central departments has been allocated on the basis of estimated time spent by officers on various services, and the cost of administrative buildings on the basis of floor area.

Summary Revenue Account

This summary shows the total gross expenditure for 1989/90. Net expenditure is arrived at by deducting income and grant.

Committee	Year ended 31 March 1990			
	Gross expenditure £'000	Income and Grant £'000	Net expenditure £'000	Net expenditure £'000
Education	465,567	62,760	402,806	396,304
Libraries, Museums and Archives	13,476	1,473	12,004	10,977
Fire Service	26,550	596	25,954	22,197
Public Protection	5,891	1,534	4,357	4,635
Planning	2,206	208	1,998	1,841
Highways & Transportation	95,468	32,949	62,519	54,285
Economic Development and Tourism	3,177	78	3,099	1,814
Amenities and Waste Disposal	9,807	2,383	7,424	6,304
Police	108,801	61,878	46,923	44,075
Policy and Resources	56,563	39,290	17,273	13,006
Social Services	103,169	17,430	85,739	74,943
Totals	**890,675**	**220,579**	**670,096**	**630,381**
Transfer to reserves			383	1,024
			670,479	631,405

Summary Revenue Account cont.

| | Year ended 31 March 1990 | | |
	Gross expenditure £'000	Income and Grant £'000	Net expenditure £'000	Net expenditure £'000
Committee				
This was financed by:				
Rate Support Grant			221,121	235,400
Rate Income			438,305	392,060
Transfer from reserves			6,029	3,945
Roll forward 1988–89			1,024	–
Transport Supplementary Grant			4,000	–
			670,479	631,405

Work in progress

Work in progress on private street works is entered in the accounts at a valuation based on cost price and this forms the major part of the work in progress total. In addition the Council operates its own printing and furniture production units, work in progress in these units is valued at cost price.

Stocks and stores

Stocks and stores are maintained in some departments, covering such items as stocks held in Kent County Supplies central warehouse, stocks of materials used for maintenance and improvement of Highways and food stocks.

Where stocks are maintained and recorded they are shown on the balance sheet at the lower of cost, or net realisable value.

Accounting for Value Added Tax

VAT is separately accounted for in accordance with SSAP 5 and is not included as income or expenditure of the County Council, except where it is not recoverable, e.g. the purchase of motor cars.

Notes to the Summary Revenue Account

1 Interest

Interest paid on internal and external borrowings which has been charged to Committees and included as expenditure in the summary revenue account amounted to £26,275,538. Interest credited to Revenue account in respect of temporary investment of surplus funds was £4,348,762.

2 Precepts

The following precepts were paid during 1989–90:

	£
Southern Water Authority	5,347,474
Kent and Essex Sea Fisheries Committee	73,000
Sussex Sea Fisheries Committee	5,947
	5,426,421

3 Trading operations

The County Council operates a central supplies department which provides purchasing and supply facilities to County Services. The service is also used by other local authorities.

	1989–90 £'000	1988–9 £'000
Turnover	62,604	76,808
Net surplus (deficit)	(6)	28

4 Section 137–Local Government Act 1972

Section 137 empowers local authorities, subject to various conditions and limits, to incur expenditure which in their opinion is in the interests of their area or any part of it, or all or some of its inhabitants. Under this section, the County Council's limit for any such expenditure was £4.4m in 1989–90. The actual expenditure was:

	£
Grants and Loans for Economic Development and Tourism	2,123,172
Administrative costs supporting the above activities	231,029
	2,354,201

5 Agency

The County Council incurs expenditure on behalf of the following bodies which is fully reimbursed.

- The Department of Transport in respect of motorways and trunk roads, where the amount of expenditure involved in 1989–90 was £253,372,000.
- The Training Commission in respect of various training initiatives, where the expenditure in 1989–90 amounted to £4,816,609.

6 Publicity

Publicity is defined by the Local Government Act 1986 as any communication in whatever form, addressed to the public at large or to a sector of the public. However, a number of areas are exempt from inclusion in the account e.g. stautory publication and publicity approved by or on behalf of the Chief Constable.

The County Council expenditure on publicitiy in 1989–90 was:

	£'000
Staff advertising/recruitment	2,124
Staffing costs of publicity	209
Other advertising and publicity costs	498
	2,831

Capital expenditure 1989–90

The main items of capital expenditure during the year were:

	£'000
Highways Schemes	
Thanet Way	7,189
A2070 Beaver Road, Ashford	1,827
Albion Place/Mote Road, Maidstone	4,376
Faversham Western Link	1,861
Reconditioning Schemes	2,735
Acquisition of Land and Property	6,528
Education Schemes	
Rochester Girls' Grammar School	1,808
Rochester Warren Wood Secondary School	2,985

Financing of capital expenditure 1989–90

The capital expenditure was financed as follows:

	£'000
Loans	30,838
Capital receipts	28,224
Grants & contributions	5,241
	64,303

Consolidated Balance Sheet

The consolidated balance sheet shows the financial position of the County Council as a whole at the end of the year. Balances on all accounts are brought together and items which reflect internal transactions are eliminated. Some of these include amounts borrowed by service committees from the Consolidated Loans Fund.

	Notes	31 March 1990 £'000	31 March 1990 £'000	31 March 1990 £'000	31 March 1990 £'000
Net Fixed Assets					
Capital outlay comprising of:					
The total expenditure on provision of land, buildings other permanent assets			568,310		522,729
This expenditure has been largely financed by borrowing but there is currently a debt free amount of:	1		(332,029) 236,281		(303,575) 219,154
Deferred charges representing expenditure for which no tangible asset is held	1		1,439		224
Investments which cost			51		55
Long term debtors	3		2,682 240,453		1,782 221,216
Current Assets					
Short-term investments which cost		39,745		64,294	
Stocks of material in hand and work in progress		6,137		5,244	
Written down values of cars on lease		7,649		9,887	

Consolidated Balance Sheet cont.

	Notes	31 March 1990 £'000	£'000	31 March 1990 £'000	£'000
Amounts owed to the Council by debtors	3	62,070 **115,601**		46,159 **125,584**	
Less: current liabilities					
Amounts owed by the Council to creditors	4	(95,659)		(74,160)	
Cash balances overdrawn		(11,597)		(16,112)	
Net current assets			**8,345**		**35,312**
Net assets			**248,798**		**256,528**
The net assets of the County Council are represented by:					
External borrowing	5	197,668		186,826	
Unused capital receipts	6	14,682		27,404	
Provisions and reserves	7	25,830		25,022	
Balance on the General County revenue fund	8	10,618		17,276	
			248,798		**256,528**

Notes to the Accounts

1 Fixed assets

Movements in fixed assets during the year were as follows:

	Balance at 1 April 1989 £'000	Expenditure £'000	Disposals £'000	Capital discharged and adjustments £'000	Balance at 31 March 1990 £'000
Unanalysed at 1 April 1987	75,361		(2,642)	(7,679)	65,040
Land and buildings	29,189	21,031	–	(12,174)	38,046
Infrastructure	104,916	33,529		(16,395	122,050
Vehicle, plant, furniture and equipment	9,688	9,743	–	(8,286)	11,145
Total net fixed assets	21,9154	64,303	(22,642)	(44,534)	236,281

The County Council's asset records to not provide an analysis of capital expenditure prior to 1 April 1987.

The column headed capital discharged and adjustments includes the writing down of the value of assets as debt is repaid.

Capital expenditure 1989–90

The main items of capital expenditure during the year were:

	£'000
Highways Schemes	
Thanet Way	7,189
A2070 Beaver Road, Ashford	1,827
Albion Place/Mote Road, Maidstone	4,376
Faversham Western Link	1,861
Reconditioning Schemes	2,735
Acquisition of Land and Property	6,528
Education Schemes	
Rochester Girls' Grammar School	1,808
Rochester Warren Wood Secondary School	2,985

Financing of capital expenditure 1989–90

The capital expenditure was financed as follows:

	£'000
Loans	30,838
Capital receipts	28,224
Grants & contributions	5,241
	64,303

Analysis of major asset holdings

	31 March 1990	31 March 1989
Schools	775	777
Further Education Colleges	8	7
Libraries (Full Time)	56	60
Fire stations	65	65
Police stations	32	30
Police houses and flats	496	475
Magistrates Courts	17	17
Smallholdings	88	92
Homes and Day Centres for the Elderly	71	71
Family Support Centres	15	15
Facilities for the mentally ill and handicapped	39	34
Recreation sites	19	17
Waste Disposal sites	27	31
County roads	8,500 Km	8,313 Km
County offices	32	31

Future capital expenditure commitments

At 31 March 1990 contractually committed capital expenditure to be in incurred in 1990–91 and later years includes the following major projects:

	£m
Highway Scheme	
Albion Place/Mote Road Maidstone	2.9
Education Schemes	
Rochester Warren Wood Secondary School	2.2
Margate Holy Trinity Church of England Primary School	1.3
Rochester St Peter's and St Margarets Church of England Primary School	1.5
Sheerness Sir Thomas Cheyne and Lady Anne Cheyne Middle School	1.7

2 Deferred charges

Equivalent to outstanding loan debt on assets sold, and premature loan repayment expenses.

	£'000
At 31 March 1989	224
Additions	1,324
Amounts written off	109
At 31 March 1990	**1,439**

3 Amounts owed to the Council by Debtors

	At 31 March	
	1990	1989
	£'000	£'000
Long Term Debtors:		
Housing Act Advances	960	1,202
Public bodies	1,722	581
	2,682	**1,783**
Other debtors:		
Staff advances	610	615
Government Departments	7,286	7,661
Precepts	2,551	756
Payments in advance	5,082	6,565
General debtors	46,494	30,643
Leasing debtors	47	(81)
	62,070	**46,159**

4 Amounts owed by the Council to creditors

	At 31 March	
	1990	1989
	£'000	£'000
Kent and Essex Sea Fisheries	81	113
Receipts in advance	514	412
General creditors	77,053	52,346
Other Local Authorities	308	732
Government Departments	14,649	14,389
Leasing Creditors	3,054	5,405
	95,659	**73,397**

5 External borrowing

The external debt of the County Council can be analysed as follows:

	At 31 March	
	1990	1989
	£'000	£'000
Public Works Loan Board	191,891	170,699
Money Market Loans	2,000	12,000
European Investment Bank	3,000	3,000
Local Bonds	777	1,127
	197,668	**186,826**

The European Investment Bank loan is secured by a floating charge on the County Council's revenues.

These loans are repayable within the following periods.

	£'000	£'000
■ Less than 1 year	9,321	11,122
■ between 2 and 5 years	53,728	60,829
■ between 6 and 10 years	10,492	9,366
■ more than 10 years	124,127	105,509
	197,688	**186,826**

6 Unused capital receipts

	£'000
Balance at 1 April 1989	27,404
Add: Receipts from sales	22,085
Less: Capital receipts used to finance expenditure, to repay debt and transferred to Renewal and Repair Fund	(34,807)
Balance at 31 March 1990	**14,682**

7 Provisions and reserves

	1 April 1989 £'000	Income £'000	Expenditure £'000	31 March 1990 £'000
Renewal and Repairs Fund	16,947	14,003	14,231	16,719
Insurance Fund	3,263	2,135	5,482	(84)*
Information Technology Fund	492	3,541	1,333	2,700
Other Special Funds	4,320	6,974	4,799	6,495
	25,022	26,653	25,8445	25,830

* Payment to the Insurance Fund in respect of claims totalling £4.0m was outstanding at 31 March 1990 from insurance companies.

Provisions
Renewal and Repairs Fund
Established for the purpose of financing the renewal and repair of buildings, plant, vehicles and equipment, for which annual contributions are made by committees from their revenue budgets.

Insurance fund
Established to provide cover internally against various specified risks.

Reserves
Information Technology Fund
Established to provide funds for investment in information technology in the authority.

Other Special Funds
Established to finance exceptional and non-recurring items of expenditure (e.g. repairing flood damage or clearing up of air pollution), to finance the initial costs of relocation schemes etc. that are intended to produce long-term savings or benefits, to facilitate the implementation of policy

changes, to fund expenses in connection with the BR Channel Tunnel Rail Link proposals, to develop transfrontier initiatives and to provide funds for employment creating initiatives.

8 General County Revenue Fund

The County Council operates a rolling budget facility whereby underspendings on committee revenue accounts may be carried forward into the following year by transferring them to reserves. Underspending in 1988–9 amounting to £1,024,000 was rolled forward and utilised during 1989–90. £383,000 in respect of underspending in 1989–90 has been rolled forward and transferred into the general county revenue fund. In addition, £7,029,000 has been transferred from the fund to finance revenue expenditure in excess of income in 1989–90. As a result of these transfers, the balance on the general county revenue fund has reduced to £10.6 million.

9 Leases

The County Council has made use of finance leasing to acquire vehicles and equipment. The capital value of assets acquired during the year using this method of funding was £2,958,092. Lease rentals paid during the year in respect of all current finance leases amounted to £5,637,282.

Outstanding commitments in respect of both finance and operating leases at 31 March 1990 are as follows:

	£'000
1990–1	7,269
1991–2	3,651
1992–3	802
1993–4	659

10 Rate Support Grant – Block Grant

Although the accounts of the County Council for 1989–90 have been closed, under the Block Grant System, the final amount of grant to be received by the County Council will not be known until all Local Authorities' final expenditure has been reported to the Government. The amount brought into the accounts is therefore based upon the latest modification as follows:

	£'000
Block Grant 1989–90	220,946
Adjustment for prior year	175

11 Superannuation Fund

The assets and liabilities of the Superannuation Fund are shown separately from those of Kent County Council although the legal position is that they are all in the ownership of the Kent County Council. This accounting treatment has been adopted because, once credited to the Superannuation Fund, monies may only be used to provide for the statutory determined pension and other payments attributable to staff covered by the Fund. However, any actuarial surplus or deficit is apportioned to the constituent member bodies of the fund.

12 Contingent Liability

The County Council has provided a guarantee in respect of loans raised by the developer of Kings Hill Business Park, West Mailing. At 31 March the maximum liability under the guarantee was £5m.

Consolidated Statement of Revenue and Capital Movements

The Consolidated Statement of Revenue and Capital Movements shows where the County Council's money came from in 1989–90 and how it was spent.

	1989–90		1988–9	
	£'000	£'000	£'000	£'000
Revenue expenditure				
Employment costs	524,597		507,951	
Other operating costs	313,665		281,270	
Interest and Leasing charges	23,315		22,653	
		863,577		811,514
Capital expenditure				
Acquisition of fixed assets	64,303		56,179	
Long term investments	–		1	
		64,303		56,180
Total revenue and capital expenditure		927,880		867,694
Revenue income				
Rate Income	438,305		392,060	
Government Grants and Contributions	319,810		326,921	
Charges for goods and services and other income	125,890		104,588	
		884,005		823,569
Capital income				
Sales of assets	22,085		26,661	
Government capital grants	4,978		6,060	

Consolidated Statement of Revenue and Capital Movements cont.

	£'000	1989–90 £'000	£'000	1988–9 £'000
Other	(187)			2,721
		26,876		**35,442**
Total revenue and capital income			910,881	**859,011**
Excess of expenditure over income financed from:			(16,999)	(8,683)
Net new long term borrowing	10,842			28,531
Net change in short term indebtedness	20,034			(44,867)
		30,876		**(16,336)**
Changes in other short term assets/liabilities increase/decrease in:				
provisions and reserves	808			2,422
creditors	21,499			16,226
debtors	(15,911)			(9,654)
stocks and works in progress	(893)			201
General County Revenue Fund	(6,658)			(1,671)
Unused capital receipts	(12,722)			129
				7,653
		(13,877)	(16,999)	**(8,683)**

Note: Reconciliation of revenue expenditure 1989–90

	£'000
Revenue expenditure shown	863,577
Add: Internal charges not resulting inoutflow of funds	27,481
Less: transfer to reserves	(383)
Revenue expenditure as shown in the Summary of Revenue Account	890,675

Superannuation Fund Accounts

This is an extract from a more detailed published statement, a copy of which is available for inspection at County Hall.

Under the provisions of the Local Government Superannuation Regulations, 1986, a Superannuation Fund has been established and is administered by the Kent County Council for the purpose of providing pensions and other benefits for the pensionable employees of the County Council, of the district councils in Kent, and of other minor bodies established within the county area. Teachers, Police and Firemen are not included as they have their own national pension schemes.

There is a year by year surplus of contributions and investment income over pensions and benefits payments. The fund is maintained by investing this surplus in stock market securities, both in this country and overseas, and in real property. Contributions are made to the Fund by employees at the rate of 6% of remuneration for offices and at 5% for manual workers as required by the Regulations. The rate of employers' contributions is determined by the Fund's actuary at the level necessary to keep the Fund solvent having regard to existing and prospective liabiities. This rate is currently 165% of the employees rate.

The Fund has been accepted by the Inland Revenue as an 'exempt approved scheme' under the Finance Act 1970 and, as such, qualifies for exemption from tax on investment income, underwriting commission and gains on selling transactions.

Administrative costs of paying pensions, allowances and other benefits, maintaining employees' records, arranging transfer values etc. are now borne by the Fund. This follows amended Regulations introduced with effect from 1st April 1987. Costs relating to the investment of the fund continue to be charged in this way.

The accounts comply in all material respects with Statement of Recommended Practice Number (SORP1): Pension Scheme Accounts published by the Accounting Standards Committee in May 1986. The principal change has been to include investments at market value rather than at cost.

Notes

1 *Currency Accounts:* currency deposit accounts established to facilitate settlement of overseas investment transactions.

2 *Cash:* a small part of the daily cash balance of the Fund is used by the County Council as part of its temporary borrowing requirements. The County Council is required to credit the Fund with interest on such monies at not less than 7 days notice money market rates. The remaining cash is held by the external fund managers on deposit for interest until it is required.

3 *Transfer Values:* cash payments representing the value of employees' pension rights which are transferred between the Fund and other pension funds or schemes on changes of employment.

Revenue Account for the year ended 31 March 1990

Income	1990 £'000	1989 £'000
Contributions from employees and employers	33,142	30,679
Dividends, interest, rents and other investment income	32,363	25,254
Transfer values received	5,027	4,501
Additional Voluntary Contributions	87	33
Total income	**70,619**	**60,467**
Expenditure		
Pensions, allowances and other benefits	39,436	35,306
Return of contributions etc.	326	1,072
Transfer values paid	6,291	4,096
Additional Voluntary Contributions	88	33
Other miscellaneous expenditure	2,006	1,682
Total Expenditure	**48,147**	**42,189**
Net new money available for Investment	22,472	18,278

Net Assets Statement as at 31 March 1990

	1990 £'000	1989 £'000
Investments at market value	564,679	531,896
Cash	45,431	44,746
Currency accounts	1,890	1,226
Current assets (debtors)	10,162	8,019
	622,162	**585,887**
Current liabilities (creditors)	(6,089)	(7,413)
Net assets	**616,073**	**578,474**

Reconciliation of movement in net assets of the Fund for the year ended 31 March 1990

	1990 £'000	£'000	1989 £'000	£'000
Net assets at 1 April		578,474		479,409
New net money invested		22,472		18,278
Change in market value of investments				
Realised	35,071		31,501	
Unrealised	(199,94)		49,286	
		15,127		80,787
Net assets at 31 March		**616,073**		**578,474**

Investments at market value as at 31 March 1990

Investments	Value of Investments at 31 March 1990 £'000	Value of Investments at 31 March 1989 £'000
British Government Stocks	22,285	30,698
Index Linked Stocks	26,236	23,745
Public Boards	146	171
Foreign Stocks	927	1,372
UK Company:		
Debenture/Loan Stocks	5,333	3,245
Equities/Convertibles	299,428	283,415
Overseas Government Stocks	10,783	9,357
Overseas Company:		
Equities/Convertibles	127,256	102,295
Property	72,285	76,968
	56,679	**531,896**

In-house Contractors

The County Council operates four In-house contractors run on a fully commercial basis which in accordance with statutory requirements tender for the work they carry out for the County Council in competition with private sector companies.

The In-house contractors are:

- *Highways Direct Works Organisation* – Provides Highways construction and maintenance service.
- *County Transport Workshops* – Provides a repair and maintenance service for the County Council's fleet of vehicles.
- *Landscape Services* – Provides a construction and maintenance service for the grounds of schools and other County Council property.
- *Abacus Catering* – Provision of the school meals service and catering facilities at some other County Council establishments.

The Trading results of the In-house contractors were as follows

	Highways DWO £'000	County Transport Workshops £'000	Landscape Services £'000	Abacus £'000
Income	13,824	1,004	3,936	9,277
Expenditure	14,413	974	3,593	9,774
Surplus/(Deficit	(589)	31	343	(497)
Assets employed	4,538	339	2,103	711
Rate of return on	(13.0%)	9.03%	16.30%	(69.9%)

Notes

1 The results shown for County Transport Workshops and Abacus are for the period 1 August 1989 (when these IHCs were established) to 31 March 1990.
2 Accounts are maintained on a current cost accounting basis.
3 Legislation relating to In-house contractors requires that charges made should allow for a specified rate of return on capital employed (at present 5%).
4 Abacus Catering have an outstanding contractual claim of £606,000. Any potential income resulting from this claim is not reflected in the financial results shown above.

9

The National Health Service

Introduction

This chapter is divided into three parts. The first part is intended to provide the reader who is unfamiliar with the National Health Service (NHS) with a general idea of its size, structure, funding and current problems. The second part considers recent developments designed to strengthen financial management control, so making both managers and clinicians more accountable for the services that they provide. These particularly concern the health service reforms outlined in the white paper *Working for Patients* (Cm.555). The reforms were subsequently embodied in the NHS and Community Care Act 1990, which came into operation on 1 April 1991. The final part examines the important aspect of presenting financial information.

Overview

As is generally well known, the NHS was established in 1948 with a mandate that promised unlimited, free medical care of the best possible standard to the entire population. However, in the very next year something completely different was to replace this promise. Costs soared out of control in Nye Bevan's first year as Minister of Health and when Stafford Cripps announced his 1948 budget he stated that henceforth the Treasury would set an annual ceiling on NHS spending – the British public would thus be allowed as much free health care as could be afforded within this economic limit. Ever since, over the last 44 years, an undersupply of medical health care has led to rationing. In England, the Department of Health changed its title to that of the Department of Health and Social Security (DHSS) in 1968. Mr

Richard Crossman was then Minister of Health and, by combining his post with that of Minister of Pensions, he acquired a seat in the Cabinet and the new title of Secretary of State for Social Services. In 1990, the DHSS was split into two with the re-creation of the Department of Health and the newer, separate, Department of Social Security. Both departments are headed by a Secretary for State.

The National Health Service (NHS) comprises:

- Hospital and community health services, providing all hospital care and a wide range of community health services;
- family health services (FHS), formerly family practitioner services, providing general medical, dental and dispensing services, some ophthalmic services and covering the cost of medicines prescribed by general practitioners;
- central health and miscellaneous services, providing a limited number of services most effectively administered centrally. Examples include the Special Hospitals Service Authority and the Health Education Authority.

At the time of writing the NHS is undergoing a number of key reforms, in particular:

- major changes in the roles of health authorities and hospitals following on from the separation of the purchaser and provider functions;
- the introduction of general practice fundholders as purchasers of secondary and providers of primary health care;
- major changes in the arrangements for the management of family health services.

These changes came at the end of two decades of major structural reorganization within the NHS.

The NHS was reorganized in 1974 in order to rationalize an organizational structure for health care that had to this point split responsibility between hospital authorities, local government (responsible for community services), and executive councils (responsible for administering the contracts, but not managing, self-employed general dental and medical practitioners, pharmacists and opticians). The reforms of 1974 determined that community services and hospital services became the responsibility of new regional and district health authorities, who also had some responsibility (via family practitioner committees, the successors to the executive councils) for self-employed practitioners. Health authority boundaries were designed wherever possible to approximate to local government boundaries so as to facilitate liaison with local authority social service departments. The hierarchy of administration that was created went, in descending order, from department, to region, to area and to district. In 1981 the area tier of management was removed. There are now 14 regional health authorities (RHAs) and 194 district health authorities (DHAs). 1981 also saw the introduction of performance indicators and compulsory competitive tendering for hospital support services.

During the 1980s the pace of management reforms in the NHS quickened. The NHS Management Inquiry (DHSS, 1983a), the Griffiths Report, was very critical of the consensus management approach adopted throughout the NHS. Griffiths believed this management structure to be weak on determined and consistent execution of authority decisions, with no focus of executive authority at regional and district levels. He saw too much emphasis on administration organized along discipline lines, and not enough activity based management. Following the Griffiths Report the government issued health circular HC(84)13. It required the implementation of the Griffiths recommendations which included the appointment of some 1800 general managers at regional, district and unit levels – units being subdivisions within a district. Other issues concerned the involvement of clinicians in the management process and budgeting; more attention to quality improvement and consumer participation; the introduction of cost improvement programmes; and the introduction of better personnel management – including appraisal, manpower planning and the operation of incentive schemes. Following the reforms of the 1970s and 1980s, and the work of Griffiths, the overall structure was as presented in figure 9.1. This structure existed immediately prior to the publication in early 1989 of the white paper *Working for Patients* (Cm.555).

Within the Department of Health, chaired by the Secretary of State, were a health services supervisory board, which set overall objectives and the broad strategy for the service, and a management board, whose role was to implement the supervisory board's recommendations. Both regional and district health authorities are statutory bodies whose members are appointed to serve on a part-time and, excepting the chairperson, on an honorary basis. All of the Griffiths general managers are appointed on short-term rolling contracts, the renewal of which is dependent upon annual appraisals of their performance. General managers may also receive performance related pay. Other health authority staff are responsible to general managers, although the status of consultants is slightly ambiguous. In most cases consultants

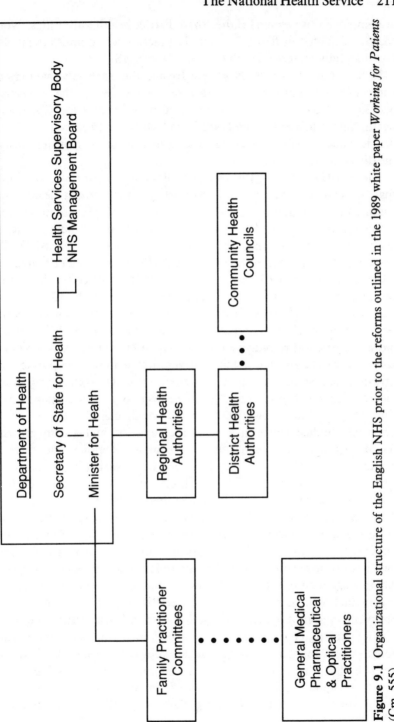

Figure 9.1 Organizational structure of the English NHS prior to the reforms outlined in the 1989 white paper *Working for Patients* (Cm. 555)

are employed by regional rather than district health authorities. Note that, as depicted in figure 9.1, family practitioner committees appear less than fully integrated with the rest of the NHS.

In Scotland, Wales and Northern Ireland there are only two tiers of control in the provision of health care. These are: (1) the respective Secretary of State; and (2) district health authorities for Wales and health boards in Scotland and Northern Ireland. In these counties both districts and boards have exactly the same role and responsibilities as the districts in England.

Klein (1989) noted, with respect to *Working for Patients* (Cm.555), that 'never before had any government document about health care commanded so much space and time in the media'. He also noted that a policy review launched in an attempt to devise new funding systems ended up saying nothing about how to finance the NHS. While Cm.555 reaffirmed commitment to the NHS and the key principles of a service available to all, free at point of use and financed mainly from taxation, it gave encouragement to a mixed economy of health care – an economy that would create a system of internal markets in which NHS care institutions would compete with each other in order to produce a more efficient and responsive service to its users. The mixed economy approach would also allow for joint ventures between the public and private health sectors and give tax relief to the over sixties for private medical insurance premiums. With respect to central management, Cm.555 proposed a new policy board, which includes a number of prominent industrialists in a part-time capacity, and a management board to replace the management executive. Regional and district health authorities have reduced in size with, surprisingly, no local authority representation. Each authority is now composed of five executive and five non-executive members. The philosophy is that districts will be responsible for ensuring access to services, setting targets and monitoring performance. While they will provide care services these will mainly be in the form of contracts issued to their own or outside hospitals, including those in the private sector. Day-to-day management of the districts' own hospitals is now to be via quasi-contractual 'management budgets' – see below. Major hospitals were given the option of applying for self-governing trust status, free from district control, employing their own staff, including consultants, and able to raise capital in the private sector subject to an external financial limit (EFL). Financial reforms were also introduced, including a new weighted capitation formula for the distribution of revenue in place of the Resource Allocation Working Party (RAWP) system, and the introduction of capital asset accounting. The Family Health Services Authority service (FHSA) has replaced the family practitioner committees. The FHSA is managerially much stronger and is integrated into the NHS structure by now being accountable to the respective regional health authority.

Harrison et al. (1990) note that the intellectual basis of Cm.555, that of internal markets, owes much to the ideas of Enthoven (1985). Enthoven considered that the separation of the purchasing and providing roles in health care would mean that purchasers 'could buy services from producers who offered good value' and that the 'bargaining leverage' of being able to buy outside would produce better performance from the internal providers. The creation of internal markets entails the separation of two functions that were previously conflated in the role of the districts: the 'provision' of hospital and community health services, entailing the ownership of health care institutions and the employment of direct care staff, and the 'purchase' (or commissioning) of care, that is, the allocation of funds to providing institutions so as to ensure that the needs of the district's population are met. It should be noted that Cm.555 applies to the whole of the United Kingdom and it now seems clear that the role of the English regional health authorities will be reduced to that of ensuring the implementation of central government policy. Their role as providers of common services to district authorities will diminish. A summary of these and other changes instituted as a result of Cm.555 is as follows

Departmental level:	(a)	Policy Board replaced the Supervisory Board
	(b)	Management Executive replaced the Management Board
Regional level:	(a)	Core role of ensuring the implementation of central government policy
	(b)	Role as providers of service reduced
	(c)	Family practitioner service now accountable to regional health authorities
District level:	(a)	Primary role is that of purchasers of health care for their resident population
	(b)	Relinquish control of day-to-day management of the institutions they own by means of quasi-contractual management budgets

'Self-Governing'   (a) Institutions, principally hospitals, can
Status: apply to the Secretary of State to become
                       'self-governing trusts', and hence released
                       from 'ownership' by a district health
                       authority

                   (b) Such freedom will allow trusts: to deter-
                       mine their own terms and conditions of
                       service and to accumulate financial service
                       for reinvestment. With respect to the
                       latter, capital charges will be set to ensure
                       a return of a proportion of such surpluses
                       to government

GP fundholding: (a) This will apply to the larger general
                       pratices. If they wish, and qualify accord-
                       ing to the terms set out, they can apply to
                       their regional authority for 'practice funds'.
                       Such a budget includes elements for pres-
                       cribing and grants for staff salaries and
                       premises improvements received by
                       ordinary practices, in addition to an amount
                       reflecting the practice's potential hospital
                       referrals to outpatients, to pathology and
                       X-ray, and for specified elective surgical
                       procedures

                   (b) The amount for referrals, etc. is deducted
                       by the regional health authority from its
                       allocation to the relevant district health
                       authority

Figure 9.2, adapted from Harrison et al. (1990) is not a conventional
organizational chart but rather an attempt to illustrate the major NHS
funding flows as from 1992–3. Appleby et al. (1990) recognize that
the proposals of Cm.555 amount to a revolution in management
practice within the NHS. They state (p. 30):

Theoretical translation of policy into practice is not simply a
matter of replacing one set of autonomous rules with another,
but, rather it involves considerable reorientations of attitudes and
cultural environments. Given the distinct lack of detailed
prescription in the NHS reforms, the tight implementation
timetable and the scope of change, the attitudes and cultural

upheavals will be particularly acute in the NHS. Health authorities and their managers, clinicians and others, face a radical change intheir roles if the ideas of the reforms are to become a reality.

What we are faced with, therefore, is a tension between the theory underlying health markets and the practical problems of bringing these reforms into practice. While economic theory states that perfectly competitive markets will lead to an efficient allocation of resources, it has to be recognized that the market for health care is far from perfect. Key amongst the imperfections that exist are possible provider monopoly, the uncertainty of demand and a scarcity of financial information relevant for decision-taking. Glynn et al. (1992) note that the recent initiative of general practice fundholding has led to a number of budget ploys by both providers and purchasers. The public sector health market is still subject to an overall cash limit and hospitals are subject to stringent central regulations with respect to the important questions of pricing, capital investment and the range of services to be offered.

In a 1984 health survey carried out by the *Economist* (28 April 1984) it was stated that:

90 per cent of perceived episodes of ill-health in Britain are sensibly dealt with by the slightly sick people themselves. Of the remaining one tenth, over 90 per cent came to the family doctors. These then remitted over one in ten of their cases (i.e. just over 1 per cent of all cases of illness) to a hospital. Together with the 0.5 per cent or so of all British people who went to hospital directly, this meant that under 2 per cent of ill Britons ended up in a hospital bed. These few hospitalised Britons absorb around two thirds of the costs of the NHS.

The NHS employs almost one million people, with many more in supporting industries. The total planned central government expenditure on the NHS in 1991–2 for the UK is £30 billion. This NHS funding comes mainly from general taxation (circa 85 per cent) and national insurance contributions (circa 15 per cent). Other sources of finance come from prescription charges, other receipts (mainly land sales, but including some private patient income) and donations (for general use or in accordance with the terms of a bequest or trust). Each year, as part of its negotiations with the Treasury, the Department of Health calculates the actual increase in expenditure that it estimates

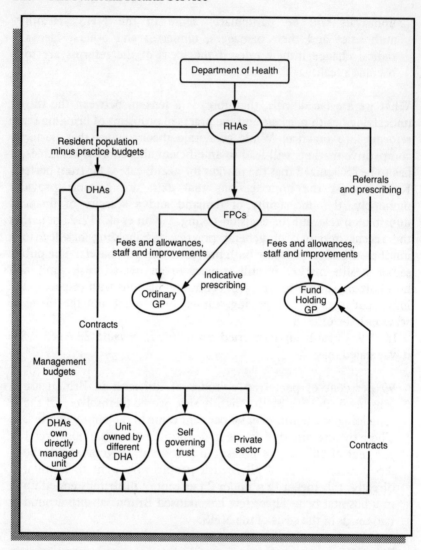

Figure 9.2 Proposed major NHS funding flows, 1992–3
Source: adapted from Harrison et al. (1990)

will be necessary to meet its requirements. Harrison et al. (1990) suggest that the most important single demographic change is the increasing number of very elderly, those of 75 years and over. In 1991 it is estimated that four million people were 75 years and over (7 per cent of the population). By the year 2001 this figure will increase by another half per cent (based on *Social Trends*, No. 18, 1988). This increase might at first seem modest but its financial consequences are not. The average person in this age band consumes something like nine times the volume of health care resources used by the average person of working age, or five times the average for all ages (DHSS, 1983a). The *Fourth Report* of the Social Services Committee (1986) concluded that health authority budgets need to increase in real terms by roughly 1 per cent per annum. As the Healthcare Financial Management Association (1990) note, one of the major debates surrounding the adequacy of NHS finance relates to national revenue allocations and finance. The Association states (1990, p. 3):

Depending on the inflation index used, differing conclusions can be drawn regarding the real purchasing power of Health Authorities. In recent years, cost improvement programmes, or so-called internally generated funds, also need to be considered, producing at least three commonly used measures of growth in NHS resources:

(a) real terms increase, using a measure of inflation in the economy as a whole, e.g. GDP deflator,
(b) real terms increase, using a health service specific price index,
(c) (a) or (b) plus cost improvement programmes.

Each of these measures is compared with a target growth figure based on the estimated percentage real change in expenditure necessary to cope with changes in demographies, advances in medicine and the funding implications of government policies.

The 1980s represented a decade of very tight funding for the NHS, when expenditure on the cash-limited hospital and community health services (representing around 70 per cent of total spending) grew at less than 1 per cent in volume terms; that is, cash increases adjusted by the NHS pay and price index. The settlement for 1990–1 represented an increase of nearly 5 per cent in volume terms, while the 1991–2 increase is estimated at about 3.5 per cent. The Chancellor's 1991 autumn statement suggests a growth of around 3 per cent in volume terms for 1992–3. While this change in direction by the government is to be welcomed it has to be remembered that the growth in demand for health care from an ageing population and the high costs of new medical technology will erode much of this growth in money.

Revenue allocations to RHAs between 1977 and 1989 were on a basis established by the Resource Allocation Working Party (RAWP), which reported in 1976 (DHSS, 1976, 1980). The objective of the RAWP allocation formula, amended over the years, was to allocate hospital and community service resources in a way which would eventually provide equal access to care for people in equal need. The formula did reduce some of the disparities between the better provided and the less well provided parts of the country. The gap between the region furthest above target and furthest below target reduced from 26 per cent in 1977–8 to 11 per cent in 1988–9. Some aspects of the RAWP formula were subject to criticism and the (then) NHS Management Board reviewed the operation of the formula, reporting in July 1988. The changes recommended were superseded by *Working for Patients* (Cm.555), which recommended from 1990–1 onwards a move to resident population based funding. In summary the base for determining an RHA's funding is as follows:

1 Each region's population is 'weighted' to reflect the demands on its health services by different age groups. These 'capitation rates' are based on estimates of expenditure per head per age group.
2 The age weighted populations are adjusted by the standardized mobidity ratio (SMR).
3 Certain geographical supplements are added to these allocations:

   (a) London weighting, for staff working in the London area;
   (b) market forces, to reflect regional variations in staff costs;
   (c) Thames supplement – 3 per cent for the Thames Regions to reflect the higher costs and demands on services within these regions.

Cross-boundary flows are not taken into account in allocations; they now form the subject of inter-authority contracts. It had been the government's intention that full weighted capitation funding would be achieved at regional level by 1992–3 but in the allocations for 1991–2 it was announced that this process would have to be at a slower rate in order that all regions received a minimum level of growth. While regions have some discretion in determining their own sub-regional allocation formula they are expected to be 'broadly on the same basis' as the national formula. GP fundholders receive their allocation direct from their region and the funds so allocated are deducted from the funds otherwise available to their district health authority.

Capital expenditure is still currently allocated between regions on a RAWP based formula. Regions, in turn, allocate to districts in line with their strategic programmes. Capital expenditure by NHS Trusts is financed through accumulated depreciation, surpluses and borrowing.

Family health service expenditure currently remains largely non-cash limited. However, expenditure on practice staff, premises and computing are subject to cash limits, as are FHSA administrative costs.

From the Department of Health's point of view, RHAs' internal accountability is monitored within a cycle of planning, monitoring and review which is operated by the management executive. This cycle is as follows (Masters, 1990, p. 31):

December	Department issues allocation to regions
February	Regions submit short-term programmes showing in outline how they expect to perform in the following year
March	The management executive agrees with regions their objectives for the following year
March	Individual authorities finalize their budgets based on their short-term programmes
July	Detailed planning statements submitted by regions; these contain detailed outturn reports for the previous year and detailed plans for the current year (updating the short-term programmes and budgets)
July, October January & April	Regions submit quarterly and annual income and expenditure monitoring returns within 15 days of the period end
August, November, February & May	Regions submit quarterly and annual activity returns within two months of the period end

As Masters (1990, p.31) points out:

From a region point of view, the cycle of interaction with the Management Executive is supplemented by its own series of interactions with its districts. Each of the main elements of the cycle has a financial aspect. The main financial report used in each of the planning and monitoring phases is a table which analyses the marginal changes in the authority's affairs. This table is always expressed in terms of the forecast outturn for the year in question; as the year progresses a greater proportion of the forecast is based on actual results achieved.

The marginal analysis table referred to by Masters (1990, p.31) is reproduced as table 9.1. In part this table is a reflection of that fact that annual income and expenditure statements are partially deficient.

Table 9.1   Marginal analysis table

Additional recurrent resources allocated in excess of the general cash uplift to allow for GDP inflation	×
Resources generated from cash-releasing cost improvements and income generation	×
Other recurrent resources	×
Less:	(×)
Additional costs of maintaining existing services	
Additional pay and price costs (over that allowed for in the general cash uplift)	(×)
Service developments	(×)
Use of recurrent resources non-recurrently	(×)
Net (over) or under commitment of recurrent resources	×
Net surplus or deficit of non-recurrent resource	×
Net change in working balances for the year	×

Financial Management

As outlined above, the very large sums of money spent on the NHS mean that management must at all times be able to demonstrate that funds are prudently allocated, expenditure strictly controlled, and performance critically examined. In this section we review three important developments in the area of financial management:

1 speciality costing;
2 management budgeting
3 contract management.

Speciality costing

The report from the Körner Committee (DHSS, 1984) sought to make available improved financial information to assist management to carry out these tasks. The aim of Working Group F (Financial Information) was to provide more refined and meaningful cost information. This was no mean achievement, since an effort was made to strike a sensible balance between information structured to a common national format, and information reflecting the great diversity of local management arrangements.

The working group on financial information was set up in March 1981 by the steering group on health service information. It was given two tasks:

1 to propose a minimum set of management accounting data for budget setting, and for the planning and cost control of NHS health care provision; and
2 to work closely with other information working groups to ensure that the recommendations about accounting data are compatible with and complementary to those about activity and manpower statistics.

As the introduction to this report states:

The management processes introduced by the reorganis-ation of the NHS in 1974, and the devolution of functions and responsi-bilities within districts in the restriction of services in 1982, require not only that appropriate and adequate information be available at district level, but also at unit and operational levels, and particularly to clinicians who play a crucial role in the management of resources.

Figure 9.3, from the report, depicts the way money is used day by day in the hospital service, and how this is related to the terms 'subjective', 'departmental' and 'patient care' analyses. There are similar processes in the community, patient transport and other services.

The working group highlighted five criticisms of the (then) existing financial information systems:

1 financial information did not provide the cost of treating different groups of patients (i.e. translating the *input* of resources into the *outputs* of health care);
2 costs produced in the uniform departmental (functional) analysis generally did not reflect local budgetary responsibilities due to inconsistent analysis;
3 hospital classification, under the costing system, did not account for the substantial variations in case-type which existed between hospitals of the same type;

Financial input

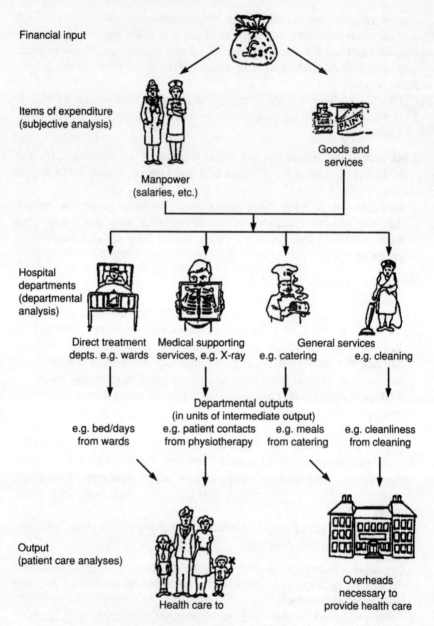

Items of expenditure
(subjective analysis)

Manpower
(salaries, etc.)

Goods and
services

Hospital
departments
(departmental
analysis)

Direct treatment   Medical supporting   General services
depts. e.g. wards   services, e.g. X-ray   e.g. catering   e.g. cleaning

Departmental outputs
(in units of intermediate output)

e.g. bed/days   e.g. patient contacts   e.g. meals   e.g. cleanliness
from wards   from physiotherapy   from catering   from cleaning

Output
(patient care analyses)

Health care to

Overheads
necessary to
provide health care

Figure 9.3 Day-to-day expenses in the NHS
Source: DHSS (1984)

4 financial information was often of suspect validity, particularly when apportionment was required to produce patient care analysis;
5 lack of timeliness of information – particularly serious for budget holders who require information for control purposes.

Various approaches to costing were considered: patient costing; diagnostic group costing; clinical team costing; and speciality costing. Of these the team considered that speciality costing commended itself to providing useful information at moderate cost. Speciality costing has been under consideration for some time. It has been tested in a variety of situations and has been gaining increased support. A wide section of NHS management is familiar with its underlying concepts and intentions. While there are more than 50 specialities currently recognized by Royal Colleges, the report (Annex G) recommended that, for management purposes, the minimum data set should consist of 20 specialities. A speciality cost can be defined as the average cost of treating patients within a speciality or group of specialities.

The recommendations of this report (detailed in the previous section) present a considerable challenge to those who use, analyse and interpret financial data. Both finance and administrative officers face a major technical task and, even more importantly, the task of reiterating and refocusing their own and their authorities' interest and attention on the outputs of the services for which they are responsible. All personnel with spending responsibilities will require training and education in order to use effectively use the information provided. As the report states (para.1.5):

Reliable financial data and well structured financial analyses are an essential tool of management: to enable managers to account for past expenditure, control present expenditure and allocate future resources. Financial data analysed in conjunction with activity and manpower statistics are essential for planning.

There are three main approaches to speciality costing:

1 The 'sampling' approach, considered by the Körner working group and based on the work of Professor Charles Magee of Cardiff University. As Perrin (1988, p. 73) states:

Magee speciality costing was designed to provide cost information of a sufficient accuracy for use in financial and operational planning, and in general performance reviews. But accuracy was not nearly 100%, such as should be sought for any system of speciality costing used to report performance against speciality or clinical budgets.

2 The 'continuous' approach, which has been described as simply an evolutionary development from Magee's speciality costing approach. The principles are the same but the differences are that workload data is continuously collected and recorded, rather than sampled. This approach is more accurate and progress reports are more readily and regularly available.

3 The 'statistical' approach, which arose from the interest of health economists and econometricians in analysing the cost structure of health care by means of statistical regression techniques.

For a more detailed discussion on the history and development of speciality costing see Hillman (1984) and Perrin (1988).

Management budgeting

The present impetus for management budgeting (also known as clinical management budgeting) arises out of a recommendation of the Griffiths Report – the NHS Management Inquiry (DHSS, 1983a). It is an approach to budgeting which has the following characteristics:

1 the unit should be the focal point for management delegation;
2 clinicians should be involved in the budgeting process;
3 clinicians' budgets should include costs directly controlled by the clinician, and charges for the use of other services;
4 budget holders should be involved in setting and controlling their budgets (they should be encouraged to increase the effectiveness of services by having powers to retain and reallocate a proportion of any savings which can be achieved);
5 the system developed should emphasize management and not accounting.

The broad framework for management budgeting involves six main areas: revised budget structure; improved budget setting procedures; incentives for involvement; budget holder reporting; improved information systems and an established review procedure. This revised budget structure recognizes three classes of budgets. They are for:

1 functions: diagnostic or support departments here the budget holder is the respective head of department;
2 facilities: physical locations such as wards, theatres and clinics where the budget holder is a ward sister or nursing officer;
3 specialities: where the budget holder is the relevant clinician.

Once budget holders have been identified, items of expenditure are assigned, as far as possible, to those who are able to influence the level of expenditure. For example, dressings and central sterile service department (CSSD) packs would be assigned to a facility budget holder while drugs would be assigned to a speciality: to a nursing officer in the former case and a consultant in the latter case. The system is designed to reflect more clearly the pattern of decision-making within the hospital, but it does require participation, agreement to decisions on expenditure, and commitment. In such a system re-charged costs would need to be made at a standard charge. This enables simple variance analysis so that expenditure can be divided into an element of volume, incurred by the user, and cost, incurred by the provider.

Presently there are a number of pilot schemes under way to further develop the principles of management budgeting. If this system is to become more widely adopted it will require increased delegation in order to allow budget holders greater discretion over how they manage their various activities. Paragraph 19 of the Griffiths Report states:

We believe that urgent action is required, if Units are to fulfil their role and provide the most effective management of their resources. This particularly affects the doctors. Their decisions largely dictate the use of all resources and they must accept the management responsibility which goes with clinical freedom. This implies active involvement in securing the most effective use and management of all resources. The nearer that the management process goes to the patient, the more important it becomes for the doctors to be looked upon as the natural managers. This should be more explicitly recognized:

- in the doctors' training – undergraduate, postgraduate, in-service, and in preparation for particular clinical management posts; and
- in constructing the system of management budgets in a way which supports this work and meets the medical requirement and interest.

Outside the pilot schemes, hospital budgets continue on a functional basis: nursing, pharmacy, physiotherapy, catering, etc. Budget holders have to satisfy the demands made upon them by clinicians for their patients, while at the same time attempting to keep within their budgets. The 1982 NHS reorganization has not yet resulted in the devolution of real decision-taking to the unit and hospital level. Wickings et al. (1983) discuss the clinical accountability, service planning and evaluation (CASPE) research and other projects concerned with the closer involvement of clinicians in budgeting. Bevan (1984, p. 52) states:

Giving budgets to clinicians may satisfy the canons of budgetary control and the criteria of economic efficiency. It may be necessary given that the old concordat can no longer work. But it does mean that, when we go to hospital for treatment, we cannot expect the clinician to pretend that the cost does not matter.

It is generally considered that it takes around four years to introduce a management budget system into hospitals. This is because all patient, administrative and workload information, and costing systems, have to be upgraded and computerized at least to a level as defined by the Körner working group. Perrin (1988, p. 107) states that management budgeting:

> is the next evolutionary stage of NHS financial development beyond speciality costing. . . [It] involves hospital consultants taking a share of responsibility in planning and monitoring the distribution of hospital resources amongst the different specialities or individual clinicians. Historically doctors have not sought this role, although willing to take part collectively through advisory committees and representation on management teams and authority boards.

Even while speciality costing and management budgeting still remain very much at the development stage, research is taking place to evaluate the practicality of adopting another costing and budgetary system, based on diagnosis related groups (DRGs). This approach was pioneered by Professors Thompson and Fetter of Yale University in the USA. UK experience is reported in the *Diagnosis Related Groups Newsletter* published by the King Edwards Hospital Fund for London. In the USA DRGs are used as the basis for reimbursing hospitals for patients treated under the Medicare insurance programme.

Contract management

The final development discussed in this section is that of contract management. Speaking in the House of Commons, Kenneth Clark, Minister of Health, stated (Hansard, 4 July 1984, col.589):

> The Government's policy is that the National Health Service should contract out all services where this can be shown to be cost-effective and operationally sound.

DHSS circular (83) 18, issued in September 1983, is the main document that outlines NHS policy on what is usually referred to as competitive tendering. The circular advised health authorities to submit, by spring 1984, a full programme for putting out all cleaning, catering and laundry work to open tender by September 1986. However, this policy has, to the government's annoyance, met with varying degrees of acceptance by the health authorities, with many showing a continuing preference for their existing workforce. Undaunted, the government has now embarked on a much broader and far more comprehensive approach, that of 'managed' competition.

The government's White Paper *Working for Patients* (Cm.555) contained two important changes to the provision of health care. These were:

1 the separation of the responsibilities for service planning and managing the provision of services; and
2 the introduction of competition, largely through an internal market in health care provision.

Each health district is now to receive a purchasing budget based on the size and age structure of its resident population with some adjustments for mortality rates. Districts will have sole responsibility for ensuring that their own resident population has access to an adequate range of health care services. (Note though, as stated earlier, that some GP practices will become independent fundholders and purchasers of health care, thereby reducing the global funds available to their districts). As Appleby et al. (1990, p. 28) note:

Contracts will be the method by which purchasers and providers do business; setting out prices, treatment levels and quality standards. . . 'spending' thus becomes 'billing' in the new health care market.

The new health care market is therefore composed of district health authority and GP fundholding purchasers and a range of providers consisting of the new self-governing hospital trusts, DHA managed hospitals and private and voluntary care hospitals.

Purchasers now have to prepare service specifications which must set out the range, volume and quality of services its residents need. DHAs will need to ensure that they have appropriate clinical advice from GPs about patterns of referrals. Providers, on the other hand, will have to assess the services they can provide and ensure the commitment of their consultants, clinical and support staff in providing these. Indeed, at the time of writing, many providers are preparing prospectuses that set out the range of services on offer, together with statements on all the associated 'quality management' aspects, waiting times etc. The Healthcare Financial Management Association and the Institute of Health Services Management (1990) have produced a discussion paper, *Making Contracts Work: The Practical Implications*, which outlines the principles surrounding this new contracting process, together with discussion on a number of practical issues. Figure 9.4 outlines the overall contracting process now being initiated.

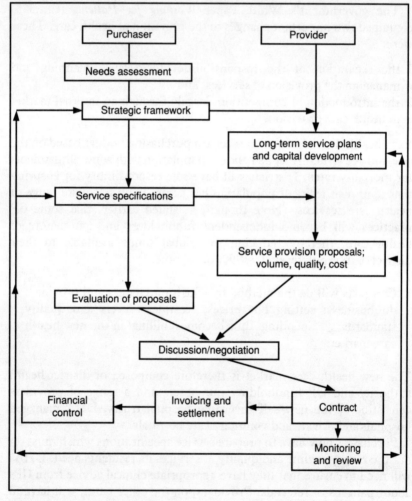

Figure 9.4 The contracting process

Cm.555 envisages three types of contract:

1 Block contracts	–	when the provider is paid an annual fee, in instalments, for a defined range of services.
2 Cost/volume contracts	–	when the provider receives a guaranteed minimum sum for treating a minimum number of cases and additional funds for treating additional cases to an agreed maximum level.
3 Cost per case	–	when the purchaser agrees a price for the treatment of an individual patient.

Block contracts, although a simple basis of contractual agreement, could prove problematic for purchasers since there is little control over the efficient use of resources. They could also prove problematic for providers because of unpredictable demand. Cost/volume contracts afford the purchaser some measure of financial control, though contingency reserves will have to be maintained throughout the year. Providers have a guaranteed minimum level of funding. Cost per case contracts are, in certain respects, disadvantageous to both purchasers and providers due to the high level of administration required. However, as payment is only made if a patient receives treatment there is the ability for the purchaser to contract for very specific types of treatment. For providers there are opportunities for making best use of spare capacity and thereby adjusting prices to reflect changes in cost or clinical practice.

For DHAs in particular there are, as a result of these changes, major changes in organizational culture that pose major organizational challenges. As Appleby et al. (1990, p. 32) note:

> Not only will districts be acting as both purchaser of services for their resident population and provider of services in relation to directly managed units, but they will also need to focus on health needs assessment and the planning, procurement and monitoring of services designed to meet those needs for the district's residents.

Since 1 April 1991, a new scheme of capital charges has come into operation. The objectives of this scheme are:

- to increase the awareness of health services managers of the costs of capital (previously treated as a 'free' good);
- to improve efficient capital management; and
- to ensure that capital costs are fully reflected in the pricing of hospital services.

This latter objective is to promote both fair competition within the NHS and between the NHS and private sector providers. Capital charges apply to all NHS assets except for those acquired by donation (though these are depreciated) and those used for administrative purposes (though these too are depreciated on the balance sheet – see below).

Capital charges consist of two elements – depreciation (based on a schedule of notionally determined standard lives) and interest (based on the opening value of assets) (currently 6 per cent in real terms).

The introduction of capital charging has posed problems for those hospitals occupying expensive sites and for the districts purchasing services from them. In 1991, these problems were largely avoided because each district received a revenue allocation which had been adjusted in line with the capital charges it was expected to meet from the hospitals and other units providing it with services. As each district purchaser received sufficient cash to meet its own individual capital charges bill the overall effect of capital charging in 1991 was neutral. In the longer term the system is not intended to be neutral. As Robinson (1992 p. 98) notes:

> For capital charges to influence the way in which capital assets are used, it will be necessary to remove the protection presently received by providers with above-average capital costs. This will be achieved by allocating revenue expenditure to districts on the basis of national *average* capital charges instead of the actual charges they incur. In this way, districts purchasing from high-cost providers will find that they are able to buy a lower volume of services than comparable districts facing lower-cost providers.

Clearly, too rapid a move to such a system would provide highly disruptive. The DOH has therefore developed transitional arrangements to phase in capital charging over a number of years. Inner London hospitals provide one example of those needing transitional assistance as their capital charges are over 50 per cent higher than those incurred by comparable hospitals in the remainder of the south east (Akehurst et al. 1991).

Financial Accounting and Reporting

Unlike local authorities and public corporations, individual health authorities are not required by statute or regulation to publish annual accounts. DHAs generally only report internally to RHAs and the DoH. One notable exception to this general rule is the West Glamorgan Health Authority's annual report and accounts. Indeed the authority's 1984–5 report was commended by the Chartered Institute of Public Finance and Accountancy as a model for other authorities to achieve. As Perrin (1983, p. 194) states:

It is of course a moot point how far there is a need for, or benefit from, detailed reporting of financial performance at the local level. Given that NHS expenditure is funded centrally, with no burden on the rates, it is a reasonable supposition that the degree of local interest in the details of NHS expenditure is relatively limited. It also seems likely that many members of health authorities are unable to evaluate the detail of financial reports. . . This might suggest that local reporting is a waste of time. Alternatively, it may suggest that the challenge to the local treasurer is all the greater – to produce financial, accounting and activity information in a form, with appropriate visual aids, that even members without previous financial experience can begin to understand.

From 1948 to 1974 the (then) Ministry of Health required every health authority in England and Wales to report by the end of each month the previous month's expenditure on all the main 'subjective' headings, and the cumulative expenditure from 1 April compared with an appropriate proportion of the approved annual budget. Half-way through the year, revised estimates were called for which could be adjusted to take account of over- or underspendings which could not be avoided. For 26 years these forms were used, subject to periodic minor modifications. The subjective analysis of expenditure had the merit of being simple to update as, for example, all cleaners' wages were collectively grouped under the heading 'domestic salaries and wages'. No attempt was made to classify costs by departments or functions so that there was no clear picture of the pattern of expenditure incurred by a diverse range of activities.

With the reorganization of 1974 came the introduction of 'functional' accounts, that is by activity: renal dialysis, catering and so on. The arguments for adopting the functional system were that:

1 the consumption of resources would be classified by function, thereby showing who had been responsible for using them;
2 by adopting standardized functions comparisons between districts might be facilitated;

3 functional budgets would give managers a sense of responsibility.

Even though functional accounting had been adopted, subjective accounts were not abolished. They were still regarded as a useful control mechanism and the information they provided was used by the DHSS to construct usage and price indices. As under the previous system, cost statements still tended to lag seriously behind the financial accounts.

Section 98(2) of the National Health Act 1977 provides that health authority accounts and audit should be in a form required by the Secretary of State with the approval of the Treasury.

The recent NHS reforms, outlined above, have also meant that the content of DHA annual accounts and financial returns are becoming more structured on commercial practice. The accounting year is from 1 April to the following 31 March. Annual accounts are required to be completed within three months of the financial year end. There are three summary statements:

1 revenue income and expenditure account, which provides information on the purchasing and managing roles of the DHA;
2 balance sheet, which is a statement of assets and liabilities at the beginning and end of the financial year;
3 sources and application of funds statement, which is a return which determines the DHA's outturn against cash limit.

DHAs are also required to complete a set of financial returns that provide more detailed analyses of expenditure. Fourteen such returns were required for 1991–2. These ranged from catering and patient transport services to hospital and community health services departmental analysis and capital assets. The accounts must be accompanied by a statement of accounting practice and must be certified by the director of finance and by the chairman.

For the new NHS, the format of accounts will be largely based on the requirements of the Companies Acts in order to show 'a true and fair' view of the trust's financial affairs. FHSAs are, as with DHAs, required to produce three main statements. In their case, the balance sheet is substituted by a statement of working balances. These statements are supported by notes on a range of issues including accounting policy and expenditure by functional areas. General practice fundholders have to operate a budgeting and accounting system as outlined in *GP Fundholders' Manual of Accounts* (DOH, 1990). They must also report on budgetary performance monthly to the FHSA.

Conclusion

This chapter has mapped out a number of important and major changes designed to reform the management of the NHS. The impetus for these changes has recently been reinforced by the publication of a government consultative document, *Health of the Nation* (June 1991). Though not itself part of the NHS reform programme, it sets the context within which purchasing and other strategies need to be developed. The strategy in this document is to select a number of key areas where targets for the improvement of health can be specified and progress towards these targets can be monitored. Target areas range from cases of substantial mortality, such as coronary heart disease, to cases that involve substantial ill-health, such as diabetes, and factors which contribute to unhealthy living, such as smoking.

This document aims to move the debate on the adequacy of our health care system away from a preoccupation with health services *per se*, focusing instead upon the promotion of health. Such a strategy will require the development of joint policies between the NHS and other government departments and agencies. At a local level DHAs will need to establish 'health alliances' with social services departments, voluntary service organizations, private sector employers and others. In due course the government intends to publish a white paper to legislate for these reforms, which will require further management reform and new chains of accountability.

10

The Nationalized Industries

Introduction

The intervention by the state in a large and diverse number of trading and quasi-trading activities has been a feature of most of the twentieth century, and is by no means unique to the United Kingdom. Such intervention has been achieved either by the creation of nationalized industries or by holding equity share capital in certain private sector companies. While in theory intervention was supposed to be an arms-length relationship, in practice governments have tended to exert strong influence in controlling the destiny of such industries. The UK has been no exception.

The intention in these opening paragraphs is to discuss in general terms the overall sphere of government influence in such organizations before concentrating discussion upon the control and regulation of the nationalized industries.

Nationalized industries represent those industries taken into public ownership or control for a variety of economic, political and social reasons. Traditionally they have been thought of as comprising those industries that dominate four strategic sectors of economic activity: energy; public transport; communications; and iron and steel. In the words of the 1978 white paper, *The Nationalised Industries* (Cmnd. 7131, para. 52):

They supply the basic goods and services to industry, and essentials of life to individual consumers. They are themselves major customers of the capital goods industries, and the scale of their purchases means that some of these supplying industries are heavily dependent on their strategic decisions and investment. In short, the nationalized industries have a pervasive influence thoughout the economy on investment, employment, industrial costs, and on the cost of living. The share of national resources going to them, and the efficiency with which they use these resources, are matters of major importance.

On the one hand, nationalized industries are expected to follow best commercial practice; they adopt, for example, full accruals basis accounting and adjust their trading results for the effects of inflation. On the other hand they have also been expected to accommodate additional social obligations, which have often conflicted with strict commercial criteria. For example, the Post Office has a duty to provide postal services to every part of the country at a uniform rate regardless of the fact that additional costs are incurred through servicing rural areas.[1]

The nationalized industry sector grew rapidly following the election of the first Labour government after the Second World War. First to be nationalized were the coal industry and the principal transport undertakings. By contrast, the 1980s proved to be the decade of privatization. This trend has continued into the 1990s. Forty-six major (and dozens of smaller) companies have been privatized since 1979. By the middle of 1990 the nationalized industries' share of GDP had fallen to just over 3 per cent, down from 9 per cent in 1979. Over the same period the numbers employed in nationalized industries have more than halved to 660,000 and more than 920,000 jobs have been transferred to the private sector (Foreign and Commonwealth Office, 1992). There are now only nine main nationalized industries. We list these in table 10.1, together with their financial performance targets. The question of privatization concludes this chapter.

The managing boards of nationalized industries are not civil servants. The boards are appointed by ministers who have the power to give general directions but are not involved in day to day management. The current government believes that nationalised industries should act as commercial enterprises and has laid down policies with which they are expected to perform. The policies involve:

- clear government objectives for each industry;
- regular corporate plans and performance reviews;
- agreed principles relating to investment appraisal and pricing;
- financial targets and performance aims;
- external financing limits;
- systematic monitoring.

External scrutiny of the nationalized industries' efficiency is conducted by the Monopolies and Mergers Commission (MMC). Where appropriate, investigations may also be undertaken by private firms of management consultants. House of Commons Select Committees, such as the Treasury and Civil Service Committee, also scrutinise these industries' performance.

The Political, Economic and Financial Framework for Nationalized Industries

As stated in the introduction, the political debate on nationalization really started after 1945. Prior to this, the late nineteenth century saw many service industries coming under municipal ownership. This municipalization of utilities was usually justified on the grounds that they were either natural local monopolies or required regulation of competition in order to meet particular standards of service. Municipalization was relatively free from political controversy. Those industries nationalized before 1945 were brought under state control not only because they were seen as a logical extension to municipalization, but also because of economy of scale arguments. For example, in 1926 the Central Electricity Board was set up in order to achieve nationwide economies of scale which had, by then, become technically feasible.

Political arguments in favour of nationalization have not altered significantly over the past 60 years or so. These viewpoints have been summarized in *A Study of UK Nationalised Industries: their role in the economy and control in the future* (Natinal Economic Development Office (NEDO) 1976, appendix volume, p.76) as follows:

(a) a belief, often supported by investigatory committees, that increased government ownership and/or control is required in certain industries: to promote greater efficiency; or to achieve an inevitable reduction in size with less harmful impact on employees and local communities; or to achieve economic survival and development in an industry of strategic or regional importance where sufficient private risk capital is not forthcoming;
(b) a belief that nationalisation of basic industry is an essential prerequisite of national economic planning;
(c) recognition that certain services to the public constitute natural local or national monopolies and/or require considerable regulation in order to ensure acceptable levels of service, prices and safety; and a belief that in these circumstances there is significantly reduced justification for continued private ownership competition;

Table 10.1   Nationalized industries' financial targets

Industry	Current target	Latest achievement[1]
British Coal	Sustainable profitability	1990–91: Profit of £78 million
British Rail	By 1992–93: Public Service Obligation (PSO) grant for Regional down to £345 million and Network South East to be out of grant. [2] Objectives now under review	1990–91: PSO grant £600 million
British Waterways Board	1991–92: Breakeven after grant	1990–91: Breakeven after grant
Caledonian MacBrayne[3]		
Civil Aviation Authority	1989–90 to 1991–92: 8 per cent average[4][5]	1985–86 to 1988–89: 7.7 per cent average [4][5]
London Transport	By 1992–93: £70 million operating surplus[6]	1990–91: operating deficit £100 million
Nuclear Electric	1991–92: Profit[7] target ranges from 1.9 per cent to 3.0 per cent	1990–91: Profit[7] of 1.9 per cent

Table 10.1 cont.

Industry	Current target	Latest achievement[1]
Post Office	1989–90 to 1991–2: 6.4 per cent[8] average[8]	1990–91: 1.5 per cent[8]
Scottish Nuclear	1991–92: 2.8 per cent[7]	1990–91: Breakeven

(1) On same basis as current target, except where specified.
(2) In 1989–90 prices, separate targets for BR non-supported sectors of: 1992–93 profits of £95 million for Inter-City and £50 million for Railfreight.
(3) Targets being set.
(4) Current cost accounting return on average net assets.
(5) Excludes activities where CAA's charges are determined by international agreement. The Highlands and Islands Airports are also excluded. Latest achievement against target of 7 per cent average for the period.
(6) Before depreciation and renewals
(7) Current cost accounting return on net current costs.
(8) Return on capital employed after interest and exceptional items and before tax. Group target; separate targets are set for the Letters, Parcels and Counters business. Capital measured on modified historic cost basis, broadly equivalent to current cost.

Source: Cm. 1920, Table 6.1

(d) conviction in the trade union movement that in certain industries, such as coal mining, employees' legitimate rights could not be obtained without nationalisation;

(e) a belief made explicit in Clause IV (S.4) of the Labour Party constitution, that the most equitable distribution of income is dependent upon 'common ownership of the means of production, distribution and exchange'.

The motivations and political ideologies of the political parties and governments over the decades have differed widely. A major platform of the present Conservative administration is the release of resources from the public to the private sector thereby reducing the size of the public sector and spreading private shareholding more widely. It is also felt that privatization increases competition and improves service efficiency. Privatization has also raised valuable income for the government though there has been some concern at the prices at which certain industries have been sold off. The issue of nationalization will always remain controversial.

Responsibility and control

The duties of each nationalized industry are set out in separate statutes. They are usually described in general terms with little guidance on relative priorities or the means of reconciliation when potential conflicts arise. Often political compromise or expediency has resulted in much ambiguity in the legislation (a reflection of the inherent conflict in the purposes of nationalization). Two examples serve to illustrate this point. First, Section 9(1) of the Post Office Act 1969 is ambiguous since it charges the Post Office 'to meet the social, industrial and commercial needs of the British Isles'. Second, Section 1 of the Coal Industry Nationalisation Act 1946 requires the National Coal Board to serve the public interest in the following terms:

making supplies of coal available, of such qualities and sizes, in such quantities and at such prices, as may seem to them best calculated to further the public interest in all respects, including the avoidance of any undue or unreasonable preference or advantage.

The chain of responsibility for individual nationalized industries is clearly structured. It is the Secretary of State for each respective sponsoring department who is formally responsible to Parliament for the implementation of the legislation concerning each industry. It is to him that the auditors report rather than to management or directly to Parliament. In practice the minister, while answering questions in the

House of Commons relating to the industries in his charge, leaves primary supervision to the civil servants in his department. Senior officials from each sponsoring department look after their industries' interests in discussions with the Treasury and other government departments. Only on rare occasions are the problems of a particular industry so serious that a debate is instigated on the floor of the House of Commons.

The strategic objectives of the main nationalized industries are as follows (Cm.1920, pp. 77–8):

British Coal   The corporation's overall objective is to develop a mining business that achieves sustainable profitability. To this end the corporation is required to increase productivity and reduce costs as rapidly as possible. Safety must remain the corporation's overriding concern.

British Rail   In December 1989, the then Secretary of State for Transport set British Rail objectives for a three-year period from April 1990 to cover safety, quality and finance. They flow from the existing statutory and financial duties to provide railways and related services in Great Britain, having regard to efficiency, economy and safety. The government is reviewing British Rail's financial objectives, which are no longer attainable within the original timescale.

British Waterways Board   The Board's objectives are to promote the fullest practicable use of the waterways for leisure, recreation, amenity and frieght transport. The Board should act commercially, achieve value for money and an adequate return on investment, and increase private sector participation in the business.

Caledonian MacBrayne   Its strategic objectives are to provde cost-effective lifeline services to remote island commuities, with the ultimate objective of maintaining island populations and economies.

Civil Aviation Authority   The Authority's main objectives are to secure a high standard of safety in United Kingdom aviation; to continue to operate as an efficient regulatory body for the air traffic system; and to develop an air traffic control system to meet demand as far as is practicable. The Authority will also seek greater integration and compatibility of international, and especially european, air traffic management, communications systems and navigational techology.

London Transport   In December 1989, the then Secretary of State for Transport set quality of service objectives to be met by the end of March 1992. New quality of service objectives will be set in March 1992. London Transport's own safety objectives were endorsed by the Secretary of State at the same time. In April 1990, London Transport were given financial objectives for the period to 1992–3. These objectives supplement the statutory duty to provide, or secure the provision of, public transport services for London, Having due regard to efficiency, economy and safety of operation.

Nuclear Electric In October 1991, the Secretary of State for Energy set company objectives for Nuclear Electric

The Company must seek to:

(a) increase profit and reduce total and unit costs;
(b) achieve a continued increase in electricity generation, provided that it is economically justified;
(c) achieve a progressive reduction in the company's dependence on the levy;
(d) complete Sizewell B to time and costs; and
(e) achieve a reduction in the costs of reprocessing, decommissioning and waste disposal and greater certainty about these costs.

All of these objectives should be achieved while maintaining the company's excellent safety record.

Post Office Its objectives are to continue to work towards the separation of its businesses, and to seek to secure maximum efficiency through sustained and detailed cost control. The Post Office aims to make a profit each year in each of its constituent businesses and to ensure that its price structure is sensibly related to costs and avoids cross-subsidy, particularly from monopoly to competitive activities.

Scottish Nuclear The primary objectives of Scottish Nuclear are the safe and economic operation of its Advanced Gas Cooled Reactor nuclear power stations at Hunterston B and Torness, including the final commissioning of the fuel route at latter, and the successful decommissioning of Hunterston A Magnox station. A further objective is to reduce the costs of nuclear power through examination of ways of reducing waste management costs and decommissioning liabilities.

The oversight of nationalized industries' control has a chequered history. Until 1980 the Select Committee on Nationalized Industries (SCNI) had a mandate to oversee the control of all public corporations. Originally established in 1952, this backbench committee of the House of Commons faced the same problem as other similar committees in seeking to establish an authoritative voice in Parliament. The SCNI was replaced by a system of Select Committees, each of which covered a main government department. The Select Committee responsible for a particular industry is therefore the one that covers its sponsoring department. These committees tend to be interested in matters of general policy, including matters of finance, but they usually do not take issue on matters of accounting practice. Even the Public Accounts Committee (PAC) has generally been more concerned with individual votes involving subsidies and grants of public money to nationalized industries rather than accountancy issues. The PAC relies heavily on the reports that it receives from the National Audit Office (NAO). The NAO's investigatory powers with respect to nationalized industries are somewhat limited. Schedule 4 of the National Audit Act 1983 specifically excludes these industries from value for money reviews by the Comptroller and Auditor General's staff (see chapter 6).

Under provisions in the Competition Act 1980 the Monopolies and Mergers Commission (MMC) can be asked to report on the efficiency of enterprises in the public sector. Originally established in 1984, the MMC had previously reported critically on the performance of certain public sector enterprises under the Fair Trading Act 1973. Under Section 11 of the 1980 Act the Secretary of State for Trade is empowered to direct the MMC to examine questions of costs, efficiency and standards of service, as well as possible abuses of monopoly power by the nationalized industries. Examinations made so far under this section of the Act are noteworthy both for their comprehensiveness and the relatively short time in which reports are prepared. The reports relating to the London and South East Commuter Services, operated by British Rail, and the Central Electricity Generating Board were prepared in five and nine months respectively. Section 12 of the 1980 Act gives ministers the power to order an industry to produce a plan to remedy 'a course of conduct which operates against the public interest'.

Collins and Wharton (1984) reviewed and summarized the first 12 reports of the MMC after the provisions of the 1980 Act were introduced. The major problem with the MMC's work is that there is no formal mechanism for its reports to be responded to. Table 10.2 provides a summary of the findings of four of these reports.

The most common headings under which the Commission's reports on nationalized industries have been prepared have included: management structure; financial control; use of manpower; pricing policy; investment appraisal; performance indicators; and abuse of monopoly power. The Commission has often recommended that part-time board members play a more active 'outside director' role and that they, together with the chairman, should constitute an audit committee. The audit committee's role is to supervise and review the work of the internal audit department. The Commission has often criticized the

Table 10.2 MMC reports: terms of reference and findings, 1980–84

	Year of publication	Months taken	Terms of reference	Main findings
British Rail (London and south east commuter services)	1980	6	Costs and efficiency; service provided	*Objectives*: directive on public service obligation not clear *Overcapacity*: need better matching of provision to demand *Management structure*: need for senior post responsible for computer services *Use of manpower*: extend coverage of measured standards *Investment appraisal*: 'appraisal optimism' and lack of ordered priorities *Performance indicators*; publish quality of service indicators
National Coal Board (production and supply of coal)	1983	15	Costs and efficiency	*Overcapacity*: excessive stocks had built up and marginal pits were highly unprofitable

Table 10.2 MMC reports: cont.

	Year of publication	Months taken	Terms of reference	Main findings
				Management structure: appoint part-time board members from outside the industry; too many departments and committees at HQ
				Financial control make each pit 'business unit'
				Pricing policy: questionable policy of exporting at well below domestic price
				Investment appraisal: appraisal optimism: should evaluate proposals against genuine 'do nothing' alternative
				Performance indicators: undue emphasis on production targets
Caledonian MacBrayne (shipping services)	1983	7	Costs and efficiency; service provided; possible abuse of monopoly	*Abuse of monopoly*: had given discriminatory discounts to a haulage subsidiary
				Overcapacity: scope for savings

Table 10.2 MMC reports: Cont.

	Year of publication	Months taken	Terms of reference	Main findings
				through reducing fleet *Management structure:* should appoint full-time chief executive
London Transport Executive (maintenance of buses and coaches)	1984	10	Costs and efficiency	*Financial control:* should incorporate cost reduction targets in budget-setting; should develop a cost-accounting system with garages as cost centre *Use of manpower:* agreed manning levels not related to measured standards; actual time to do jobs not recorded; production planning weak in both works and garages
Post Office (letter service in Glasgow, Belfast and Cardiff)	n/a	n/a	Costs and efficiency; the service provided	Investigation not yet completed

Source: Adapted from Collins and Wharton (1984), pp. 16–17. Published in *Public Money*, the research journal of the Chartered Institute of Public Finance and Accountancy 'incremental' approach to budgeting, preferring instead the adoption of a budgetary process that more closely relates to physical plans. Delegation of budget responsibility to the lowest practicable level in the management hierarchy is also recommended. In the case of the National Coal Board (now renamed British Coal), the MMC recommended that each mine should have its own profit and loss account and balance sheet, rather than operating profit statements that took no account of the cost of capital. As we noted in chapter 3, Berry et al. (1985) argued that British Coal should consider the contribution, rather than the profitability, of each pit.

Pricing policy

As far as pricing policy is concerned, the MMC expects industries to follow the simple guidelines set out in the 1978 White Paper (see below). Despite the existence of Treasury guidelines on investment appraisal, the MMC found much to criticize. Major problems arose not from applying the principles of discounted cash flow techniques but in estimating parameters, selecting options for appraisal, exploring the sensitivity of results and determining priorities. In analysing the projects completed by the National Coal Board, the Commission found that some areas had consistently overestimated the productivity of proposed projects and underestimated the time taken to complete them. Collins and Wharton (1984) suggest that for the MMC to be more effective, it should work more closely with the Select Committees of the House of Commons; the formal powers provided under Section 12 have yet to be exercised. They noted that during the debates on the Parliamentary Control of Expenditure (Reform) Bill in 1982, many backbenchers wished to replace the MMC in its role of investigating nationalized industries. A compromise offered by the government was to retain the Commission but to involve the PAC in choosing subjects for investigation. If this were implemented it would make the MMC more independent since it would no longer only investigate subjects chosen by the government. The government also suggested that the PAC and other Select Committees should become more involved in following up the Commission's reports. For the present, though, there is no mechanism for formally reviewing whether proposed changes are implemented. Cm.1920 (p. 77) states:

> For some industries prices are largely market determined. For those with scope for setting their prices, the financial target will

determine the level of prices in the light of general objectives and the need to cover the continuing costs of supply, including an adequate return on capital.

Policy Guidelines Through White Papers

To date three White Papers have been issued which discuss government policy towards the nationalized industries. These are:

1 *The Financial and Economic Obligations of the Nationalised Industries* (Cmnd. 1337), issued in 1961;
2 *Nationalised Industries: A Review of Economic and Financial Objectives* (Cmnd. 3437), issued in 1967; and more recently
3 *The Nationalised Industries* (Cmnd. 7131), which was issued in 1978.

The 1978 White Paper was the government's response to the 1976 NEDO report. The government did not entirely accept all the recommendations of this report, but did recognize the need to establish a financial and economic framework for the nationalized industries. The NEDO report highlighted certain features of the relationship between government and the nationalized industries (p. 8):

– there is a lack of trust and mutual understanding between those who run the nationalised industries and those in government who are concerned with their affairs;
– there is confusion about the respective roles of the boards of nationalised industries, ministers and Parliament, with the result that accountability is seriously blurred;
– there is no systematic framework for reaching agreement on long-term objectives and strategy, and no assurance of continuity when decisions are reached;
– there is no effective system for measuring the performance of nationalised industries and assessing managerial competence.

The report went on to call for a framework to be established within which management could plan with confidence. These criticisms were highlighted by a study, commissioned by NEDO, in which Coopers and Lybrand Associates Limited examined why the 1967 White Paper guidelines were unsuccessfully applied in four major industries. This report regarded the principles underlying the 1967 white paper as too simplistic. NEDO called on the government to base its relationship with the nationalized industries on three basic concepts: trust, continuity and accountability.

The 1978 White Paper tends to focus on financial rather than economic variables; this is more in line with the provisions of the 1961 white paper. Many writers (Foster, 1971; Heald, 1980) have thought that, in retrospect, the 1967 White Paper was far too ambitious in its attempts to specify a general framework that would be applicable to all nationalized industries. Each of these three white papers marks different attempts by government to devise a system of control over the public enterprise sector. We will now review the impact of the most recent white paper under four headings: (1) the move from the test discount rate to the required rate of return; (2) financial targets and controls; (3) pricing policy; and (4) non-financial performance indicators.

Moving from the test discount rate (TDR) to the required rate of return (RRR)

Whereas the 1961 White Paper gave no explicit guidance on investment criteria, the 1967 white paper instructed the nationalized industries to appraise their investment projects using the net present value for discounting net cash flows by a test discount rate (TDR) of 8 per cent in real terms. This rate was raised to 10 per cent in 1969. The method of calculation of the TDR was to survey a selection of large firms in order to establish the ex-ante real rate of return sought by them for marginal, low risk projects. The rationale for using the TDR was that it was deemed a necessary condition for welfare maximization, and that the marginal rate of return on new investment projects in the public sector should equal those in the private sector. The TDR was therefore seen as a measure of marginal opportunity cost to the public sector (an attempt to prevent decreases in welfare due to a reallocation of investment resources).[2] In summary, the proposed application of the TDR had two major failings: (1) it ignored the problems of risk and capital rationing; and (2) investment programmes classified as 'necessary' or 'replacement' were not evaluated. The general economic difficulties of the late 1960s and early 1970s led to many examples of cuts in public expenditure irrespective of prospective returns. It was evident from the NEDO report and the 1978 White Paper that the TDR was never fully implemented. Consequently, it had only a marginal impact on the total of public sector investment.

The 1978 White Paper substituted for the TDR an overall 'real rate of return' (RRR) set at 5 per cent in real terms before tax. The important distinction between these two approaches is that while the TDR was to be applied to each individual project, the RRR was to be applied to a nationalized industry's investment programme as a whole. The stress on economic, allocative efficiency was removed and an overall financial target was introduced. The 1978 White Paper states that 'the main evidence used to determine the RRR, albeit modified by less tangible factors, was a projection of the pre-tax real rate of return on assets achieved by private companies in recent years' (appendix I, para. 15). Heald (1980) stated that three points should be noted (p. 248):

> First, whereas the TDR was based on ex-ante returns sought by the private sector, the RRR is based on ex-post returns achieved in the private sector. The TDR is thus a forward-looking measure and the RRR a backward-looking measure (as any attempt to 'project' it forward can be little more than speculative). Second, whereas the TDR was an attempt to measure marginal returns in the private sector, the RRR is an average. If the RRR were thought to measure opportunity costs accurately, it would remain a measure of the average and not the marginal opportunity cost of capital to the public sector. Third . . . accounting ratios are an imperfect basis for deriving a discounted cash flow rate of return. . . Such calculations are plagued by measuring profit and capital stock.

The 1978 White Paper insists that the RRR is a measure of the opportunity cost of capital to nationalized industries. This is quite wrong; the RRR approach is simply an accounting ratio for the purposes of financial control; it says nothing else. Indeed the nationalized industries may now choose their own 'operating methods of investment appraisal' (Cm.7131) after consultation with their sponsoring department. The withdrawal of TDR, therefore, ends the application of one uniform discount rate for nationalized industry investment. The lack of such a rate precludes a necessary condition for a welfare-maximizing approach to the allocation of investment funds between the different public sector industries. For example, the application of non-uniform discount rates between competing nationalized fuel industries will distort investment choice. Indeed the application of different rates could lead one industry to reject a proposal that is accepted by another. Only at paragraph 64 of the 1978 White Paper is there a specific requirement for nationalized industries to use the RRR for individual project evaluation. That is when they are 'solely concerned with the choice of the best techniques for producing a given output or with issues concerning the phasing of capital expenditure'. Paragraph 64 also provides limited, and inadequate, guidance for the treatment of risk and uncertainty when it states that nationalized industries 'will consult their sponsor departments on those methods including, for example, the choice of discount rates, and allowance for risk and for appraisal optimisation'. Currently the RRR is set at 8 per cent, a rate determined in April 1989.

Financial targets and controls

Paragraph 73 of the 1978 White Paper states that financial targets:

> will take account of a wide range of factors. These will include the expected return from effective, cost conscious management of existing and new assets; market prospects; the scope for improved productivity and efficiency; the opportunity cost of capital; the implications of the Public Sector Borrowing Requirement; counter-inflation policy; and social and sectional objectives, e.g. the energy and transport industries.

Financial targets are set by the relevant minister of each industry's sponsoring department. They usually take one of three main forms. The first of these measures, the return on net assets, is the most common. The 1978 White Paper considered this ratio to be the 'main form' target; it is set at different levels depending upon the individual circumstances of individual profitable industries. It is normally calculated on a current cost basis (see below) before the deduction of interest and tax. This is because it is deemed inappropriate to calculate the ratio on a net-of-interest basis; management have had little or no responsibility for the financial structure of their industry. Labour intensive industries, such as the Post Office, use an alternative measure: the percentage return on turnover; while ailing industries, such as British Rail, are required to meet a target profitability or loss.

Another measure commonly reported by nationalized industries is the self-financing ratio, though it is rejected by government as being an inappropriate measure of performance. Two different measures are used and care needs to be taken to understand whether an industry is referring to the proportion of its capital expenditure that it has financed internally or whether it is the proportion of total funds financed internally.

Many public sector economists view the application of financial targets with far less enthusiasm than do politicians, civil servants and the nationalized industries themselves. Financial targets *per se* say nothing about allocative efficiency. They can also distort investment because they bias management towards less capital intensive programmes and account rules which write off net assets more quickly than strictly necessary. The Price Commission (1978) criticized the (then) South of Scotland Electricity Board for the accelerated depreciation of assets and for charging the interest on power stations under construction to revenue rather than applying the usual accounting convention of capitalizing these payments as part of the cost of the asset. Bates and Fraser (1974) have also argued that nationalized industries view financial objectives as the major factor in determining their pricing policy. The 1978 White Paper is very disappointing in that it fails to tackle issues of accounting policy, the choice of which can transform the published results of an industry. It is difficult to see how government can expect to control and hold the nationalized industries accountable if accounting policies are left entirely to management. One would have logically expected the Treasury to have taken on this responsibility.

Pricing policy

The 1978 White Paper withdrew the guidelines, established in the 1967 White Paper, whereby the nationalized industries were instructed to adopt long-run marginal cost pricing policies. (This instruction was qualified by an insistence that accounting costs should be covered in full and that financial targets should be met.) The primary role for deciding pricing policy now rests with each individual industry subject to a requirement that arbitrary cross-subsidization is avoided and that, where applicable, tariffs reflect differences between peak and off-peak periods. Paragraph 68 states, in part, that: 'the government believes that it is *primarily* for each nationalized industry to work out the details of its prices with regard to its markets and its overall objectives, including its financial target' [emphasis added]. This statement emphasizes therefore that the RRR and the financial target will be the major influences on the pricing decision. Just as the 1967 White Paper seemed to have been too ambitious in expecting industries to apply the TDR for project evaluation, so too did it prove to be the case that most industries failed to make any progress at all towards achieving a long-run marginal costing pricing structure. The Coopers and Lybrand study (1967) clearly identified this lack of progress in the four industries that they reviewed.

Non-financial performance indicators

Another provision of the 1978 white paper was a requirement that each nationalized industry agree non-financial performance indicators with their sponsoring departments and publish them. Lapsley (1984) considers the usefulness of the non-financial indicators adopted by British Rail. He notes that the British Rail indicators focus primarily on efficiency in the use of inputs and that as such they are (approximate) mirror images of certain of the financial indicators produced. Measures such as 'passenger miles per member of staff employed' say nothing about the quality of the service provided; rather they relate, in this instance, to the major operating cost of labour. As a contrast Lapsley (1984) considers non-financial indicators compiled by Baumol (1975) for the Amtrak railway network in the United States. Though reservations could be made about this scheme, he thought that 'its potential application to the UK is evident' (p. 226).

Financing the Nationalized Industries

Until 1977 nationalized industries' capital investment was included in the public expenditure totals in the annual public expenditure white paper. Since that time only revenue subsidies, such as those provided to British Rail, and borrowings from the Exchequer count as part of public expenditure. Since 1976 a cash limit has been set annually for each nationalized industry's external financing requirements. The sources of this finance consist of loans which bear fixed interest at the rate prevailing when the funds are borrowed, public dividend capital, grants; and leasing. This limit is commonly termed an external financing limit (EFL). Industries can borrow on both the home and overseas markets, the latter when terms are more favourable and providing that government policy at the time allows them to do so. Because the normal practice is that loans are guaranteed by the government, they are therefore counted as part of government financing despite the fact that the funds do not come directly from public monies. With overseas borrowings the Treasury operates a scheme, for which the industries pay a premium, whereby they are insured against losses arising if sterling depreciates against the foreign currency in which the loan was taken out.

Public dividend capital (PDC) was originally introduced in 1966, when it was termed Exchequer dividend capital. Its introduction represented a wish to provide a proxy to equity capital in the private sector and thereby negate the effect of fluctuating gross earnings on profits after interest.

The 1978 White Paper rejects the NEDO (1976) contention that there are no convincing principles that underlie the use of PDC. The 1978 white paper states (at paragraph 86) that its application is restricted to 'fully viable' industries which are 'especially subject to cyclical fluctuations in their returns as a result of their trading conditions and the nature of their assets'. PDC was statutorily eligible for both British Shipbuilders and the British Steel Corporation until they were privatized, although one wonders in what sense either of these industries could they have been said to be have then been fully viable. At best the attempt by government to have a private sector analogy for part of the capital structure of certain nationalized industries has been generally regarded as cosmetic. All the introduction of PDC does is to reschedule payments to the Exchequer over time. Both debt and PDC are funded from the same source, either public sector borrowings or savings.

EFLs are first published for each industry before the beginning of the financial year, usually in November. They subsequently also appear in the financial statement and budget report (FSBR), published each year at the time of the Budget. Information concerning the actual cash provided in a particular year is to be found in the succeeding year's FSBR, in the public expenditure white paper and also in the annual reports of each industry.

While technically the government has no statutory power to prevent an industry from exceeding its EFL for the year, it does have a tremendous amount of indirect influence which it can bring to bear. For example, ministers can withhold their agreement for major investment decisions or borrowings. Having said this, however, EFLs should not be thought of as being analogous to an overdraft facility granted by a commercial bank to a private sector firm. EFLs are much less rigid following an accord reached in 1980 between the Treasury and representatives from the Nationalized Industries Chairmen's Group. Under this accord there can be some flexibility granted, on the basis of discussions, where there is either a danger of damage to an industry's medium-term commercial interests or a danger of damage to explicit government objectives (*Hansard*, cols. 41–2, 4 July 1981). An additional 'fine-tuning' formula was also agreed whereby additional borrowings of 1 per cent of the total of the turnover and capital expenditure for the year over and above the EFL would be allowed. However, if this amount is actually borrowed it is to be deducted from the limit determined for the succeeding year. EFLs are therefore the result of detailed negotiations. They reflect a compromise between the claims made by the industry chairmen and the government's desire to promote individual spending programmes while, at the same time, wishing to keep contain total public expenditure under control.

In the past few years there has been a growing emphasis on the self-financing of investment programmes. Government has wanted to reduce the claims made by the nationalized industries on the Exchequer resulting from large revenue deficits that accumulated as a result of price restraint policies in the early 1970s. Heald (1980, p. 256) quotes as an example the decision in December 1976 to require the (then nationalized) British Gas Corporation to repay £100 million of net borrowings in the financial year 1977–8 as a method of reducing the PSBR. Cm.1920 asserts that where an industry generates a positive cash flow, after financing new investment, it is expected to repay outstanding debt, or if no debt is outstanding, to invest in financial assets which are liabilities of the public sector. Some industries are set negative EFLs, which reduce the planning total.

There is also a growing realization by nationalized industry management that the more investment they can finance internally the less intervention there is likely to be from departmental sponsors or the Treasury. Foster (1971) and NEDO (1976) both confirm the extent to which nationalized industries in receipt of revenue subsidies receive closer supervision than do the profitable industries.

The Annual Reports and Accounts

The enabling legislation for each industry stipulates that a report and accounts be produced each year. The typical annual report runs to between 50 and 100 pages. While generally comparable to the reports of large private sector companies, the amount of detail provided is in some cases superior. Each Act generally requires that the particular industry follow either 'best commercial practice' or produce accounts showing a 'true and fair view' of its results and financial position. The requirement that nationalized industries' accounts should conform to best commercial practice means that each industry must consider, though it is not necessarily bound to comply with, the Companies Acts, Stock Exchange requirements and general accounting conventions and practice. In addition there is usually provision for ministerial direction on the form and contents of the report and accounts, and an assumption that full accruals accounting will be adopted. For example, the accounts of British Rail are drawn up in accordance with the Transport Act 1962 and a direction issued by the Secretary of State for Transport in 1981. This direction requires that a 'true and fair view' of affairs be reflected by the accounts and that, except as specifically directed, there should be no less information than if they had been prepared under the Companies Acts. The direction further specifies that accounting standards are to be followed and stipulates how the Board's non-railway businesses are to be dealt with in its accounts. There is also a requirement to provide a breakdown of the major categories of expenditure between classes of business. The direction therefore obliges British Rail to disclose much more information than might be expected from a private sector organization. Ministerial directives vary both in length and detail. The direction issued in 1975 to British Coal simply asked that the operating profits of coal mines be broken down into individual mining areas.

Accounting standards relating to the treatment of a wide variety of items are issued. Only in the case of SSAP 16, which concerned accounting for inflation, have the nationalized industries been specifically mentioned (see below). The Nationalized Industries Chairmen's Group also acts as a forum for discussion on accounting matters that are of particular interest to their industries.

Not all the legislation is clear in its meaning, with the result that conflicts of interest can arise between an industry's chairman and its respective minister. A notable example was the former requirement that British Gas set aside reserves. The Gas Act 1972 stated that (Section 14):

shall be the duty of the corporation. . . to secure that, taking one year with another, the combined revenues of the corporation and its subsidiaries are not less than sufficient

(a) to meet the total outgoings of the corporation and its subsidiaries properly chargeable to revenue account, and
(b) to enable the corporation and its subsidiaries to make such allocations to reserve as the corporation considers adequate.

Conflict could have arisen if the chairman and minister disagreed about how much should have been allocated to reserve.

The accounts of the nationalized industries consists of three major statements: the balance sheet; profit and loss account; and statement of sources and application of funds. The balance sheet is a statement of assets, current liabilities and sources of capital as at the last day of the financial year end. Most industries follow the same format by reporting figures of net assets or capital employed. This sum represents assets minus current liabilities. The profit and loss account summarizes the income received and the expenses incurred over the year, the net difference being reported as either a profit or loss. The same industries have referred to this statement as the revenue account. While the profit and loss account is prepared on an accruals basis, the statement of sources and application of funds represents the flow of funds in and out of a corporation between two balance sheet dates. This statement lists the sources of funds and the application of these funds in purchasing fixed assets or repayment of loans. Any resulting difference is explained by the movement in working capital over the period.

Copies of the report and accounts are available direct from each industry or through HMSO. In addition to their obvious interest to government, they are also generally required by Parliament as both equity investor and loan-creditor. The public too have shown increasing individual and collective interest in these accounts; in the latter case various bodies have been set up specifically to look after the consumers' interests in a particular industry – The Nationalized Industries Consumer Councils (NICCs). Relationships between individual NICCs and their respective industries vary. For example, the Post Office Users National Committee (POUNC) meets quarterly with senior postal management and issues its own annual report on the state of the UK postal service.

Inflation Accounting

The subject that has aroused most controversy in recent years in the field of accounting, for both the public and private sector, is the treatment of accounting for inflation. It is a debate that has bedevilled the accounting profession for more than a decade. Until 1978 major differences existed between the different industries as to how best to account for inflation. While the Post Office had charged supplementary depreciation since 1974, other industries had made no significant adjustments at all. The 1978 white paper stated that financial targets would in future normally be set on the basis of current cost accounting (CCA) figures. This resulted in a variety of accounting presentations being adopted, including;

1 historic cost accounts which incorporated an additional/supplementary depreciation provision to reflect the impact of inflation on fixed assets;
2 historic cost accounts presented as the main accounts, with supplementary current cost accounts;
3 current cost accounts as the main accounts, with supplementary historic cost accounts;
4 current cost accounts as the only accounts accompanied by adequate historical information.

While the traditional historic cost convention measures the cost of resources consumed in generating revenue in terms of prices paid for those resources at the time they were acquired, the CCA method was designed to reflect the impact of changing prices on the maintenance of capital. In 1981, the nationalized industries adopted for the first time a common set of rules for taking account of inflation based on Statement of Standard Accounting Practice (SSAP) 16, issued by the (then) Accounting Standards Committee in 1980. The provisions of this standard were modified by a ministerial policy statement issued in the form of a Parliamentary written answer by John Biffen (Chief Secretary to the Treasury) (*Hansard*, col. 454, 21 December 1979) and the *Code of Practice for Current Cost Accounting in the Public Sector Corporations* issued by the finance panel of the Nationalized Industries Chairmen's Group in January 1981. The Biffen statement, though made before the standard was issued, anticipated it by specifying that nationalized industries should follow whatever standard came out 'in general' and in particular should:

1 publish current cost balance sheets 'whenever possible';
2 if they were potential candidates for privatization 'adopt the gearing adjustment embodied in the final standard';
3 if unlikely to be privatized and remain in the public sector 'not make a gearing adjustment in the accounts, though they should show in a footnote the effect of such an adjustment if it had to be made'.

The code of practice asked the nationalized industries to follow SSAP 16 though it did allow them some flexibility. However, it did specify:

1 a different set of presentation options (outlined as methods (2)–(4) above);
2 that although the gearing adjustment would not be included in the profit and loss account, with certain exceptions the effect of the gearing adjustment was to be included in the notes to the current cost accounts.

Taking into account these provisions, the general principles of CCA require that historical cost profit is subject to three operating adjustments:

1 a cost of sales adjustment to reflect the replacement cost of goods sold;
2 a depreciation adjustment that reflects the additional cost of consuming fixed assets as a result of price changes since their date of acquisition;
3 a monetary working capital adjustment to the reflect the extent by which net monetary working capital must be increased in order to support the same physical volume of sales.

Private sector companies were also obliged to provide a gearing adjustment which recognizes the gain made by equity investors arising from funding in the form of long-term debt. This arises in a period of inflation because debt, finance, denominated in monetary terms, is fixed. Since the gain on the proportion of assets financed by borrowing does not accrue to lenders it must pass to the owners of the residual interest, that is, the equity investors. It is a gain that represents a transfer of wealth between these two classes of investor. As discussed above, there is only a cosmetic difference between PDC and debt so it is argued that the gearing adjustment is inappropriate for nationalized industries. Likierman (1981) surveyed 18 nationalized industries in the first year of reporting under the SSAP 16 conventions. He discovered that three industries reported CCA results as their only or main operating statements (British Airports Authority, British Gas and the Electricity Council). Fourteen industries gave supplementary CCA information and only one (British Waterways) declined to produce a full CCA analysis.

Likierman (1983) also examined evidence relating to accusations that nationalized industries had manipulated their profitability by adjustments for inflation over the period 1976–81. His investigation was prompted from the large number of criticisms that were made both in the popular press, with such headlines as 'Shoot the Nationalized Industry Auditor – No One Would Notice' (*Economist*, 29 July 1978), and by academics such as Heald (1980). In Likierman's (1983) view (p. 30):

There was a large variety of criticisms put forward, virtually all concerned with the manipulation of the profit figure. Manipulation is of course an emotive word. It implies a deliberate attempt to deceive and is hardly likely that finance directors would admit to trying to do anything of this kind.

It has been charged that the auditors of the nationalized industries have been somewhat lax in their certification of the accounts of these bodies. However, Wright (1985) concludes 'that accusations that auditors of nationalized industry accounts are not doing their job appear to be ill-informed'. Indeed he found that there was in fact a far higher level of qualification and comment than in the private sector. Such qualifications do not necessarily mean that nationalized industries 'bend the rules'; rather Wright (1985) suggests the usual case is that the nationalized industries have to operate within a more complex environment than their private sector counterparts, with the result that they do sometimes find it difficult to comply with some parts of generally accepted accounting practice.

In the introduction to SSAP 16 it was stated that:

It is the intention of the ASC, as far as possible, to make no change to SSAP 16 for three years so as to enable producers and users to gain experience in dealing with practical problems and interpreting the information.

Following further consideration the (then) ASC decided to replace SSAP 16 with an exposure draft (ED35) *Accounting for the effects of changing prices*. This was issued in August 1984. ED35 proposed that companies produce CCA information either as part of their main accounts or in the form of notes that supplement historic cost accounts. While ED35 was supposed to counter protests over the complexity of producing CCA accounts, the objection was raised that its provisions were so open ended that it was not really a standard at all. For example, ED35 left it optional as to whether the cost of sales and monetary working capital adjustments were shown separately or combined into one working capital adjustment. ED35 also dismissed the requirements of a SSAP 16 style balance sheet. Instead only two adjustments were required: the current cost of fixed assets and stocks were required to be shown. ED35 was withdrawn and in June 1985 paragraphs 2–6 of SSAP 16 were likewise withdrawn, the effect being to make the standard non-mandatory. Indeed the Stock Exchange estimated that, prior to this announcement, less than 20 per cent of private sector companies were complying with the provisions of SSAP 16. Must then the nationalized industries continue to produce CCA annual reports?

It is clear that the former ASC failed in its endeavours to produce a suitable accounting standard for the treatment of inflation in company accounts. There is currently disagreement as to whether another standard should be issued at all; some have proposed that a Statement of Recommended Practice (SORP) be issued instead. While the debate on the need for an appropriate accounting standard continues within the profession, the Treasury expects that the nationalized industries should continue reporting in accordance with the provisions of SSAP 16. Professional economists employed by the Treasury support CCA and rates of return made on this basis since they best approximate definitions of real (inflation adjusted) profit in the economic literature. In Sherer's (1984, p.9) view:

> the CCA reporting framework is consistent with the government's policy objective towards the public sector, which of itself derived from its ideological commitment to unfettered market forces as the sole means of achieving economic prosperity . . . CCA is one of a panoply of accounting controls (others include cash limits and value for money auditing) currently employed to create a new regime which emphasizes profit, efficiency and productivity. Such a regime may contribute directly to a reduction in public sector spending in either of two ways: enterprises may be induced by adherence to CCA profit targets, to become more efficient and hence less dependent on government financing; or the inability to record CCA accounting profits may provide the justification for closing down 'inefficient' enterprises.

To be efficient, so the government would claim, means that the nationalized industries must produce accounts that reflect the maintenance of 'physical' capital. In practice some industries have found reasons to supply only the minimum of supplementary current cost information. In the 1990 annual report and accounts for British Coal it was stated that full current cost accounts would not in future be prepared because the current cost operating adjustments made in the past had been comparatively immaterial, with the exception of those relating to depreciation. Because fixed assets other than land and non-specialist buildings had been written down at March 31 1990 to reflect their estimated recoverability out of future earnings by way of a provision for permanent diminution in value, the difference between historic cost depreciation and that calculated for current cost accounts was also now immaterial. Only information on the current cost book amount of tangible fixed assets was provided.

Privatization

As stated in the introduction to this chapter, one of the main policies of the present Conservative government is that of privatization. The government has adopted a variety of approaches to privatization. For major industries such as British Telecom and British Gas, it opted for the large scale sale of shares at a fixed price. In some instances, industries have been sold by private treaty, such as with the sale of Rover cars. The National Bus Company was sold as over 60 subsidiaries in order to develop competition. The principal aim of the proponents of privatization is to improve by competition the performance of the economy as a whole. It is believed that monopoly positions can lead to inefficiencies, a lack of motivation by management and employees, and a restriction of consumer choice. These proponents also cite political interference and trade union closed shop operations, particularly throughout the 1970s, as additional deficiencies within public enterprises (Shackleton, 1984). It has also been argued that, given the government's desire to reduce the public sector borrowing requirement (PSBR), the income received greatly enhances this aim. The problem is, though, that in pursuing such a policy the government has had to ensure that asset values are protected. This they have done in the case of British Telecom.

In the case of British Telecom, privatized in 1985, the government has essentially substituted a private monopoly for a state one. The enthusiasm of its senior management for privatization lay in the fact that they could operate better as a private rather than a state monopoly. Despite union opposition one licence was granted to a competitor (Mercury), but this company seems unlikely to be a major threat in competitive terms. Because there is likely to be little stimulus to competition the government established the Office of Telecommunications (OFTEL) to ensure that restrictive practices are detected. (It is interesting to note that, just as this regulatory body was established, its counterpart in the USA was scrapped because it was unable to fulfil such a role.) The receipts from privatizing British Telecom are estimated at some £4 billion.

In an effort to counter the charge of merely transferring monopoly power from the public to the private sector, the government has refused simply to transfer shares en masse to the highest bidder. The government has attempted to follow a policy of preferential allocations to small investors and employees. Shackleton (1984) points out that the small investor tends only to purchase such shares for a short-term gain and that, within a fairly short space of time, the institutional investors consolidate their control of these industries. He states (p.67):

> When British Aerospace (in 1980) made its appearance on the London Stock Exchange it had 158,000 individual shareholders. Amersham International (in 1981) received 65,000 successful applications for shares. By October 1983 there were 26,000 shareholders in British Aerospace and 7,500 in Amersham International. It seems that the bulk of shares in privatized enterprises are ending up in the portfolios of the major institutional investors who dominate the market.

Only in the case of the National Freight Consortium staff buy-out could the government claim any success with this policy. Each employee was only required to contribute, on average, £700. In August 1985 the government disposed of their remaining 49 per cent holding in Britoil. Some 60 per cent of shares were earmarked for British institutions and overseas investors. The remaining 40 per cent was four times oversubscribed. The merchant bankers, Lazard Brothers, complied with the government's wish by favouring the small investor. Requests for more than 1,400 shares were not taken up while those for small amounts were restricted to a pro-rata maximum of 150 shares. Employees only applied for about 3.4 million shares, or about 22 per cent of their preferential allocation of 6.2 per cent of shares issued. The sale of Britoil shares added some 450,000 shareholders to the (then) existing register of 40,000 shareholders. Table 10.3 summarizes stock market flotations of nationalized industries over the period 1979–91.

Marsh (1991) provides an interesting review on the aims of privatization. He notes that even when some industries have been nationalized government can, via regulatory bodies (OFTEL, OFWAT, OFGAS, etc.) and the MMC, retain some control. This has also been facilitated by the retention of a 'golden share'. Golden shares allow the government the option of outvoting all other shareholders on specific issues, such as takeovers. British Telecom is an example of one industry covered by this control. Even though the Conservative government has generally chosen not to interfere, the powers remain and could be used should a future administration be committed to greater intervention in the supply side of the economy. Estrim el al. (1990) have noted the high costs associated with stock market flotations. In the case of the 1986 flotation of British Gas total costs were established at £381 million. Half of this cost represented direct incentives to shareholders in the form of bonus shares and bill

Table 10.3 Asset sales 1979–91

Company	Financial year of initial flotation	Golden share	Net proceeds to HMG (£ millions)	Times oversubscribed (under-subscribed)	Discount on share price (%)
British Petroleum	1979–80	No	6,149	N/A	–
British Aerospace	1980–81	Yes	390	N/A	–
Cable and Wireless	1981–82	Yes	1,024	5.6	17
Amersham International	1982–82	Yes	60	24.0	26
Britoil	1982–83	Yes	53	(0.3)	N/A
Associated British Ports	1982–83	No	97	34.0	21
Enterprise Oil (British Gas subsidiary)	1984–85	Yes	382	(0.4)	N/A
Jaguar (British Leyland subsidiary)	1984–85	Yes	–	8.3	6
British Telecom	1985–86	Yes	3,681	3.0	21
TSB	1986–87	No			
British Gas	1986–87	Yes	7,731	4.0	11
British Airways	1986–87	Yes	850	23.0	29
Rolls-Royce	1987–88	Yes	1,028	9.4	25
British Airports Authority	1987–88	Yes	1,183	8.1	12
10 Water Companies	1989–90	Yes	3,480	2.8	17
Electric Companies	1990–91	Yes	5,200	10.7	21
2 Electricity Generating Companies (Powergen and National Power)	1991–92	Yes	2,000	4.0	37

Source: Marsh (1991)

vouchers. Ten per cent funded the preferential treatment of British Gas employees in the form of free and discounted shares. Forty per cent went in the form of direct flotation costs – underwriting, broking, commissions, etc.

There have also been accusations that the price for which nationalized industries have been sold is far too low. These critics have included the National Audit Office. Its report on the private sale of the Rover Group plc makes interesting reading.

On 1 March 1988, the Secretary of State for Trade and Industry announced that the government had entered into exclusive negotiations with British Aerospace plc to sell them the government's majority shareholding in Rover Group plc. The sale was completed on 12 August 1988 for £150 million, after the government had made a cash injection of £547 million into Rover Group. The National Audit Office (NAO) examined the factors influencing the government's decision to deal exclusively with British Aerospace, the arrangements for the sale and their financial implications, and the achievement of the government's objectives for the sale.

The main findings of the NAO's examination were:

1 The government's decision to grant exclusive negotiating rights to British Aerospace up to the end of April 1988 was based on the view that the benefits of competition were outweighed by the risk to Rover Group's prospects arising from the uncertainty that would be associated with a competitive sale.

2 The announcement of the government's intention to negotiate exclusively with British Aerospace for two months for the sale of Rover Group prompted approaches from four other companies. The Department of Trade and Industry told them that if negotiations with British Aerospace did not lead to an agreement, alternative proposals would be considered.

3 The Department's initial expectation was that, after a cash injection to wipe out financial debt, the net cost to the taxpayer of selling Rover Group might be between £420 and £500 million.

4 In the absence of competition, the NAO found it difficult to determine a fair price for a Rover Group substantially relieved of debt. The Department pointed out that the consideration of £150 million was the most that British Aerospace were prepared to pay.

5 For £150 million, British Aerospace obtained:

   (a) A going concern whose profit for 1987 was £27.9 million which, on the basis of the price/earnings ratio of 5:1 cited by the

Secretary of State, suggested a minimum value of some £140 million.

(b) Tax benefits worth between £33 million and £40 million, available to reduce the business's future tax liabilities.

(c) Surplus sites, not required for the running of the business, subsequently estimated by the NAO's advisors as worth £33.5 million at the time of the sale.

(d) Holdings in the nine associated companies, some of which they could sell without detriment to the rest of the business, and from which in two cases they have already raised £126 million, significantly more than the £48 million to £60 million foreseen at the time of the sale.

The NAO concluded that the Department had substantially met three of the four objectives set by the government for the sale of Rover Group, i.e:

1 To privatize Rover Group within the lifetime of the current Parliament. This objective was successfully fulfilled.

2 To relieve the taxpayer of potential liabilities on the best possible terms. Successive Secretaries of State had given assurances in Parliament that Rover Group would not be left in a position where they could not meet their obligations to creditors. British Aerospace provided an indemnity against any such reasonably foreseeable claims. However, since the sale price was well below the NAO's valuation of the company at the time of the sale, the NAO questioned the Department's assertion that no better terms could have been secured.

3 To achieve a clean break without further risk to the taxpayer. This objective has been met as far as is practicable.

4 To avoid damage to Rover Group through privatization. The company's declared results show that it has been trading profitably since privatization; indeed profits were substantially higher than forecast in the 1988 corporate plan.

Conclusion

The history of the nationalized industries has been chequered, with excessive interference in their operations by both Labour and Conservative administrations. As Price (1986, p. 19) states, when reviewing the reasons for wanting to privatize British Gas:

To substitute a single, poorly controlled private company for a public monopoly seems as unsatisfactory as nationalizing an industry and then subjecting it to political interference. But in the final analysis all these relatively esoteric points have doubtless carried little weight besides the government's overriding need – augmented by rapidly falling oil prices – to raise as much revenue as possible as quickly as possible.

In the last decade the scale of privatization has been immense. The legacy of the Thatcherite era has been a been a significant shift in the balance between the public and private sectors.

For those industries that are to remain within the public sector domain, the government intends to legislate in due course to update aspects of nationalized industry statutes. The Treasury is co-ordinating the process of consultation between various sponsoring departments and their respective industries. It is the government's view that the existing statutes of nationalized industries, some of which are nearly 40 years old, have not kept in line with policies developed by successive governments. In due course it is proposed to draft a bill that would set out a core framework that could be applied to all remaining nationalized industries. Such a bill would incorporate many provisions from existing statutes and would also reflect developments in the relationship between these industries and the government since their statutes were originally enacted. It is proposed that the resultant Act and accompanying legislation would provide clear guidelines within which these industries would have the freedom to operate as successful commercial businesses. Parliament, industries and the government would know exactly where they stand. The Treasury (1985) has summarized some of these proposals under four headings: borrowing and guarantees; accounts, report and audit; financial targets and balance sheets.

The Citizen's Charter (1991, Cm.1599) contains proposals for improving the quality of service provided by nationalized industries, including better information on performance standards and outturns, and improved procedures for redress. These are being taken forward by individual industries.

At present there is considerable doubt as to whether privatization has increased efficiency. Critics claim that the policy of privatization has proven costly to the taxpayer. Indeed some have likened the government's policy to 'asset stripping'.

Notes

1 See House of Commons, First Report from the Select Committee on Nationalised Industries, Session 1966–67, *The Post Office*, Volume 11, HC 340 (1967), p. 596.
2 It should be noted, though, that there are those against this rationale who would argue for public sector discounting at the social time preference rate. See chapter 5.

11

Concluding Comments

Introduction

In this short book an attempt has been made to illustrate the distinct nature and problems of accounting and financial control in the public sector. Such a task has not been easy given the diversity of activities undertaken in the public sector and the fact that public sector organizations have been subject to more management reforms in the last decade than at any other time this century. This concluding chapter briefly considers two concerns – that most financial management reform has been based on the growing separation of the 'policy' and 'agency' roles in government; leading to new contractual relationships for the provision of public services, and that there is therefore need to reform the Westminster model of government accounting.

As explained in chapter 2, the concern of this book has been with financial accountability and how it is achieved externally, through financial reporting, and internally, through managerial accountability. The need for those entrusted with the provision of services to be financially accountable has received even greater emphasis since government began its drive to gain greater efficiency from the resources available. However, it is necessary for those involved with policy and agency roles to reflect on whether the government's structural reforms, and their associated management reforms, have been applied pragmatically or solely as an act of political faith.

New Contractual Relationships

Throughout this book we have largely been concerned with financial management issues related to a number of new contractual relationships for the provision of public sector services. The 1980s saw the introduction of compulsory competitive competition. The Local Government Planning and Land Act 1980 and the Local Government Act 1988 made competitive tendering compulsory for a range of services provided by manual workers. A consultation paper suggested that a wider range of services could also be similarly provided. In the NHS the approach has been similar although, rather than by legislation, the process began with a circular in 1983 which called on health authorities to subject their ancillary services to tendering. Central government too has made use of competitive tendering. One can think of this process as 'mandatory market testing' (Flynn, 1990). This change towards contractual relationships means that the quality, level and costs of services are made explicit and formally agreed. It has also meant that managers have had to change the way they work. These new arrangements divide management functions into three – a 'policy/strategy' function (deciding overall policy and resource allocation), a 'buyer' function (writing specifications in compliance with policy) and a 'contractor' function (providing services to clients). The first two management functions remain in-house, but are usually separated, while the third may or may not, depending on who is awarded a particular tender.

The Griffiths (1988) proposals on community care effectively place local authority social service departments in the role of brokers between their clients and the providers of the services they require. While the White Paper on community care, Caring for People (Cm.849), explicitly excludes compulsory tendering, the net effect is the same since contracts of service will be written and costs taken into account when deciding to award contracts. Health service reforms follow similar lines whereby district health authorities buy services from hospitals that they once directly managed or from the private sector. Opting out general practitioners have a similar role.

The costs of this process are not negligible. While competition may well reduce the cost of service provision, indirect costs increase as the buying side of the organization needs to employ people to specify, supervise, monitor and police the contractors. It seems to many observers that this process of competition only produces a one-off reduction in costs. In the longer term, costs in real terms may well rise back to or beyond those that existed before the advent of tendering. As the process of tendering continues *ad infinitum* there is a danger that the establishment of relationships with suppliers on matters such as quality assurance and alternative service delivery is reduced or lost. As Flynn (1990, p. 42) states: 'Such relationships require trust on both sides, and can only be established over long periods. The use of competition and a contractual style of relationship leads to inflexibility.'

He goes on to state (p. 43):

> The overt objective for competitive tendering is increased efficiency. This will be achieved by reducing employment and increasing productivity, which will achieve two subsidiary objectives which are to reduce the number of people employed in the public sector and to reduce the power of the public sector unions. But it may also be the case that competitive tendering is a step in the direction of true privatisation. Once services are provided by contractors and are bought and sold, then it is a relatively small step to move to private purchasing, whether individually or collectively, through insurance schemes.

This view is to see government as an enabler and not as a direct provider.

The more recent introduction of the Next Steps agencies further illustrates the government's moves to being an enabler rather than a provider. If we are to believe the government's account, the Next Steps initiative was an incremental extension to the Financial Management initiative (FMI). In fact the Next Steps initiative would not have been launched if the FMI had been a success. Fry (1988, p. 430) writes that the FMI lost its direction and that government had 'to deal with the reality that philosophies represented by the FMI were incompatible, certainly with the existing structure of government'. If we review a number of government schemes for improved efficiency, we can find various reasons for their not being entirely successful. A common problem is that often objectives are not clearly stated which means that it is then difficult to agree measures of performance which adquately reflect the tasks to be done and the results achieved. Such criticisms have a marked similarity to the criticisms of PPBS and ZBB in the 1960s and 1970s. We discussed these earlier.

Certainly it can be claimed that the shift from the FMI to the Next Steps initiative represents a change from a very comprehensive, some would say paper-hungry system, to a simpler one of accountable management where targets are negotiated and chief executives are judged against these targets. The FMI has become bureaucratized. The creation of Next Steps agencies represents a half-way house to privatization and is already leading to a number of concerns. Jordan (1992) points out that the Next Steps initiative raises a constitutional issue with respect to earlier notions of public sector accountability. In his introduction to the Annual Review (Cabinet Office, 1991) the Minister of State described the 'quiet revolution' that saw: 'Chief Executives put in charge to see that the job is done properly; and Chief Executives [made] accountable to a Minister for the agency's performance.'

Jordan (1992) considers that the revolution is not only quiet but silent on the real impact of accountable chief executives. He states (p. 13):

There is a deliberate or accidental ambiguity. We are told ministerial accountability remains. But in reality it is now accountability to the Minister by the Chief Executive rather than accountability of the Minister to the House of Commons that is now on offer: these are different. If there is no accountability 'problem' why has the National Health Service Management Executive not been given agency status? Precisely because it was thought agency status removed a politically sensitive matter too far from accountability.

There is much rhetoric, most of it political, concerning the benefits of managerial freedom afforded to agencies. More broadly, the experience of 40 years of public corporations shows that ministers will intervene if they deem it necessary and that this will be particularly likely if agency management develop policy objectives of their own. Many Next Steps agencies were initially considered, but rejected, as candidates for privatization. The Treasury remains as banker of last resort. Certainly the justification for agencies, as with the related policy of contracting out, needs to be more realistic. By and large agencies are set performance targets as a substitute for markets. Such arrangements ought to be recognized as antithetical to the genuine article.

All of these management reforms within central government, local government and the NHS represent what Pollitt (1990, p. 56) depicts as the current British administrative fashion with 'neo-Taylorism'. Taylor (1911) was one of the fathers of the scientific management movement that promotes the setting of clear targets, the development of performance indicators and the reward/promotion of those individuals who get 'results'. More modern writers, such as Peters and Waterman in their *In Search of Excellence* (1982), reject what they call this 'old rationality'. An underlying assumption behind many of the government's reforms is that it is somehow possible to separate 'administrative questions' from 'political questions'. Woodrow Wilson, writing more than a century ago (*The Study of Administration*, *1887*), took the view that the notion that such a separation is possible has long been the Aunt Sally of political scientists.

The question to be asked is: was structural change necessary in order to achieve management reform? To many it would appear that the current political ideology that smaller government leads to better government is not necessarily proven. Arguments for selling off one part of the public sector, the programme of de-nationalization, cannot necessarily be generalized into arguments for selling off the rest of the public sector. Management reforms are in danger of being associated with constitutional change, not by a pragmatic process but rather as a result of political faith. Management reforms tend, therefore, not to be evaluated in their own right. Good management is a politically neutral concept.

Reforming the Westminster Model of Government Accounting

The Treasury performs two roles: the provision of economic policy and advice and the development of financial management and control. However, as previously stated, there is a marked tendency for the former role to dominate the latter. One possible solution would be to adopt the approach of the Commonwealth of Australia – the Canberra model. This change from the previous Westminster model was designed to broaden and strengthen the sources of advice to government and facilitate more effective budgetary management. Since 1976 the Commonwealth Department of Finance has been responsible for financial management and control, while the Department of the Treasury has retained its role of economic planning. Hardman (1982, p. 39) states:

The development of the Canberra model of government accounting. . . has highlighted the importance of financial management and control in general, and the government accounting function in particular. The establishment of a separate Department of Finance facilitates the mobilisation and independence of accounting resources and sharpened the financial focus, in contrast to the antecedent diffused pattern in which the government accounting function had to co-exist with – and, to some extent, compete with – the government economic function in the same department, i.e. the antecedent Department of the Treasury.

Under the Canberra model, additional importance has been given to the government accounting function by the confirming of cabinet status on the Minister of Finance. A similar structure exists in Canada and reform is long overdue in Britain. Appendix 11.1 outlines the functions of the Departments of the Treasury and Finance.

Conclusion

The ten preceding chapters have outlined many of the changes that are currently taking place in order to improve financial control and accountability in the public sector. If past history is anything to go by, some of these developments will prove useful, others will evolve or be repackaged at some future date whilst the remainder will be abandoned. Nevertheless, important inroads are being made into improving the quality, reliability and usefulness of financial information in all areas of the public sector. In this concluding chapter two points have been made. First it is often difficult to evaluate the usefulness of management reforms in isolation from the structural changes that took place at the same time. Many of the financial management reforms discussed in earlier chapters could just as easily have been introduced without structural reform. Second, brief consideration was given to whether it is time to discard the traditional Westminster accounting model in favour of another, such as the Canberra model.

Appendix 11.1

Functions of the Department of the Treasury and Finance
Department of Treasury
The Department of the Treasury is responsible for advice on and the administration of:

1 Economic, fiscal and monetary policy, involving the continuous assessment of current and future economic conditions and the provision of advice on resource allocation, including:

   (a) budgetary policy – matters relating to expenditure, revenue and deficit/surplus and means of achieving overall budgetary objectives;
   (b) monetary policy – matters relating to the control of the money supply and official interest rates;
   (c) taxation policy – matters relating to the structure and level of taxation in relation both to budgetary needs and effects on resource allocation; and

(d) income and prices – providing advice on trends in income and price levels and on their bearing on broad economic objectives.

2 External economic relations, i.e. matters relating to external financial and economic policy issues, including the balance of payments, overseas reserves, the working of the international economic and monetary systems, Australia's role in international financial affairs, Australia's membership of various international organizations, Commonwealth/State financial relations including the provision of financial assistance to the States and local authorities and the sources of State and local authority revenue.

3 Matters relating to the raising, redemption or conversion of Australian government loans in Australia and overseas, administration of the Financial Agreement and the Gentlemen's Agreement, and the operations of the National Debt Commission.

4 Financial and economic aspects of policy matters concerning the structure and functioning of the banking system and other financial institutions in the Australian capital market, Australian capital investment abroad, exchange control, coinage and aspects of company law bearing on company structures and financing.

5 Matters relating to foreign investment in Australia.

Department of Finance

The Department of Finance is reponsible for advice on the the administration of:

1 The Public Account (Consolidated Revenue Fund, Trust Fund and Loan Fund) which also includes prescribing rules for central and departmental accounting within the requirements of the Audit Act 1901 and other related legislation and research into management accounting techniques, accounting policy and the operation of the Commonwealth accounting system.

2 The collection, preparation and financial analysis of forward estimates of departmental expenditure.

3 The preparation of Appropriation Bills.

4 Expenditure review.

5 The general oversight of the finances of departments and authorities financed from the Budget.

6 Participation in evaluations of the effectiveness of expenditure programmes in meeting government-determined objectives.

7 Financial evaluation of expenditure proposals and programmes in the field of social services, veterans' affairs, health, education, housing, immigration, science, recreation, arts and culture, aboriginals, the environment, employment and Australian government employment.

8 Financial evaluation of expenditure proposals and programmes relating to air, land and sea transport and internal and international communications, assistance to manufacturing, mining, rural, fishing and tourist industries – for example, by way of reconstruction schemes, payment of bounties and subsidies and assistance to research and promotion.

9 Financial aspects of the legislation and operation of statutory authorities of the Australian government.

10 Financial evaluation of expenditure proposals and programmes relating to defence, budgetary aspects of the defence five year rolling programme, and services pay and conditions, defence works, civil works and related programmes, foreign aid, and mainland and external territories.

11 Financial evaluation of expenditure proposals and programmes relating to urban and regional development, irrigation, transport and other development projects.

Glossary of Terms

Accounting Officer The title of the post held by the permanent secretary at the head of a central government department. The accounting officer is responsible to his/her respective minister for the funds voted to a department by Parliament. By tradition he/she also liaises with the Public Accounts Committee on all aspects of financial management.

Accruals accounts The accruals convention makes the distinction between the receipt of cash and the right to receive cash, and the payment of cash and the legal obligation to pay cash. Under this accounting principle, all income and costs relating to a financial period are taken into account, regardless of the date of receipt or payment. This matching principle is recognized by Statement of Standard Accounting Practice 2 (compare with the cash basis of accounting).

Balance sheet A statement of the assets, liabilities and funding of an organization at a particular date. While public sector organizations' long-term funding is provided by loans, private sector companies use a combination of shares and loans.

Billion A thousand million.

Block grant The major element of the rate support grant. Its distribution broadly reflects the needs and resources of individual authorities.

Budget An estimate of future operations which is usually measured in monetary terms but can also be measured in terms of quantities.

Capital Budget A budget that sets out the proposed acquisition of fixed (or long-term) assets and their financing.

Cash accounting Recording the transactions by which revenue and expenses are reported in the period in which the related cash receipts and payments occur. The widespread use of cash accounting in the public sector results from the government's historically based requirement for financial information that shows fiscal compliance. Although chapter 1 refers to the growing support for the wider adoption of accruals accounting, this method has traditionally only been mandatory for the nationalized industries and a small number of other public corporations.

Cash block   Central government support for local authority expenditure is divided into a number of different cash blocks, which reflect the arrangements for monitoring and controlling this expenditure.

Cash budget   A budget of cash receipts, payments and periodical balances.

Cash limits   The limit on the amount of money the government proposes to spend or authorize on certain services or blocks of services during a financial year. Cash limits as a means of control over cash spending in the year ahead were introduced generally in 1976. The nationalized industries' contribution to public expenditure is controlled by means of external financial limits (q.v.), which are a form of cash limit for individual industries.

Clinical budgeting and costing   A system where resource use and patient care workload planning are based on the clinician as controller or admissions and of decisions on the volume of diagnostic tests, drugs, etc.

Community charge   A charge payable by all adults, with certain limited exemptions, as a payment towards the cost of services provided by local authorities. It replaced domestic rates from April 1989 in Scotland and April 1990 in England and Wales.

Consolidate fund   The government's main account with the Bank of England. Most of central government is financed from this fund and the government's tax revenue and other current receipts are paid into it.

Contracting out   Taking a service/function, typically within local government or the NHS, and offering it on precise contract terms (of standards of quality and of efficiency) to the lowest bidder who meets the standards.

Contribution   The excess of income or revenue over related variable costs which contribute to the payment of an organization's fixed costs, and if sufficiently large, to a profit or surplus from operations.

Contribution margin   Income or revenue less related variable costs.

Cost-benefit analysis (CBA)   An economist's technique for assessing the overall or 'net' merit of a particular activity, organzation or service. Net merit includes an evaluation of social benefits.

Credit approvals   Central government permissions for individual local authorities in England and Wales to borrow or raise other forms of credit for capital purposes.

Current cost accounting   A system of accounting that is based on the matching or current revenues with current costs and the maintenance of physical capacity. Valuations are usually made in terms of current replacement costs. It is a system widely adopted by the nationalized industries.

Decision package   Terminology used in the application of zero base budgeting. It refers to the documentation (typically a pro-forma) that is used to describe a decision unit and its cost of operation. A decision unit is an organizational entity, which could be a project or a cost centre, that has an identifiable manager with the necessary authority to establish priorities and prepare budgets for all activities within the unit.

Depreciation   The measure of the loss in value of a fixed (long-term) asset in an accounting period resulting from use, the passage of time or obsolescence.

Diagnosis related groups (DRGs)   The name given to a system of classifying acute, non-psychiatric in-patients according to diagnostic characteristics and related health care resource requirements. The system was originally developed in the USA.

Differential cost   Synonym for marginal cost.

Direct labour organization (DLO)   An organization within a local authority undertaking maintenance and construction work. Separate accounts and an annual report are statutorily required for the DLO.

External financing limits (EFLs)   Cash limits imposed by government on external finance.

Financial Management initiative (FMI)   A system designed to develop better management information systems in central government, introduced about 1980.

Fixed (long-term) asset   An asset, such as land, building or equipment, held for use for a period that extends beyond one financial year. All other assets are classified as current assets.

Fixed cost   A cost that does not vary with the level of activity.

Functional budget   A budget that allocates costs (or inputs) to particular functons or activities. Also termed programme budget.

Fund accounting   Accounting arrangements whereby a self-balancing set of accounts are provided for specific purposes. Fund accounting is typically operated on a cash basis. for example, the two main fund accounts operated by central government are the Consolidated Fund and the National Loans Fund. Chapter 8 discusses the fund accounts normally associated with local authorities.

Gross domestic product (GDP)   (at market prices) is the value of the goods and services provided by UK residents, including taxes on expenditure on both home produced and imported goods and services and the effect of subsidies. No deduction is made for depreciation of existing assets.

Gross national product   Gross domestic product plus the income accruing to domestic residents arising from overseas investment less income earned in the domestic market accruing to investors from overseas. Gross national product measures the total flow of goods and services produced by the economy during the financial year.

Historic cost accounting   The traditional system of accounting that is based on valuations made in terms of the prices reigning when transactions took place. In practice this process is modified by the concept of prudence and the possible revaluation of fixed (long-term) assets. Prudence is one of the four fundamental accounting concepts embodied in Statement of Standard Accounting Practice 2; the other three concepts are: going concern, accruals and consistency.

Income and expenditure account (or statement)   A financial account or statement that shows the surplus of deficit or funds arising from the operations of a non-trading organization in an accounting period. Whilst such statements are commonly associated with public sector entities, they are also prepared by certain private sector entities such as charities. The counterpart to this statement for a trading organization is the profit and loss account.

Incremental budgeting   A system in use prior to the introduction of cash limits (q.v.). Under this system the size of the existing budget was not usually challenged in volume terms and formed the baseline for negotiating the next year's budget, typically additions to cover inflation.

Line-item budget   A budget that lists costs in terms of imputs or items of expenditure such as salaries, stationery, materials and so on. Also termed subjective budgeting.

Management budgeting   A major recommendation of the Griffiths Inquiry Report. The general concept was that budgets should become more active management tools – it was recommended that clinicians should become their own budget holders, with their own clinical management budgets (CMBS).

Management by objectives (MBO)   A system for focusing a narrow spotlight on a few managerial objectives or activities at any one time. MBO is a complement to budgeting, not a substitute.

Marginal cost   The amount by which total costs increase if an extra unit of output is produced. Marginal cost is thus dependent upon the change in variable costs, as opposed to fixed costs, which do not change with the level of activity.

National Loans Fund   The government's account with the Bank of England set up under the National Loans Fund Act 1968. All government borrowing transactions, including the payment of debt interest, and most lending transactions are handled through this fund account.

Non-domestic rates   The contribution towards the cost of local authority services paid by the occupiers of non-domestic property. The rate bill depends on the rateable value and the poundage for the year in question. In England and Wales, from April 1990, the poundage is set by central government at a uniform rate throughout each country – the so-called uniform business rate. The rates are collected by local authorities, paid into a central pool, and redistributed to authorities as an equal amount per chargepayer.

Opportunity cost   The value of the next best opportunity forgone by deciding upon one course of action rather than another. For example, the opportunity cost of using a vehicle that would otherwise be sold is the loss in value arising from the deferred sale.

Outcome measure   A measure designed to gauge the effectiveness of an activity or programme. For example, the impact made on unemployment statistics as a result of a regional development grants programme or the impact on the incidence of a particular disease following an innoculation programme. Outcome measures should not be confused with output measures. The former measures are relative to intended objectives of activities or programmes, where as the latter measures are simply absolute measures of activity.

Output measure   A measure of the quantity of service produced. For example, the number of grant application processed or the number of innoculations given. Such measure can be useful in guaging the efficiency of those involved with the provision of service.

Pareto optimal   A group welfare concept originated by the early twentieth-century Italian economist Vilfredo Pareto. A Pareto optimum is said, in theory, to exist when no event can increase the well-being of one person without decreasing the well-being of someone else.

Planning, programming, budgeting (PPB)   A system of programme budgeting, originally developed in the USA, which seeks to establish the goals and objectives for each major area of an organization's operations. Priorities are determined for the attainment of goals and objectives by executive management and conveyed to operational managers who, in turn, develop possible alternative programmes. The total cost of each programme is related to the total benefits that would be derived from the programme to determine the efficiency of the programme. The most effective and efficient programmes are selected, integrated into a comprehensive programme, and implemented. It is a top-down approach; the zero-base budgeting system is a bottom-up approach.

Profit and loss account   A financial account that shows the profit or loss arising from the operations of a trading organization. The counterpart to this statement for a non-trading organization is the income and expenditure account.

Programme budget   A budget that allocates costs (or imputs) to particular functions or activities. Also terms functional budget.

Public dividend capital   A form of long-term government finance for certain public corporations on which government is paid dividends rather than interest. Often used in those industries where trading activities are subject to cyclical fluctuations and where it is difficult for the industry to meet regular interest payments.

Public expenditure survey (PES)   The annual review of public expenditure plans undertaken by central government.

Rate support grant   A grant paid by central government to aid local authority expenditure. It is made up of block grant and a grant to reduce the rates paid by domestic ratepayers. Superseded by revenue support grant (q.v.) in Scotland in 1989–90 and England and Wales in 1990–1, alongside the introduction of the community charge.

Revenue budget   A budget that shows the deployment of resources in order to carry out the day-to-day activities of an organization.

Revenue support grant   The unhypothecated grant to supplement local authorities' own finances. It replaced the rate support grant (q.v.).

Semi-accruals accounting   Analogous to the accruals basis of accounting except that no provision is made for the depreciation of fixed (long-term assets).

Speciality costing and budgeting   The process of allocating or apportioning all hospital costs to each separate speciality according to the actual level of workload it has imposed on wards, theatres, clinics, X-ray, laboratories and other support services. Originally developed by Professor C. Magee in Wales.

Statement of source and application of funds   This statement is designed to explain the difference between two successive balance sheets. A variety of formats can be used but all attempts to summarize the cash flows that have occurred from both revenue and capital transactions. Under the provisions of Statement of Standard Accounting Practice10, this statement is normally prepared by private sector companies, nationalized industries and certain other public sector corporations.

Statement of Standard Accounting Practice (SSAP)　Accounting standards issued by the Accounting Standards Committee on behalf of the six members of the Consultative Committee of Accountancy Bodies in the UK and Ireland. Each SSAP is preceded by one or more exposure drafts (EDs). While primarily designed to facilitate the harmonization of financial reporting by private sector companies, certain standards are being increasingly recognized as applicable to a large number of public sector entities. Nationalized industries, being generally expected to follow best commercial practice, are particularly expected to adopt SSAPs in their financial reporting. Table 2.2 lists those SSAPs issued as at October 1986, together with their applicability to local authorities, health authorities and nationalized industries.

Subjective budget　A budget that lists costs in terms of inputs or items of expenditure such as salaries, stationery, and so on. Also termed line-item budget.

True and fair view　What constitutes a true and fair view is defined neither by statute nor by case law, yet it is the overriding external financial reporting principle for UK private sector companies. This requirement overrides the detailed requirements of company law and statements of Standard Accounting Practice.

Uniform business rate　See Non-domestic rates.

Variable cost　A cost that varies in direct proportion to activity. Accountants usually assume that variable costs are constant over a relevant range of activity and as such equal to marginal cost (compare fixed cost).

Westminster model of government　Based on the assumption of centralized financial and economic authority. In this model the two separate functions of macroeconomic policy and planning and financial management and control are centralized in one entity – the Treasury. Such a model can be contrasted with other models, such as the Canberra model which is based on the assumption of decentralised financial and economic authority. At the Commonwealth level in Australia, the Department of Finance is responsible for financial management and control, whereas economic policy analysis and advice to government remains with the Treasury.

Zero-base budgeting (ZBB)　A system of programme budgeting, originally developed in the USA, which seeks to establish the goals and objectives for each major area of an organization's operations. It is a system designed for non-trading organizations and was originally conceived in an era of resource constraint. Its approach is to commence at the lowest administrative tier of the organization and to ask those responsible to rank the importance of their activities in a series of decision packages. At each successive tier in the hierarchy, packages are grouped and reranked until the overall priorities of the organization are determined. It is a bottom-up approach; the planning programming budgeting system is a top-down approach.

References

AAA (1970–1), American Accounting Association, 'Report of the Committee of Concepts of Accounting Applicable to the Public Sector, *The Accounting Review, pp. 76–108.*

AAA *(1975)*, American Accounting Association, 'Report of the Committee of Nonprofit Organization's, *The Accounting Review*, Supplement to Vol. XLX, pp. 1–39.

Accounting Standards Steering Committee (1975), *The Corporate Report*, London.

Accounts Commission (1984), *Standards for the External Audit of Scottish Local Authorities*, Edinburgh.

AHST/CIPFA (1985), *Managing Capital Assets in the National Health Service*, London: the Association of Health Service Teasurers Incorporated in the Chartered Institute of Public Finance and Accountancy.

Akehurst, R., Hutton, J. and Dixon, R. (1991), *Review of the Evidence of Higher Costs of Healthcare Provision in Inner London and a Consideration of the Implications for Competitiveness*, University of York – Health Economics Consortium.

Anthony, R. N. (1977), 'Zero-base budgeting: a useful fraud?', *The Government Accountants Journal*, Summer, pp. 19–26.

Anthony, R. N. (1978), *Financial Accounting in Nonbusiness Organisations*, Financial Accounting Standards Board, Stanford, Conn.

Anthony R. N. and Young, D. W. (1984), *Management Control in Non-Profit Organisations*, USA: Richard D. Irwin Inc.

Appleby, J., Robinson, R., Ranade, W., Little, V. and Salter, S. (1990), 'The Use of Markets in the NHS: The NHS Reforms and Managed Competition', *Public Money and Management*, Winter 1990, pp. 27–33.

Aristotle, *The Politics*, translated by T. A. Sinclair, Penguin, 1984.

Ashworth, M. and Forsyth, P. (1984), *British Airways*, Institute of Fiscal Studies, Report Series No. 12.

ASSC (1975), Accounting Standards Steering Committee, *The Corporate Report*, London (ICAEW).

Audit Commission for Local Authorities in England and Wales (1983), *Improving Economy, Efficiency and Effectiveness in Local Government*, London.

Audit Commission (1985), *Capital Expenditure Controls in Local Government in England*, London.

Audit Commission (1990), *Report and Accounts*, London.

Audit Commission (1991), *Competitive Councils*, London.

Auditor General of Canada (1976), *1976 Annual Report of the Auditor General*, Ottawa: Government Publishing Centre.

Auditor General of Canada (1981), *Audit Guide: Auditing of Efficiency*, Canada: Ottawa.

Australian Audit Office (1985), *Annual Report of the Australian Auditor General 1984-5*, Canberra: Australian Publishing Service.

Australian Audit Office (1986), *Elements of Efficiency Auditing: A Basic Guide*, Canberra: Australian Publishing Service.

Bains, M. (1978), *Management Reform in English Local Government*, Centre for Research on Federal Financial Relations, The Australian National University, Canberra, Research Monograph no. 24.

Barton, A. (1985), *The Anatomy of Accounting*, (third edition), University of Queensland Press.

Bates, R. and Fraser, N. (1974), *Investment Decisions in the Nationalised Fuel Industries*, London: Cambridge University Press.

Baumol, W. J. (1965), *Economic Theory and Operations Analysis*, (second edition), New York: Prentice-Hall.

Baumol, W. J. (1975), 'Payment by performance in rail passenger transportation: an innovation in Amtrak's operations', *Bell Journal of Economics*, Spring, pp. 281–98.

Berry, T. et al., (1985), 'NCB accounts – a mine of misinformation?' *Accounting*, January, pp. 10–12.

Bevan, R. G. (1984), 'Organising the finance of hospitals by simulated markets', *Fiscal Studies*, November, pp. 44–63.

Bird, R. G., McDonald, M. G. and McHugh, A. J. (1982), *Management Accounting: Processing, Evaluating and Using Cost Data*, Sydney: Butterworths.

Bird, P. and Morgan-Jones, P. (1981), *Financial Reporting by Charities*, London: ICAEW.

Birdseye, P. and Webb, T. (1984), 'Why the rate burden on business is a cause for concern' *National Westminster Bank Quarterly Review*, February, pp. 2–15.

Blunkett, D. (1991), 'Poll Tax Review: The Parties Go On The Record', *Public Finance and Accountancy*, p. 18, 15 February 1991, London.

Bridgeman, J. M. (1973), Planning-Programming-Budgeting in the United Kingdom Central Government; chapter 11 in *Current Practice in Programme Budgeting*, ed. Novick, D., London: Heinemann.

Bromwich, M. (1976), *The Economics of Capital Budgeting*, Harmondsworth: Penguin.

Brown, C. V. and Jackson, P. M. (1983), *Public Sector Economics*, (second edition), Oxford: Martin Robertson.

Byrne, T. (1986) *Local Government in Britain*, Harmondsworth: Penguin.

Butt, H. and Palmer, R. (eds) (1985), *Value for Money in the Public Sector – The Decision-Maker's Guide*, Oxford: Basil Blackwell.

Cabinet Office (1991), *Annual Review 1991*, London: HMSO.

Canada (1979), *Royal Commmission on Financial Management and Accountability: Final Report*, Ottawa: Government Publishing Centre.

Canadian Institute of Chartered Accountants (CICA) (1983), *Terminology for Accountants*, Ottawa.

Cassels, J. (1983a), *Review of Running Costs*, Management and Personnel Office.

Cassels, J. (1983b), *Review of Personnel Work in the Civil Service*, London: HMSO.

Central Statistical Office (1988), *Social Trends No.18*, London: CSO.

CIPFA (1973), Chartered Institute of Public Finance and Accountancy, *Government and Programme Budgeting*, London.

CIPFA (1975), Chartered Institute of Public Finance and Accountancy, *Local Authority 1: Accounting Principles*, London.

CIPFA (1977a), Chartered Institute of Public Finance and Accountancy, *Capital Budgeting*, London.

CIPFA (1977b), Chartered Institute of Public Finance and Accountancy, *Local Government Finance and Macro-Economic Policy*, London.

CIPFA (1981), Chartered Institute of Public Finance and Accountancy, *Accounting Methods in Local and Public Authorities*, London.

CIPFA, (1984), Chartered Institute of Public Finance and Accountancy, *Guide to Local Authority Finance*, London.

CIPFA (1985), Chartered Institute of Public Finance and Accountancy, *Local Authority 1: Accounting Principles*, London.

CIPFA (1992), Chartered Institute of Public Finance and Accountancy, *Statements on Internal Audit*, London.

CIPFA/AHST (1982), Chartered Institute of Public Finance and Accountancy and the Association of Health Service Treasurers, *Local Accountability*, London.

Collier, P., Cooke, T. E., and Glynn, J. J. (1987) *Financial and Treasury Management*, London: Heinemann.

Collins, B. and Wharton, R. (1984), 'Investigating public industries: how has the Monopolies and Mergers Commission performed?, *Public Money*, vol. 4, no. 2, September, pp. 15–23.

Committee of Public Accounts (1987), *Eighth Report: Session 1986–87*, HC.96, London: HMSO.

Consumers' Association (1979), *Nationalised Industries Accounting Policies*, London.

Cm.375 (1988), *Financial Reporting to Parliament*, London: HMSO.

Cm.555 (1989), *Working for Patients*, London: HMSO.

Cm.849 (1989), *Caring for People – Community Care in the next decade and beyond*, London: HMSO.

Cm.918 (1990), *Financial Reporting to Parliament*, London HMSO.

Cm.1021 (1990), *The Government's Expenditure Plans 1990–1 to 1992–3*, London: HMSO.

Cm.1261 (1990), *Improving Management in Government – The Next Steps Agencies*, London: HMSO.

Cm.1291 (1990), *Improving Management in Government: The Next Steps Agencies*, London: HMSO.

Cm.1311 (1990), *Autumn Statement 1990*, London: HMSO.

CM.1520 (1990, *Public Expenditure Analysis to 1993–4*, London: HMSO.

Cm.1523 (1991), *The Health of the Nation*, London: HMSO.

Cm.1599 (1991), *The Citizens' Charter*, London: HMSO.

Cm.1729 (1991), *Autumn Statement 1991*, London: HMSO.

Cm.1730 (1991) *Competing for Quality*, London: HMSO.

Cm.1761 (1991), *The Next Steps Initiative – The Government Reply to the Seventh Report from the Treasury and Civil Service Committee (HC 496, 1991)*, London: HMSO.

Cm.1920 (1992), *Public Expenditure Analysis to 1994–5*, London: HMSO.

Cmnd. 1337 (1961), *The Financial and Economic Obligations of the Nationalised Industries*, London: HMSO.

Cmnd. 1432 (1961), *Control of Public Expenditure*, London: HMSO.

Cmnd. 3427 (1967), *Nationalised Industries: A Review of Economic and Financial Objectives*, London: HMSO.

Cmnd. 3638, *The Civil Service*, (The Fulton Report), Vols.1–5, London: HMSO.

Cmnd. 4506 (1970), *The Reorganisation of Central Government*, London: HMSO.

Cmnd. 6453 (1976), *Local Government Finance*, London: HMSO.

Cmnd. 6813 (1977), *Local Government Finance*, London: HMSO.

Cmnd. 7131 (1978), *The Nationalised Industries*, London: HMSO.

Cmnd. 7845 (1980), *The Role of the Comptroller and Auditor General*, London: HMSO.

Cmnd. 8323 (1981), *The Role of the Comptroller and Auditor General*, London: HMSO.

Cmnd. 8616 (1982), *Efficiency and Effectiveness in the Civil Service*, London: HMSO.

Cmnd. 9058 (1983), *Financial Management in Government Departments*, London: HMSO.

Cmnd. 9297 (1984), *Progress in Financial Management in Government Departments*, London: HMSO.

Cmnd. 9714 (1986), *Payments for Local government*, London: HMSO.

Connolly, D. M. (1980), 'Internal audit – the poor relation of the public service', *Australian Journal of Public Administration*, vol. XXXIX, no. 1, March.

Cooke, T. E. and Glynn, J. J. (1981), 'Fixed asset replacement in a recession', *Accountancy*, vol. 92, no. 1054, November, pp. 83–5.

Coopers and Lybrand Associates Limited (1976), 'Review of the pricing policies, investment criteria and financial objectives of four nationalised industries', in NEDO (1976), *A study of UK nationalised industries*, appendix volume, London: HMSO.

Culyer, A. J. (1973), *The Economics of Social Policy*, Oxford: Martin Robertson.

Custis, P. J., Morpeth, D. Sir, Stamp, E. and Tweedie, D. P. (1985), *Report of an independent committee of enquiry on certain accounting matters relating to the officers of the National Coal Board*, London: British Coal.

Dean, P. N. (1984), 'Nationalised industry consumer councils and the monitoring of financial performance', *Accounting and Business Research*, no. 56, Autumn, pp. 373–82.

Department of Education and Science (1970), Planning Paper No. 1, *Output Budgeting for the Department of Education and Science*, London: HMSO.

Department of the Environment (1955 with periodic updates), *The Form of Published Accounts*, London.

Department of the Environment (1980), *Publication of Financial and Other Information by Local Authorities: A Consutancy Document*, London.

Department of the Environment (1981), *Capital Programmes*, Circular 14/81, London.

Department of the Environment (1983), *Streamlining the Cities: Government Proposals for Reorganising Local Government in Greater London and the Metropolitan Counties*, Cmnd. 9063, London: HMSO.

Department of the Environment (DOE) (1984), *Draft Accounts and Audit Regulations*, London: HMSO.

Department of the Environment (DOE) (1988), *Capital Expenditure controls*, London: HMSO.

Department of the Environment (DOE) (1991), *The Internal Management of Local Authorities in England*, London: HMSO.

Department of the Environment (DOE) (1991), The Structure of Local Government in England, London: HMSO.

Department of Health (1990), *GP Fundholders Manual of Accounts*, London; HMSO.

DHSS (1976), Department of Health and Social Security, *Sharing Resources of Health in England Report*, London: HMSO.

DHSS (1980), Department of Health and Social Security, *Advisory Group on Resource Allocation*, London: HMSO.

DHSS (1981), Department of Health and Social Security, *Health Building Procedures*, HN(81) 30, London.

DHSS (1982), Department of Health and Social Security, *Investment Appraisal in the Public Sector*, HN(82) 34, London.

DHSS (1983), Circular No. 18, *Competitive Tendering*, London: HMSO.

DHSS (1983a), Department of Health and Social Security, *Report of the NHS Management Inquiry*, Chairman: Roy Griffiths, London: HMSO.

DHSS (1983b), Department of Health and Social Security, *Report of the DHSS/NHS Audit Working Group*, Chairman: Patrick Salmon, London: HMSO.

DHSS (1984), Department of Health and Social Security, *Steering Group on Health Services Information – Report F*, Chairman: Edith Körner, London: HMSO.

De Paula, F. C. and Attwood, F. A. (1982), *Auditing Problems and Practice*, London: Pitman.

Downey, D. Sir (1986), 'Public accountability: fact or myth?' *Public Money*, vol. 6, no. 1, June, pp. 35–39.

Downs, A. (1962), 'The public interest: its meaning in a democracy', *Social Research*, Spring, pp. 1–2.

Drebin, A. R. Chan, J. L. and Ferguson, L. C. (1981), *Objectives of Accounting and Financial Reporting for Governmental Units: A Research Study* (in two volumes), National Council on Government Accounting, USA: Chicago.

Drewry, D. (1984), *The New Select Committees*, London: Oxford University Press.

Efficiency Unit (1988), *Key Elements of Carrying Out Scrutinies*, London.

Else, P. K. and Marshall, G. P. (1981), 'The unplanning of public expenditure: recent problems in expenditure planning and the consequences of cash limits', *Public Administration*, vol. 59, pp. 253–78.

Enthoven, A. C. (1985), *Reflections on the management of the NHS*, London: Nuffield Provincial Hospitals Trust.

Estrim, S., Maim, A. and Selby, M. J. P., 'Conflicting aims in electricity privatisation', *Public Money and Management*, Vol. 10, No. 3, Autumn 1990, pp. 39–48.

Financial Accounting Standards Board (FASB) (1978), *Financial Accounting in Nonbusiness Organizations*, a report prepared by Anthony, R. N., Stanford, Conn., pp. 253–78.

Flynn, N. (1990), 'The Impact of Compulsory Competition on Public Sector Management: Competition within the Field', *Public Policy and Administration*, Vol. 5, Number 1, pp. 33–43.

Foreign and Commonwealth Office (1992), *Britain 1992*, London: HMSO.

Foster, C. D. (1971), *Politics, Finance and the Role of Economics*, London: George Allen & Unwin.

Foster, C. D., Jackman, R. A., and Perlman, M. (1986), *Local Government Finance in a Unitary State*, London: George Allen & Unwin, 1986.

French, E. A. (1977), 'The evaluation of the dividend law of England', in *Studies in Accounting*, ed. Baxter, W. T. and Davidson, S., Institute of Chartered Accountants in England and Wales.

Fry, G. (1988), 'The Thatcher Government, the FMI and the "new civil service"', *Public Administration*, Vol. 66(1), Spring, pp. 1–20.

Fulton, Lord John (Chairman) (1968), *The Civil Service, Report of Committee*, Cmnd. 3638, London: HMSO, 1968.

General Accounting Office, United States (1980), *Objectives of Accounting and Financial Reporting in the Federal Government*, Washington, D. C.

Glennerster, H. (1983), 'Client group budgeting: a prerequisite for efficient care, *Public Money*, December, pp. 25–8.

Glynn, J. J. (1985), *Value for Money Auditing in the Public Sector*, New York: Prentice-Hall.

Glynn, J. J., Murphy, M. P. and Perkins, D. A. (1992), 'GP Practice Budgets', *Financial Accountabiity and Management*, Summer 1992.

Gordon, M. J. (1959), 'Dividends, Earnings and Stock Prices', *Review of Economics and Statistics*, May, pp. 99–105.

Gordon, L. A. and Heivilin, D. M. (1978), 'Zero-base budgeting in the Federal Government: an historical perspective', *GAO Review*, Fall, pp. 57–64.

Gray, A., Jenkins, W. I. with Flynn, A. (1991), 'The Management of change in Whitehall – the experience of the FMI', *Public Administration*, Vol. 69(1), Spring, pp. 41–59.

Gray, A. G. and Jenkins, W. I. (1986), 'Accountable management in British central government: some reflections on the financial management initiative', *Financial Management and Accountabiity*, Autumn, pp. 171–86.

Gray, R. (1984), 'The NHS Treasurer and Accountabiity', *Public Finance and Accountancy*, April, pp. 30–2.

Griffiths, R. (1988), *Community Care: Agenda for Action*, London: HMSO.

Hale, R. (1985a), 'Rate support grant settlements', *Public Finance and Accountancy*, March, pp. 335–9.

Hale, R. (1985b), 'Capital cuts continue to offset overspend', *Public Finance and Accountancy*, May, pp. 37–8.

Hale, R. (1986), 'PEWP: local authorities', *Public Finance and Accountancy*, 28 February, pp. 13–16.

Hale, R. (1990), 'The make believe world of might have been', *Public Finance and Accountancy*, 2 March 1990, pp. 13–16.

Hardman, D. J. (1982), *Government Accounting and Budgeting*, Sydney: Prentice-Hall of Australia.

Harrison, S., Hunter, D. J. and Pollitt, C. (1990), *The Dynamics of British Health Policy*, Unwin Hyman.

Hatry, H. P. et al. (1979), *Efficiency Measurement for Local Government Services*, USA: the Urban Institute, Washington DC.

HC. 98 (1987), Committee of Public Accounts, *Financial Reporting to Parliament*, London: HMSO.

HC. 115 (1981), Commiittee of Public Accounts Report, *The Role of the Comptroller and Auditor General*, London: HMSO.

HC. 306 (1991), Report by the Comptroller and Auditor General, Use of National Health Service Operating Theatres in England: A Progress Report, London: HMSO.

HC131 (1985), Report of the Comptroller and Auditor General, *Review of The Rate Support Grant*, London: HMSO.

HC. 354 (1989), Committee of Public Accounts, *Financial Reporting to Parliament*, London: HMSO.

HC. 387 (1986), *Fourth Report from the Committee of Social Services – Public Expenditure on Social Services*, London: HMSO.

HC. 498 (1978), Price Commission Report, *South of Scotland Electricity Board*, London: HMSO.

HC. 576 (1986), Report by the Comptroller and Auditor General, *Financial Reporting to Parliament*, London: HMSO.

HC. 614 (1988), Treasury and Civil Service Committee, *Sixth Report – Financial Reporting to Parliament*, London: HMSO.

HC. 648 (1991), Report by the Comptroller and Auditor General, *Repair and Maintenance of School Buildings*, London: HMSO.

Heald, D. (1980), 'The economic and financial control of UK nationalised industries', *Economic Journal*, vol. 90, June, pp. 243–65.

Heald, D. (1983), *Pubic Expenditure*, Oxford: Martin Robertson.

Healthcare Financial Management Association (1990), *National Health Service Financial Management in context*, London: CIPFA.

Healthcare Financial Management Association and the Institute of Health Services Management (1990), *Making Contracts Work: The Practical Implications*, London.

Heclo, H. and Wildavsky, A. (1981), *The Private Government of Public Mondy*, (second edition), London: Macmillan.

Held, V. (1970), *The Public Interest and Individual Interests*, New York: Basic Books.

Henderson, P. D. (1965), 'Notes on public investment criteria in the United Kingdom', *Bulletin of the Oxford University Institute of Economic and Statistics*, vol. 27, pp. 55–89.

Henke, E. O. (1980), *Introduction to Non-Profit Organisation Accounting*, Boston: Wadsworth.

Henley, D. Sir (1983), 'External audit', chapter 7 of *Public Sector Accounting and Financial Control*, jointly authored with Holtham, C., Likierman, A. and Perrin, J., Wokingham: Van Nostrand Reinhold (UK).

Henley, D., Holtham, C., Likierman, A. and Perrin, J. (1989), *Public Sector Accounting and Financial Control*, (third edition), Van Rostrand Reinhold International.

Hepworth, N. P. (1980), *The Finance of Local Government*, (revised (sixth edition), London: George Allen & Unwin.

Hepworth, N. and Vass, P. (1984), 'Accounting Standards in the Public Sector', in *Issues in Public Sector Accounting*, edited by Hopwood, A. and Tomkins, C., Oxford: Philip Allen.

Herzlinger, R. E. (1979), 'Zero-base budgeting in the federal government: A case study', *Sloan Management Review*, Winter, pp. 3–7.

Hillman, R. (1984), *Speciality Costing in the National Health Service*, London: CIPFA.

Hirschleifer, J. (1958), 'On the theory of optimal investment decision', *Journal of Political Economy*, vol. 66, pp. 443–57.

HM Treasury (1978), *The Test Discount Rate and the Required Rate of Return on Investment*, Treasury Working Paper no. 9, London.

HM Treasury (1981), *Economic Progress Report 139*, London: HMSO.

292 References

HM Treasury (1983), *Economic Progress Report 153*, London: HMSO.

HM Treasury (1984), *Investment Appraisal in the Public Sector: A Technical Guide for Government Departments*, London: HMSO.

HM Treasury (1985), *National Industrial Legislation Consultation Proposals*, London: HMSO.

HM Treasury (1986), *Accounting for Economic Costs and Changing Prices: A report by an advisory group*, London: HMSO.

HM Treasury (1988), *Government Accounting: A guide on accounting and financial procedures for the use of Government Departments*, London: HMSO.

Holtham, C. (1985), 'Council spending is out of control', *Accountancy Age*, 25 April, pp. 14–15.

Holtham, C. (1986), chapters 3 and 4, in *Public Sector Accounting and Financial Control*, edited by Henley, D., Holtham, C., Likierman, A., and Perrin, J., Wokingham: Van Nostrand Reinhold (UK).

Holtham, C. (1989), as in Henley et al. (1989).

Holtham, C. and Stewart, J. (1981), *Value for Money: A Framework for Action*, Institute of Local Government Studies, University of Birmingham.

Hopwood, A. (1982), 'Value for money: practice in other countries', *Value for Money Audits: Proceeding of a Seminar*, Royal Institute of Public Administration.

Hopwood, A. (1984), 'Accounting and the pursuit of efficiency', chapter 9 in *Issue in Public Sector Accounting*, edited by Hopwood, A., and Tomkins, C., Oxford: Philip Allan.

Johnson, N. (1971), 'Financial Accountability to Parliament', chapter 13 in *The Dilemma of Accountability in Modern Government*, edited by Smith, B. L. R., and Hague, D. C., New York: St. Martins Press.

Joint Committee of Public Accounts of the Parliament of the Commonwealth of Australia (1982), *The Form and Standard of Financial Statements for Commonwealth Undertaking* – A Discussion Paper, Report No. 199, Canberra.

Jones, R. (1985), *Local Government Audit Law*, London: HMSO.

Jones, R. and Pendlebury, M. (1982), 'Uniformity v. flexibility in the published accounts of local authorities: the UK problem and some European solutions', *Accounting and Business Research*, Spring, pp. 129–35.

Jones, R. and Pendlebury, M. (1984), *Public Sector Accounting*, London: Pitman.

Jordan, G. (1992), 'Next Steps Agencies: From Managing by Command to Managing by Contract', University of Aberdeen: Working Paper No. 8 – *Accounting, Finance and Management*, pp. 34.

Kemp, P. (1988), 'Plans and Progress So Far', in *The Next Steps: A Review of the Agency Concept*, London: Royal Institute of Public Adminsitration.

Kemp, P. (1990), 'Can the Civil Service adapt to managing by contract?', *Public Money and Management*, vol. 10, No. 3, pp. 25–32.

Kennedy, J. A. and Sugden, K. F. (1986), 'Ritual and reality in capital budgeting, *Management Accounting*, February, pp. 34–7.

Klein, R. (1989), *Politics of the NHS*, (second edition), Longman.

Langenderfer, H. Q. (1973), 'A conceptual framework for financial accounting', *Journal of Accountancy*, July, pp. 64–76.

Lapsley, I. (1981), 'A case of depreciation accounting in UK health authorities', *Accounting and Business Research*, Winter, pp. 21–9.

Lapsey, I. (1984), 'Financial objectives, productive efficiency and the regulation of a subsidised state monopoly', *Accounting and Business Research*, Summer, pp. 217–27.

Lapsley, I. (1985), 'Investment appraisal in UK non-trading organisations', *Financial Management and Accountability*, vol. 2, no. 2 (Summer), pp. 135–51.

Lapsley, I. (1986), 'Investment appraisal in UK non-trading organisations'', CRIBA, University of Warwick.

Lapsley, I. and Prowle, M. (1978)(a) *Audit in the National Health Service: A Conceptual Perspective*, (b) *The Effectiveness of Functional Budgetary Control in the National Health Service: An Empirical Investigation*, Warwick University (CRIBA); two technical papers for the Royal Commission on the NHS.

Layard, R. (ed.) (1972), *Cost-Benefit Analysis*, Harmondsworth: Penguin.

Layfield, F. Sir (Chairman) (1976), *Local Government Finance*, Cmnd. 6453, London: HMSO.

Letzkus, W. C. (1980), 'Zero-base budgeting and planning – programming – budgeting: what are the conceptual differences?', *Government Accountants Journal*, Winter, pp. 180–2.

Likierman, A. (1979) 'Nationalised industries: accounting for inflation', *Public Money*, December, pp. 19–24.

Likierman, A. (1982) *Cash Limits and External Financing Limits*, Civil Service Handbook 22, London: HMSO.

Likierman, A. (1983), 'Evidence on accusations of manipulating profitability: adjustments for inflation by the nationalised industries 1976–1981', *Accounting and Business Research*, Winter, pp. 19–34.

Likierman, A. and Vass, P. (1984), *Structure and Form of Government Expenditure Reports – Proposals for Reform*, London: Certified Accountant Publications.

Lumby, S. (1984), *Investment Appriasal*, (second edition), Wokingham: Van Nostrand Reinhold (UK).

Marsh, D. (1991), 'Privatisation under Mrs Thatcher: A Review of the Literature', *Public Adminsitration*, vol. 69, Winter 1991.

Masters, S. (1990), 'Financial Accountability and Reporting in the NHS', *Public Money and Management*, vol. 10, No. 2, Summer 1990, pp. 29–34.

Mishan, E. (1971a), *Cost-Benefit Analysis*, London: George Allen & Unwin.

Mishan, E. (1971b), 'The ABC of cost-benefit analysis', *LloydsBank Review*, July, pp. 30–43.

National Association of Accountants (1981), *Financial Planning and Evaluation for the Nonprofit Organization*, New York.

National Audit Office (1983), *National Audit Office*, London: HMSO.
National Audit Office (1984), *Ministry of Defence: Dockyard Efficiency*, HC.277 London: HMSO.
National Audit Office (1984), *Property Service Agency: Building Maintenance Expenditure in the UK*, HC.369 London: HMSO.
National Audit Office (1985), *Department of the Environment: Operation of the Rate Support Grant System*, London: HMSO.
National Consumer Council (1976), *Consumers and the Nationalised Industries*, London: HMSO.
National Consumer Council (1979), *The Consumer and the State: getting value for money*, London: HMSO.
National Council on Government Accounting (USA) (1979), *Government Accounting and Financial Reporting and Principles*, Chicago.
National Economic Development Office (1976), *A Study of UK Nationalised Industries: Their role in the economy and control in the future*, London: HMSO.
Nationalised Industries Chairmen's Group (1976), *Accounting in the Nationalised Industries*, London.
Nationalised Indsutries Chairmen's Group (1981), *Code of Practice for Current Cost Accounting in the Public Sector Corporations*, London.
Nicholson, D. R. (1969), 'PPBS – A challenge to non-profit accounting', *Management Accounting* (US), November, pp. 12–14.
Nicholson, G. D. (1973), 'Multi-purpose budgeting', in *Programme Budgeting*, Chartered Institute of Public Finance and Accountancy, pp. 49–58.
Normanton, E. L. (1971), 'Public accountability and Audit: A reconnaissance', chapter 14 in *The Dilemma of Accountability in Modern Government*, edited by Smith, B. L. R. and Hague, D. C., New York: St Martins Press.
Normanton, E. L. (1980), 'Reform in the field of public accountability and audit: a progress report', *Political Quarterly*, vol. 51, pp. 175–99.
Office of Health Economics (1984), *Compendium of Health Statistics*, London.
Parliamentary Debates – Commons (1979), *Fifth Series – Report of Proceedings for 21 December 1979*, London: HMSO.
Pearce, D. W. and Nash, C. A. (1981), *The Social Appraisal of Projects: A Test in Cost Benefit Appraisal*, Macmillan.
Pendlebury, M. and Jones, R. (1983), 'Municipal disclosure in England: another market for excuses?', *International Journal of Accounting*, Spring, pp. 83–93.
Perrin, J. (1978), *Management of Financial Resources in the National Health Service*, Research Paper 2 for the (Merrison) Royal Commission on the National Health Service, London: HMSO.
Perrin, J. (1983) 'The National Health Service', chapter 6 in *Public Sector Accounting and Financial Control*, edited by Henley, D., Likierman, A., Holtham, C. and Perrin, J., Wokingham: Van Nostrand Reihold (UK).
Perrin, J. (1984), 'Accounting for Public Sector Assets', in *Issues in Public Sector Accounting*, edited by Hopwood, A. and Tomkins, C., Oxford: Philip Allan.

Perrin, J. (1988), *Resource Management in the NHS*, VNR International: Chapman and Hall.

Peters, T. J., and Waterman, R. H. (1982), *In Search of Excellence*, New York: Harper and Row.

Phyrr, P. A. (1970), 'Zero-base budgeting', *Harvard Business Review*, November/December, pp. 111–21.

Plowden, Lord E. (Chairman) (1961), *Control of Public Expenditure*, Cmnd. 1432, London: HMSO.

PM (1984), *Financial Management in the Public Sector: a review 1979–84*, London: Peat Marwick.

PM (1986), *Current issues in the Public Sector*, London: Peat Marwick.

Pollitt, C. (1990), *Managerialism and the Public Service*, Oxford: Basil Blackwell.

POUNC (1984), Post Office Users National Council, Report No. 24, London.

Premchaud, A. (1983), *Government Budgeting and Expenditure Controls – Theory and Practice*, Washington DC: International Monetary Fund.

Prest, A. R. (1978), *Intergovernmental Financial Relations in the United Kingdom*, Centre for Research on Federal Financial Relation, The Australian National University, Canberra, Research Monograph no. 23.

Prest, A. R. and Turvey, R. (1965), 'Cost-benefit analysis: a survey', *Economic Journal*, vol. 75, pp. 685–705.

Price, C. (1986), 'Privatising British Gas: is the regulatory framework adequate?' *Public Money*, vol. 6, no. 1, June, pp. 13–19.

Pryke, R. (1981), *Public Enterprise in Practice*, London: MacGibbon and Kee.

Public Finance and Accountancy (1985), 'Rate support grant settlements', three short articles by Hale, R., Paterson, K. and Tettenborn, R., March, pp. 35–43.

Puritano, V. and Korb, L. (1981), 'Streamlining PPBS to better manage national defence', *Public Administration Review*, September/October, pp. 569–74.

Richards, D. (1985), 'Local government without tiers', *Management Accounting*, April, p. 21.

Rigden, M. S. (1983), *Health Service Finance and Accounting*, London: Heinemann.

Robinson, R. (1992), 'Health Policy in 1991', chapter 7 in *Pubic Domain 1992*, edited by Terry, F. and Jackson, P., Public Finance Foundation.

Rutherford, B. A. (1983), *Financial Reporting in the Public Sector*, London: Butterworths.

Sabin, P. (1989), Internal paper on Management devolution in Kent County Council, Maidstone.

Shackleton, J. R. (1984), 'Privatization: the case examined', *National Westminster Bank Quarterly Review*, May, pp. 59–73.

Schick, A. (1966), 'The road to PPB: the stages of budget reform', *Public Administration Review*, December, pp. 243–58.

Schick, A. (1969), 'Systems politics and systems budgeting', *Public Administration Review*, March/April, pp. 137–51.

Schubert, G. (1960), *The Public Interest*, Glencoe, Ill: The Free Press.

Sherer, M. J. (1984), 'Current Cost Accounting as an instrument of government policy', *British Accounting Review*, vol. 1, no. 1, pp. 3–11.

Shackleton, J. R. (1984), 'Privatization: the case examined', *National Westminster Bank Quarterly Review*, May, pp. 59–73.

Smith, B., (1980), 'Control in British government: a problem of accountability', *Policy Studies Journal*, vol. 9, pp. 1163–74.

Steel, D. R. and Stanyer, J. (1980), 'Administrative developments in 1979: a survey', *Public Administration*, Winter pp. 387–419.

Street, A. (1983), 'Local authority capital spending on roads and its financing', *National Westminster Bank Quarterly Review*, November, pp. 48–57.

Sugden, R. and Williams, A. (1978), *The Principles of Practical Cost-Benefit Analysis*, Oxford: Oxford University Press.

Taylor, F. W. (1911), *Scientific Management*, Harper & Bros.

Taylor, W. B. (1983), 'Borrowing by local authorities in the United Kingdom', *National Westminster Bank Quarterly Review*, August, pp. 60–9.

Tomkins, C. (1977), 'A conceptual framework for reporting to ratepayers', *Public Finance and Accountancy*, vol. 4, pt. 6, pp. 186–90.

Tomkins, C. (1982), *The Effect of Political and Economic Changes (1974–1982) on Financial Control Process in some UK Local Authorities*, Working paper no. 40, School of Management, University of Bath.

Treasury and Civil Service Committee (1982a), *Efficiency and Effectiveness in the Civil Service*, vo. 1: Report, Session 1981/82, HC.236–I, London: HMSO.

Treasury and Civil Service Committee, (1982b), *Budgetary Reform*, Session 1981/82, HC.137, London: HMSO.

Treasury and Civil Service Committee (1987), *Second Report – Session 1987–88*, HC.292, London: HMSO.

Trimby, L. (1977), 'The accountability of local government', *The Accountant*, 15 December, pp. 755–8.

Tweedie, D. (1984), 'Breaking free of the CCA impasse', *Accountancy*, October, pp.115–20.

USA, General Accounting Office, (1978), *Exposure Draft: Comprehensive Approach for Planning and Conducting a Programm Results Review*, Washington, DC.

US Congress (1949), *Report to Congress on Budget and Accounting*, (The Hoover Commission), Washington DC.

Webb, S. and Webb, B. (1963). *The Development of English Local Government*, Oxford: Oxford University Press.

Wickings, I., Coles, J. M., Flux, R. and Howard, L. (1983), 'Review of clinical budgeting and cost experiments', *British Medical Journal*, vol. 286, pp. 575–8.

Wildavsky, A. (1964), *The Politics of the Budgetary Process*, Boston: Little, Brown.

Wildavsky, A. (1969), 'Rescuing policy analysis from PPBS', *Public Administration Review*, March/April, pp. 189–202.

Wildavsky, A. (1975), *Budgeting: a comparative theory of budgetary processes*, Boston: Little, Brown.

Wilson, W. (1887), *The Study of Administration*, Princeton U.P.

Wright, M. (1985), 'Audit qualification on the accounts of nationalised industries', *Accounting and Business Research*, Spring, pp. 134–43.

Index